Distributed Algorithms

Distributed Algorithms

An Intuitive Approach

Wan Fokkink

The MIT Press
Cambridge, Massachusetts
London, England

© 2013 Massachusetts Institute of Technology

All rights reserved. No part of this book may be reproduced in any form by any electronic or mechanical means (including photocopying, recording, or information storage and retrieval) without permission in writing from the publisher.

MIT Press books may be purchased at special quantity discounts for business or sales promotional use. For information, please email special_sales@mitpress.mit.edu or write to Special Sales Department, The MIT Press, 55 Hayward Street, Cambridge, MA 02142.

This book was set in Amsterdam by the author. Printed and bound in the United States of America.

Library of Congress Cataloging-in-Publication Data

Fokkink, Wan, 1965–
Distributed algorithms: an intuitive approach / Wan Fokkink
   p. cm
Includes bibliographical references and index.
ISBN 978-0-262-02677-2 (hardcover: alk. paper)
1. Distributed algorithms—Textbooks. I. Title.
QA76.58.F647 2013
004'.36—dc23

                                                      2013015173

10 9 8 7 6 5 4 3 2 1

Contents

Preface ix

1   **Introduction** 1

I Message Passing

2   **Preliminaries** 7

3   **Snapshots** 13
    3.1   Chandy-Lamport algorithm 14
    3.2   Lai-Yang algorithm 15

4   **Waves** 19
    4.1   Traversal algorithms 19
    4.2   Tree algorithm 23
    4.3   Echo algorithm 24

5   **Deadlock Detection** 27
    5.1   Wait-for graphs 27
    5.2   Bracha-Toueg algorithm 29

6   **Termination Detection** 37
    6.1   Dijkstra-Scholten algorithm 38
    6.2   Weight-throwing algorithm 39
    6.3   Rana's algorithm 40
    6.4   Safra's algorithm 42

7   **Garbage Collection** 47
    7.1   Reference counting 47
    7.2   Garbage collection implies termination detection 50
    7.3   Tracing 51

8 Routing 53
8.1 Chandy-Misra algorithm 53
8.2 Merlin-Segall algorithm 55
8.3 Toueg's algorithm 58
8.4 Frederickson's algorithm 61
8.5 Packet switching 65
8.6 Routing on the Internet 67

9 Election 73
9.1 Election in rings 73
9.2 Tree election algorithm 77
9.3 Echo algorithm with extinction 79
9.4 Minimum spanning trees 80

10 Anonymous Networks 87
10.1 Impossibility of election in anonymous rings 87
10.2 Probabilistic algorithms 88
10.3 Itai-Rodeh election algorithm for rings 89
10.4 Echo algorithm with extinction for anonymous networks ... 91
10.5 Computing the size of an anonymous ring is impossible 93
10.6 Itai-Rodeh ring size algorithm 94
10.7 Election in IEEE 1394 96

11 Synchronous Networks 101
11.1 A simple synchronizer 101
11.2 Awerbuch's synchronizer 102
11.3 Bounded delay networks with local clocks 105
11.4 Election in anonymous rings with bounded expected delay . 106

12 Crash Failures 111
12.1 Impossibility of 1-crash consensus 112
12.2 Bracha-Toueg crash consensus algorithm 113
12.3 Failure detectors 115
12.4 Consensus with a weakly accurate failure detector 116
12.5 Chandra-Toueg algorithm 116

13 Byzantine Failures 121
13.1 Bracha-Toueg Byzantine consensus algorithm 121
13.2 Mahaney-Schneider synchronizer 125
13.3 Lamport-Shostak-Pease broadcast algorithm 127
13.4 Lamport-Shostak-Pease authentication algorithm 130

14 Mutual Exclusion 135
14.1 Ricart-Agrawala algorithm 135
14.2 Raymond's algorithm 137
14.3 Agrawal-El Abbadi algorithm 140

II Shared Memory

15 Preliminaries 145

16 Mutual Exclusion II 147
    16.1 Peterson's algorithm 147
    16.2 Bakery algorithm 150
    16.3 N registers are required 152
    16.4 Fischer's algorithm 152
    16.5 Test-and-test-and-set lock 153
    16.6 Queue locks 155

17 Barriers 161
    17.1 Sense-reversing barrier 161
    17.2 Combining tree barrier 162
    17.3 Tournament barrier 165
    17.4 Dissemination barrier 168

18 Self-Stabilization 171
    18.1 Dijkstra's token ring for mutual exclusion 171
    18.2 Arora-Gouda spanning tree algorithm 175
    18.3 Afek-Kutten-Yung spanning tree algorithm 177

19 Online Scheduling 181
    19.1 Jobs 181
    19.2 Schedulers 182
    19.3 Resource access control 188

Pseudocode Descriptions 193

References 221

Index 225

Preface

This textbook is meant for a course on distributed algorithms for senior-level undergraduate or graduate students in computer science or software engineering, and as a quick reference for researchers in the field. It focuses on fundamental algorithms and results in distributed computing. The distributed algorithms treated in this book are largely "classics" that were selected mainly because they are instructive with regard to the algorithmic design of distributed systems or shed light on key issues in distributed computing and concurrent programming.

The book consists of two parts. The first part is devoted to message-passing communication. It evolved from a course at the VU University Amsterdam, which was originally based on the textbook *Introduction to Distributed Algorithms* by Gerard Tel. The second part is devoted to shared-memory architectures.

There are two very different ways to structure an algorithms course. One way is to discuss algorithms and their analysis in great detail. The advantage of this approach is that students may gain deep insight into the algorithms and at the same time experience in mathematical reasoning on their correctness and performance. Another way is to discuss algorithms and their correctness in an informal manner, and let students get acquainted with an algorithm from different angles by means of examples and exercises, without a need to understand the intricacies of the respective model and its underlying assumptions. Mathematical argumentations, which can be a stumbling block for many students, are thus avoided. An additional advantage is that a large number of algorithms can be discussed within a relatively short time, providing students with many different views on and solutions to challenges in distributed computing. In ten years of teaching distributed algorithms I have converged to the latter approach, most of all because the students in my lectures tend to have hands-on experience and practical interests with regard to distributed systems. As a result, the learning objective of my course has been algorithmic thought rather than proofs and logic.

This book provides a Cook's tour of distributed algorithms. This phrase, meaning a rapid but extensive survey, refers to Thomas Cook, the visionary tour operator (and not the great explorer James Cook). Accordingly, this book intends to be a travel guide through the world of distributed algorithms. A notable difference from other books in this area is that it does not emphasize correctness proofs. Algorithms are explained by means of brief informal descriptions, illuminating examples and exercises. The exercises have been carefully selected to make students well-acquainted with the intricacies of distributed algorithms. Proof sketches, arguing the correctness of an algorithm or explaining the idea behind a fundamental result, are presented at a rather superficial level.

A thorough correctness proof, of course, is important in order to understand an algorithm in full detail. My research area is automated correctness proofs of distributed algorithms and communication protocols; I wrote two textbooks devoted to this topic. In the current textbook, however, intuition prevails. I recommend that readers who want to get a more detailed description of a distributed algorithm in this book consult the original paper, mentioned in the bibliographical notes at the end of each chapter. Moreover, pseudocode descriptions of a considerable number of algorithms are provided as an appendix.

I gratefully acknowledge the support of Helle Hvid Hansen, Jeroen Ketema, and David van Moolenbroek with providing detailed solutions to the exercises in this book, and the comments by students on early versions of these lecture notes, in particular from Tessel Bogaard, István Haller, Jan van der Lugt, and Armando Miraglia. Special thanks go to Gerard Tel for his useful feedback over the years.

Wan Fokkink

Amsterdam, July 2013

1
Introduction

In this age of the Internet, wide and local area networks, and multicore laptops, the importance of distributed computing is crystal clear. The fact that you have opened this book means that no further explanation is needed to convince you of this point. The majority of modern-day system designers, system programmers, and ICT support staff must have a good understanding of concurrent programming. This, however, is easier said than done.

An algorithm is a step-by-step procedure to solve a particular problem on a computer. To become a skilled programmer, it is essential to have good insight into algorithms. Every computer science degree program offers one or more courses on basic algorithms, typically for searching and sorting, pattern recognition, and finding shortest paths in graphs. There, students learn how to detect such subproblems within their computer programs and solve them effectively. Moreover, they are trained to think algorithmically, to reason about the correctness of algorithms, and to perform a simple complexity analysis.

Distributed computing is very different from and considerably more complex than a uniprocessor setting, because executions at the nodes in a distributed system are interleaved. When two nodes can concurrently perform events, it cannot be predicted which of the events will happen first in time. This gives rise, for instance, to so-called race conditions; if two messages are traveling to the same node in the network, different behavior may occur depending on which of the messages reaches its destination first. Distributed systems are therefore inherently nondeterministic: running a system twice from the same initial configuration may yield different results. And the number of reachable configurations of a distributed system tends to grow exponentially with respect to its number of nodes.

Another important distinction between distributed and uniprocessor computing is the fact that the nodes in a distributed system in general do not have up-to-date knowledge of the global state of the system. They are aware of their own local states, but not always of the local states at other nodes or of the messages in transit. For example, termination detection becomes an issue. It must be determined that all nodes in the system have terminated; and even if this is the case, there may still be a message in transit that will make the receiving node active again.

This book offers a wide range of basic algorithms for key challenges in distributed systems, such as termination detection, or letting the nodes in a distributed network together build a snapshot of a global system state. The main aim is to provide students with an algorithmic frame of mind so that they can recognize and solve fundamental problems in distributed computing. They are offered a bird's-eye view on such problems from many different angles, as well as handwaving correctness arguments and back-of-the-envelope complexity calculations.

The two main communication paradigms for distributed systems are message passing, in which nodes send messages to each other via channels, and shared memory, in which different execution threads can read and write to the same memory locations. This book is split into two parts, dedicated to these two communication paradigms. The remainder of this chapter presents some preliminaries that are applicable to both frameworks.

Sets

As usual, $S_1 \cup S_2$, $S_1 \backslash S_1$ and $S_1 \subseteq S_2$ denote set union, difference and inclusion; $s \in S$ means that s is an element of the set S. The sets of natural and real numbers are denoted with $\mathbb{N}$ and $\mathbb{R}$. The Booleans consist of the elements *true* and *false*. A set may be written as $\{\cdots \mid \cdots\}$, where to the left of $\mid$ the elements in the set are described, and to the right the property that they should satisfy is identified. For example, $\{n \in \mathbb{N} \mid n > 5\}$ represents the set of natural numbers greater than 5. The empty set is denoted by $\emptyset$. For any finite set S, $|S|$ denotes its number of elements.

Complexity measures

Complexity measures state how resource consumption (messages, time, space) grows in relation to input size. For example, if an algorithm has a worst-case message complexity of $O(n^2)$, then for an input of size n, the algorithm in the worst case takes *in the order of* n^2 messages, give or take a constant.

Let $f, g : \mathbb{N} \to \mathbb{R}_{>0}$, meaning that the functions f and g map natural numbers to positive real numbers. We write $f = O(g)$ if f is bounded from above by g, multiplied with some positive constant:

$$f = O(g) \text{ if, for some } C > 0, f(n) \leq C \cdot g(n) \text{ for all } n \in \mathbb{N}.$$

Likewise, $f = \Omega(g)$ means that f is bounded by g from below, multiplied with some positive constant:

$$f = \Omega(g) \text{ if, for some } C > 0, f(n) \geq C \cdot g(n) \text{ for all } n \in \mathbb{N}.$$

Finally, $f = \Theta(g)$ means that f is bounded by g from above as well as below:

$$f = \Theta(g) \text{ if } f = O(g) \text{ and } f = \Omega(g).$$

So if an algorithm has, say, a worst-case message complexity of $\Theta(n^2)$, then this upper bound is sharp.

Example 1.1 Let $a, b > 0$ be constants.

- $n^a = O(n^b)$ if $a \leq b$.
- $n^a = O(b^n)$ if $b > 1$.
- $\log_a n = O(n^b)$ for all a, b.

Divide-and-conquer algorithms, which recursively divide a problem into smaller subproblems until they are simple enough to be solved directly, typically have a logarithm in their time complexity. The reason is that dividing a problem of input size 2^k into subproblems of size 1 takes k steps, and $k = \log_2 2^k$.

One can write $O(\log n)$ instead of $O(\log_a n)$. Namely, by definition, $\log_a a^n = n$, which implies $a^{\log_a n} = n$. So

$$a^{\log_a b \cdot \log_b n} = b^{\log_b n} = n.$$

Therefore, $\log_a b \cdot \log_b n = \log_a n$. So $\log_b n = O(\log_a n)$ for all $a, b > 0$.

Complexity measures will sometimes use the notations $\lfloor a \rfloor$ and $\lceil a \rceil$, meaning the largest integer k such that $k \leq a$, and the smallest integer ℓ such that $\ell \geq a$, respectively.

Resource consumption of an execution of a distributed algorithm can be measured in several ways.

- *Message complexity:* the total number of messages exchanged.
- *Bit complexity:* the total number of bits exchanged.
- *Time complexity:* the amount of time required to complete the execution.
- *Space complexity:* the total amount of space needed for the processes.

Part I, on the message-passing framework, focuses mostly on message complexity. Bit complexity is interesting only when messages can be very long. In the analysis of time complexity we assume that event processing takes no time, and that a message is received at most one time unit after it is sent.

Different executions may give rise to different consumption of resources. We consider worst- and average-case complexity, the latter with some probability distribution over all executions.

Orders

A (strict) order on a set S is a binary relation between elements of S that is irreflexive, asymmetric and transitive, meaning that for all $a, b, c \in S$: $a < a$ does not hold; if $a < b$ then $b < a$ does not hold; and if $a < b$ and $b < c$ then $a < c$. An order is total if for any distinct $a, b \in S$ either $a < b$ or $b < a$; otherwise the order is called partial. Given two sets S_1 and S_2 with orders $<_1$ and $<_2$, respectively, the lexicographical order $<$ on pairs from $S_1 \times S_2$ is defined by $(a_1, a_2) < (b_1, b_2)$ if either $a_1 <_1 b_1$, or $a_1 = b_1$ and $a_2 <_2 b_2$. If $<_1$ and $<_2$ are total orders, then so is the corresponding lexicographical order $<$.

Modulo arithmetic

The integer domain modulo a positive natural number n is represented by the elements $\{0,\ldots,n-1\}$. Each integer k has a representative modulo n, denoted by $k \bmod n$, being the unique $\ell \in \{0,\ldots,n-1\}$ such that $k - \ell$ is divisible by n. This means that integer values are wrapped around when they reach n: $n \bmod n$ is represented by 0, $(n+1) \bmod n$ by 1, and so on. Addition and multiplication on integers carry over to modulo arithmetic in a straightforward fashion: $(j \bmod n) + (k \bmod n) = (j+k) \bmod n$ and $(j \bmod n) \cdot (k \bmod n) = (j \cdot k) \bmod n$.

Exercises

Exercise 1.1 For each of the following functions f and g, say whether $f = O(g)$ and/or $g = O(f)$.

(a) $f(n) = 5n^2 + 3n + 7$ and $g(n) = n^3$.
(b) $f(n) = \sum_{i=1}^{n} i$ and $g(n) = n^2$.
(c) $f(n) = n^n$ and $g(n) = n!$.
(d) $f(n) = n \log_2 n$ and $g(n) = n\sqrt{\frac{n}{2}}$.
(e) $f(n) = n + n \log_2 n$ and $g(n) = n\sqrt{n}$.

I
Message Passing

2
Preliminaries

In a message-passing framework, a distributed system consists of a finite network (or graph) of N processes (or nodes). Each process in the network carries a unique ID. The processes in the network are connected by channels (or edges), through which they can send messages to each other. There is at most one channel from one process to another, and a process does not have a channel to itself. Sometimes a process may want to communicate a message to itself, but for this clearly no channel is needed. We use E and D to denote the number of channels and the diameter of the network, respectively.

A process can record its own state and the messages it sends and receives; processes do not share memory or a global clock. Each process knows only its (direct) neighbors in the network. The topology of the network is assumed to be strongly connected, meaning that there is a path from each process to every other process.

Communication in the network is *asynchronous*, meaning that sending and receiving a message are distinct events at the sending and receiving process, respectively. The delay of a message in a channel is arbitrary but finite. We assume that communication protocols are being used to avoid that messages are garbled, duplicated or lost. Channels need not be FIFO, meaning that messages can overtake each other.

In a *directed* network, messages can travel only in one direction through a channel, while in an *undirected* network, messages can travel either way. Undirected channels are required for distributed algorithms that use an acknowledgment scheme. Acyclic networks will always be undirected, since otherwise the network would not be strongly connected. A network topology is called *complete* if there is an undirected channel between each pair of different processes.

A *spanning tree* of an undirected network is a connected, acyclic graph that consists of all the nodes and a subset of the edges in the network. The edges of the spanning tree are called *tree edges*, and all other edges are called *frond edges*. Often the edges in a spanning tree are given a direction to obtain a *sink tree*, in which all paths lead to the same node, called the *root*; each directed edge leads from a *child* to its *parent*.

At some places we will deviate from the assumptions mentioned so far and move to, for instance, synchronous communication in which sending and receiving of the same message form one atomic event, or unreliable processes or channels, or FIFO channels, or processes without a unique ID, or processes with a probabilistic instead of a deterministic specification. This will then be stated explicitly.

Transition systems

A distributed algorithm, which runs on a distributed system, provides (usually deterministic) specifications for the individual processes. The global state of a distributed algorithm, called a *configuration*, evolves by means of *transitions*. The overall behavior of a distributed system is captured by a *transition system*, which consists of:

- a set $\mathcal{C}$ of configurations,
- a binary transition relation $\to$ on $\mathcal{C}$, and
- a set $\mathcal{I} \subseteq \mathcal{C}$ of *initial* configurations.

A configuration γ is *terminal* if it has no outgoing transition: $\gamma \to \delta$ for no $\delta \in \mathcal{C}$. An *execution* of the distributed system is a sequence $\gamma_0 \gamma_1 \gamma_2 \cdots$ of configurations that is either infinite or ends in a terminal configuration γ_k, such that:

- $\gamma_0 \in \mathcal{I}$, and
- $\gamma_i \to \gamma_{i+1}$ for all $i \geq 0$ (and in case of a finite execution, $i < k$).

A configuration δ is *reachable* if there is a $\gamma_0 \in \mathcal{I}$ and a sequence $\gamma_0 \gamma_1 \cdots \gamma_k$ with $\gamma_i \to \gamma_{i+1}$ for all $0 \leq i < k$ and $\gamma_k = \delta$.

States and events

The configuration of a distributed system is composed from the local *states* of its processes and the messages in transit. A transition between configurations of a distributed system is associated to an *event* (or, in case of synchronous communication, two events) at one (or two) of its processes. A process can perform *internal*, *send* and *receive* events. An internal event influences only the state at the process where the event is performed. Typical internal events are reading or writing to a local variable. Assignment of a new value to a variable is written as $\leftarrow$; for example, $n \leftarrow n + 1$ means that the value of variable n, representing a natural number, is increased by one. A send event in principle gives rise to a corresponding receive event of the same message at another process. It is assumed that two different events never happen at the same moment in real time (with the exception of synchronous communication).

A process is an *initiator* if its first event is an internal or send event; that is, an initiator can start performing events without input from another process. An algorithm is *centralized* if there is exactly one initiator. A *decentralized* algorithm can have multiple initiators.

Assertions

An assertion is a predicate on the configurations of an algorithm. That is, in each configuration the assertion is either true or false.

An assertion is a *safety property* if it is true in each reachable configuration of the algorithm. A safety property typically expresses that something bad will never happen. Examples of safety properties are:

- You can always count on me.
- The cost of living never decreases.
- If an interrupt occurs, a message will be printed within one second.

In particular, the last example states that never no message gets printed within one second after an interrupt.

In general, it is undecidable whether a given configuration is reachable. An assertion P is an *invariant* if:

- $P(\gamma)$ for all $\gamma \in \mathcal{I}$, and
- if $\gamma \to \delta$ and $P(\gamma)$, then $P(\delta)$.

In other words, an invariant is true in all initial configurations and is preserved by all transitions. Clearly, each invariant is a safety property. Note that checking whether an assertion is an invariant does not involve reachability.

An assertion is a *liveness property* if executions, from some point on, contain a configuration in which the assertion holds. A liveness property typically expresses that something good will eventually happen. Examples of liveness properties are:

- What goes up, must come down.
- The program always eventually terminates.
- If an interrupt occurs, a message will be printed.

A liveness property sometimes holds only with respect to the so-called fair executions of an algorithm. For example, consider a simple algorithm that consists of flipping a coin until the result is tails. Since there is an infinite execution in which the outcome of every coin flip is heads, the liveness property that eventually the outcome will be tails does not hold. However, if the coin is fair, this infinite execution has zero chance of happening; infinitely often we flip the coin with the possible outcome tails, but never is the outcome tails. We say that an execution is *fair* if every event that can happen in infinitely many configurations in the execution is performed infinitely often during the execution. The infinite execution in which the outcome of every coin flip is heads is not fair. Note that any finite execution is by default fair.

Causal order

In each configuration of an asynchronous distributed system, events that can occur at different processes are independent, meaning that they can happen in any order. The *causal order* $\prec$ is a binary relation on events in an execution such that $a \prec b$ if and only if a must happen before b. That is, the events in the execution cannot be reordered in such a way that a happens after b. The causal order for an execution is the smallest relation such that:

- if a and b are events at the same process and a occurs before b, then $a \prec b$,
- if a is a send and b the corresponding receive event, then $a \prec b$, and
- if $a \prec b$ and $b \prec c$, then $a \prec c$.

We write $a \preceq b$ if either $a \prec b$ or $a = b$. Distinct events in an execution that are not causally related are called *concurrent*. An important challenge in the design of distributed systems is to cope with concurrency (for example, to avoid race conditions).

A permutation of concurrent events in an execution does not affect the result of the execution. These permutations together form a *computation*. All executions of a computation start in the same configuration, and if they are finite, they all end in the same terminal configuration. In general, we will consider computations rather than executions.

Logical clocks

A common physical clock, which tries to approximate the global real time, is in general difficult to maintain by the separate processes in a distributed system. For many applications, however, we are not interested in the precise moments in time at which events occur, but only in the ordering of these occurrences in time. A *logical clock* C maps occurrences of events in a computation to a partially ordered set such that
$$a \prec b \Rightarrow C(a) < C(b).$$

Lamport's clock LC assigns to each event a the length k of a longest causality chain $a_1 \prec \cdots \prec a_k = a$ in the computation. It is not hard to see that $a \prec b$ implies $LC(a) < LC(b)$, so Lamport's clock is a logical clock. The clock values that Lamport's clock assigns to events can be computed at run-time as follows. Consider an event a, and let k be the clock value of the previous event at the same process ($k = 0$ if there is no such previous event).

- If a is an internal or send event, then $LC(a) = k + 1$.
- If a is a receive event and b the send event corresponding to a, then $LC(a) = \max\{k, LC(b)\} + 1$.

Lamport's clock may order concurrent events; that is, it may be the case that $LC(a) < LC(b)$ for concurrent events a and b. Sometimes it is useful to use a logical clock for which this is never the case. The *vector clock* VC has the property that
$$a \prec b \Leftrightarrow VC(a) < VC(b).$$

Let the network consist of processes $p_0, \ldots, p_{N-1}$. The vector clock assigns to events in a computation values in $\mathbb{N}^N$, whereby this set is provided with a partial order defined by:
$$(k_0, \ldots, k_{N-1}) \leq (\ell_0, \ldots, \ell_{N-1}) \Leftrightarrow k_i \leq \ell_i \text{ for all } i = 0, \ldots, N-1.$$

(In contrast to the lexicographical order on $\mathbb{N}^N$, this order is partial.) The vector clock is defined as follows: $VC(a) = (k_0, \ldots, k_{N-1})$ where each k_i is the length of a longest causality chain $a_1^i \prec \cdots \prec a_{k_i}^i$ of events at process p_i with $a_{k_i}^i \preceq a$. Clearly, $a \prec b$ implies $VC(a) < VC(b)$; this follows from the fact that $c \preceq a$ implies $c \prec b$, for each event c. Conversely, $VC(a) < VC(b)$ implies $a \prec b$. Namely, consider the longest causality chain $a_1^i \prec \cdots \prec a_k^i = a$ of events at the process p_i where a occurs. Then $VC(a) < VC(b)$ implies that the i-th coefficient of $VC(b)$ is at least k, and so $a \preceq b$. Since clearly a and b must be distinct events, $a \prec b$. The vector clock can also be computed at run-time (see exercise 2.7).

Basic and control algorithms

Several chapters will discuss distributed algorithms to provide some service or detect a certain property during the execution of a distributed algorithm. For instance, chapter 3 shows how processes can take a snapshot of a configuration in the ongoing computation, chapter 6 treats how processes can detect termination, and chapter 7 discusses garbage collection to reclaim unaccessible objects in memory. Then the underlying distributed algorithm for which we are taking a snapshot, detecting termination or collecting garbage, is called the *basic* algorithm, while the distributed algorithm put on top for executing this specific task is called the *control* algorithm.

Bibliographical notes

Lamport's clock originates from [45]. The vector clock was proposed independently in [29] and [55]. Dedicated frameworks exist to support the implementation of distributed algorithms on graphs [53, 41].

Exercises

Exercise 2.1 What is more general:

(a) An algorithm for directed or undirected networks?
(b) A control algorithm for centralized or decentralized basic algorithms?

Exercise 2.2 [76] Give a transition system S and an assertion P such that P is a safety property but not an invariant of S.

Exercise 2.3 [76] Define the union of $S_1 = (\mathcal{C}, \to_1, \mathcal{I})$ and $S_2 = (\mathcal{C}, \to_2, \mathcal{I})$ as $S = (\mathcal{C}, \to, \mathcal{I})$ with $\to = (\to_1 \cup \to_2)$. Prove that if P is an invariant of S_1 and S_2, then P is an invariant of S.

Exercise 2.4 Consider the following execution, of an algorithm involving processes p_0, p_1, p_2, and p_3; events are given in the order in which they are executed in real time:

- p_0 sends a message to p_2;

- p_3 sends a message to p_2;
- p_0 sends a message to p_1;
- p_2 receives the message from p_0;
- p_1 receives the message from p_0;
- p_2 performs an internal event;
- p_2 sends a message to p_3;
- p_3 receives the message from p_2;
- p_2 receives the message from p_3;
- p_3 performs an internal event;
- p_1 sends a message to p_0;
- p_3 sends a message to p_2;
- p_0 receives the message from p_1;
- p_2 receives the message from p_3.

Use Lamport's logical clock to assign clock values to these events. Do the same for the vector clock.

Exercise 2.5 [76] Define the causal order for the transitions of a system with synchronous communication. Adapt Lamport's logical clock for such systems, and give a distributed algorithm for computing the clock at run-time.

Exercise 2.6 Give an example where $LC(a) < LC(b)$ while a and b are concurrent events.

Exercise 2.7 Give an algorithm to compute the vector clock at run-time.

3
Snapshots

A *snapshot* of an execution of a distributed algorithm is a configuration of this execution, consisting of the local states of the processes and the messages in transit. Snapshots are useful to try to determine offline properties that will remain true as soon as they have become true, such as deadlock (see chapter 5), termination (see chapter 6) or garbage (see chapter 7). Moreover, snapshots can be used for checkpointing to restart after a failure, or for debugging.

In a centralized environment one can at any moment during a program run query the program state, consisting of the values of the program variables. In a distributed setting, this is not the case. Suppose that a process that is involved in the execution of a distributed algorithm wants to make a snapshot of a configuration of the ongoing execution. Then it should ask all processes to take a snapshot of their local state. Processes moreover have to compute channel states, of messages that were in transit at the moment of the snapshot. The challenge is to develop a snapshot algorithm that works at run-time, that is, without freezing the execution of the basic algorithm of which the snapshot is taken. Messages of the basic algorithm are called *basic messages*, while messages of the snapshot algorithm are called *control messages*.

A complication is that processes take local snapshots and compute channel states at different moments in time. Therefore, a snapshot may actually not represent a configuration of the ongoing execution, but a configuration of an execution in the same computation is good enough. Such a snapshot is called *consistent*.

One has to be careful not to take an inconsistent snapshot. For instance, a process p could take a local snapshot and then send a basic message m to a process q, where q could either take a local snapshot after the receipt of m or include m in the state of the channel pq. This would turn m into a "ghost" message of the snapshot, which was not sent according to p but was in transit or received according to q. Likewise, p could send a basic message m before taking its local snapshot, while q could receive m after taking its local snapshot and exclude m from the channel state of pq. Such incorrect snapshots clearly have to be avoided.

An event is called *presnapshot* if it occurs at a process before the local snapshot at this process is taken; else it is called *postsnapshot*. A snapshot is consistent if: (1) for each presnapshot event a, all events that are causally before a are also presnapshot; and (2) a basic message is included in a channel state if and only if the corresponding send event is presnapshot while the corresponding receive event is postsnapshot. The first property guarantees that all presnapshot events can be placed before the postsnapshot events in the actual execution by means of permutations that do not violate the causal order. This implies that the snapshot is a configuration of an execution that is in the same computation as the actual execution.

We discuss two decentralized snapshot algorithms for directed networks; the first one requires channels to be FIFO. In these algorithms, the individual processes record fragments of the snapshot; the subsequent phase of collecting these fragments to obtain a composite view is omitted here.

3.1 Chandy-Lamport algorithm

The Chandy-Lamport snapshot algorithm requires that channels are FIFO. Any initiator can decide to take a local snapshot of its state. It then sends a control message ⟨**marker**⟩ through all its outgoing channels to let its neighbors take a snapshot too. When a process that has not yet taken a snapshot receives a ⟨**marker**⟩ message, it takes a local snapshot of its state, and sends a ⟨**marker**⟩ message through all its outgoing channels. A process q computes as channel state for an incoming channel pq the (basic) messages that it receives via pq after taking its local snapshot and before receiving a ⟨**marker**⟩ message from p. The Chandy-Lamport algorithm terminates at a process when it has received a ⟨**marker**⟩ message through all its incoming channels.

Example 3.1 We consider one possible computation of the Chandy-Lamport algorithm on the directed network below. First, process p takes a local snapshot of its state (dark gray), and sends ⟨**marker**⟩ into its two outgoing channels pq and pr. Next, p sends a basic message m_1 to process q, and changes its state (to black). Moreover, process r receives ⟨**marker**⟩ from p, and as a result sends ⟨**marker**⟩ into its outgoing channel rp, takes a local snapshot of its state (white), and computes the channel state $\emptyset$ for its incoming channel pr.

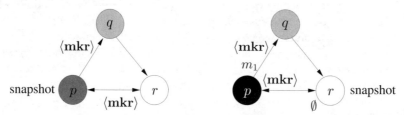

Next, p receives ⟨**marker**⟩ from r, and as a result computes the channel state $\emptyset$ for its incoming channel rp. Moreover, q sends a basic message m_2 to r. Next, q receives ⟨**marker**⟩ from p, and as a result sends ⟨**marker**⟩ into its outgoing channel qr, takes a local snapshot of its state (light gray), and computes the channel state $\emptyset$ for its incoming channel pq. Finally, r receives m_2 and next ⟨**marker**⟩ from q, and as a result it computes the channel state $\{m_2\}$ for its incoming channel qr.

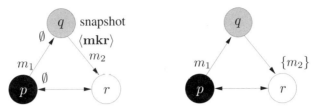

We note that the computed snapshot (states: dark gray, light gray, white; channels: $\emptyset, \emptyset, \emptyset, \{m_2\}$) is not a configuration of the actual execution. However, the sending of m_1 and the internal event at p that changes its state from light gray to black are both not causally before the sending of m_2. Therefore, the snapshot is a configuration of an execution in the same computation as the actual execution.

We argue that if an event a is causally before a presnapshot event b, then a is also presnapshot. If a and b occur at the same process, then this is trivially the case. The interesting case is where a is a send and b the corresponding receive event. Suppose that a occurs at process p and b at process q. Since b is presnapshot, q has not yet received a ⟨**marker**⟩ message at the time it performs b. Since channels are FIFO, this implies p has not yet sent a ⟨**marker**⟩ message to q at the time it performs a. Hence, a is presnapshot.

Moreover, a basic message m via a channel pq is included in the channel state of pq if and only if the corresponding send event at p is presnapshot and the corresponding receive event at q is postsnapshot. Namely, q must receive m before ⟨**marker**⟩ through pq; so since channels are FIFO, p must send m before ⟨**marker**⟩ into pq. Furthermore, q starts computing the channel state of pq after taking it local snapshot.

The Chandy-Lamport algorithm requires E control messages, and it takes at most $O(D)$ time units to complete.

3.2 Lai-Yang algorithm

The Lai-Yang snapshot algorithm does not require channels to be FIFO. Any initiator can decide to take a local snapshot of its state. As long as a process has not taken a local snapshot, it appends *false* to each outgoing basic message; after its local snapshot, it appends *true* to these messages. When a process that has not yet taken a local snapshot receives a message with the tag *true*, it takes a local snapshot of its state before the reception of this message. A process q computes as channel state of an incoming channel pq the basic messages with the tag *false* that it receives through this channel after having taken its local snapshot.

There are two complications. First, if after its local snapshot an initiator would happen not to send any basic messages, other processes might never take a local snapshot. Second, how does a process know when it can stop waiting for basic messages with the tag *false* and compute the state of an incoming channel? Both issues are resolved by a special control message, which a process p sends into each outgoing channel pq after having taken its local snapshot. This control message informs q how many basic messages with the tag *false* p has sent into the channel pq. In case q has not yet taken a local snapshot, it takes one upon reception of this control message.

Example 3.2 Consider a network of two processes p and q, with non-FIFO channels pq and qp. We apply the Lai-Yang algorithm to take a snapshot.

Let p send basic messages $\langle m_1, false \rangle$ and $\langle m_2, false \rangle$ to q. Then it takes a local snapshot of its state and sends a control message to q, reporting that p sent two basic message with the tag *false* to q. Next, p sends basic messages $\langle m_3, true \rangle$ and $\langle m_4, true \rangle$ to q. Let $\langle m_3, true \rangle$ arrive at q first. Then q takes a local snapshot of its state and sends a control message to p, reporting that q did not send any basic message with the tag *false* to p. Next, q waits until the control message from p, $\langle m_1, false \rangle$, and $\langle m_2, false \rangle$ have arrived and concludes that the channel state of pq consists of m_1 and m_2. Thanks to the tag *true*, q recognizes that m_3 and m_4 are not part of the channel state. When p receives q's control message, it concludes that the channel state of qp is empty.

Similar to the Chandy-Lamport algorithm, we can argue that if an event a is causally before a presnapshot event b, then a is also presnapshot. Again, the interesting case is where a is a send and b the corresponding receive event. Since b is presnapshot, the message sent by a carries the tag *false*. Hence, a is presnapshot.

Moreover, a basic message m via a channel pq is included in the channel state of pq if and only if the corresponding send event at p is presnapshot, and the corresponding receive event at q is postsnapshot. Namely, m carries the tag *false*, and q starts computing the channel state of pq after taking it local snapshot.

The Lai-Yang algorithm requires E control messages, and it takes at most $O(D)$ time units to complete for each snapshot.

Bibliographical notes

The Chandy-Lamport algorithm originates from [16]. The Lai-Yang algorithm stems from [43]; the special control message was suggested in [55].

Exercises

Exercise 3.1 Give an example to show that the Chandy-Lamport algorithm is flawed if channels are not FIFO.

Exercise 3.2 Propose an adaptation of the Chandy-Lamport algorithm, in which basic messages may be buffered at the receiving processes, and the channel states of the snapshot are always empty.

Exercise 3.3 Give an example in which the Lai-Yang algorithm computes a snapshot that is not a configuration of the ongoing execution.

Exercise 3.4 Adapt the Lai-Yang algorithm so that it supports multiple subsequent snapshots.

Exercise 3.5 Give a snapshot algorithm for undirected networks with non-FIFO channels that uses:

- marker messages, tagged with the number of basic messages sent into a channel before the marker message,
- acknowledgments, and
- temporary (local) freezing of the basic execution.

4
Waves

In distributed computing, a process often needs to gather information from all other processes in the network. This process then typically sends a request through the network, which incites the other processes to reply with the required information. Notable examples are termination detection, routing, and election of a leader in the network.

This procedure is formalized in the notion of a *wave algorithm*, in which each computation, called a *wave*, satisfies the following three properties:

- It is finite.
- It contains one or more *decide* events.
- For each decide event a and process p, $b \prec a$ for some event b at p.

The idea behind wave algorithms is that each computation gives rise to one or more decisions in which all processes have a say. An important characteristic of a wave algorithm is that it does not complete if any process p refuses to take part in its execution, because no event at p in the wave would be causally before the decide event.

Often a wave is initiated by one process, and in the end one decide event happens, at the initiator. If there can be concurrent calls of a wave algorithm, initiated by different processes, then usually for each wave the messages are marked with the ID of its initiator. In such a setting, if a wave does not complete, because a process refuses to take part, then typically another wave will complete successfully later on (see, for example, Rana's termination detection algorithm in section 6.3, or the echo algorithm with extinction for election in section 9.3).

4.1 Traversal algorithms

A *traversal algorithm* is a centralized wave algorithm in which the initiator sends a token through the network. After visiting all other processes, the token returns to the initiator, who then makes a decision. A typical example of a traversal algorithm is the so-called ring algorithm, in which the token makes one trip around the ring.

Traversal algorithms can be used to build a spanning tree of the network, with the initiator as the root. Each noninitiator has as parent the process from which it received the token for the first time.

Tarry's algorithm

Tarry's algorithm is a traversal algorithm for undirected networks. It is based on the following two rules:

1. A process never forwards the token through the same channel twice.
2. A process only forwards the token to its parent when there is no other option.

By applying these two rules, the token travels through each channel twice and finally ends up at the initiator.

Example 4.1 We apply Tarry's algorithm to the following network; p is the initiator.

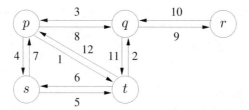

The network is undirected (and unweighted); arrows and numbers mark the consecutive steps of one possible path of the token. Solid arrows establish a parent-child relation (in the opposite direction) in the resulting spanning tree. So the resulting spanning tree of this execution is:

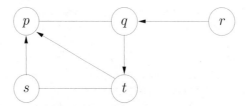

Tree edges are solid, while frond edges are dashed.

We argue that in Tarry's algorithm the token travels through each channel twice, once in each direction, and finally ends up at the initiator. By rule 1, the token is never sent through the same channel in the same direction twice. Each time a noninitiator p holds the token, it has received the token one more time than it has sent the token to a neighbor, meaning that there is still a channel into which p has not yet sent the token. So by rule 1, p can send the token into this channel. Hence, when Tarry's algorithm terminates, the token must be at the initiator. Assume, toward a contradiction, that at the moment of termination some channel pq has not been traversed by the token in both directions; let noninitiator p be the earliest visited process for which such a channel exists. Since by assumption all channels of the parent of p have been traversed in both directions, in particular, p has sent the token to its parent. So by rule 2, p must have sent the token into all its channels. Since p has sent and received the token an equal number of times, it must have received the token through all its channels. To conclude, the token has traveled through pq in both ways; this is a contradiction.

Tarry's algorithm requires $2E$ messages, and it takes at most $2E$ time units to terminate.

Depth-first search

In a depth-first search, starting from the initiator, whenever possible, the token is forwarded to a process that did not hold the token yet. If a process holding the token has no unvisited neighbor, then it sends the token back to its parent, being the process from which it received the token.

The spanning tree in example 4.1 is not a depth-first search tree, that is, it cannot be the result of a depth-first search. Namely, in a depth-first search, processes s and t would never both have p as their parent. In general, a spanning tree is the result of a depth-first search if all frond edges connect an ancestor with one of its descendants in the spanning tree (unlike the frond edge between s and t).

A depth-first search is obtained by adding one more rule to Tarry's algorithm:

3. When a process receives the token, it immediately sends it back through the same channel if this is allowed by rules 1 and 2.

Example 4.2 Consider the same network as in example 4.1; p is again the initiator. Below one possible depth-first search is depicted.

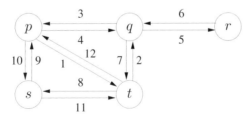

In example 4.1, when p received the token from q, it forwarded it to s. However, here p is forced to send the token back to q immediately, due to rule 3.

Depth-first search is a special case of Tarry's algorithm, so it also takes $2E$ messages, and at most $2E$ time units to terminate.

Sending the token back and forth through a frond edge, such as steps 3,4 and 9,10 in example 4.2, constitutes a loss of time. One obvious way to avoid this is by including the IDs of visited processes in the token, so that a process can determine which neighbors have already seen the token. Since the token then travels back and forth only through the $N-1$ tree edges, the message complexity is reduced from $2E$ to $2N-2$ messages, and similarly the time complexity to at most $2N-2$ time units.

The drawback, however, is that the bit complexity goes up from $O(1)$ to $O(N \log N)$ (assuming that $O(\log N)$ bits are needed to represent the ID of a process).

An alternative is to let a process p that holds the token for the first time inform its neighbors (except the process that sent the token to p and the process to which p will send the token) that it has seen the token. In Awerbuch's depth-first search algorithm, p waits for acknowledgments from all those neighbors before forwarding the token, to ensure that they cannot receive the token before p's information message. A process marks a channel as frond edge as soon as it has received an information message through this channel and the token through another channel. A process never forwards the token through a frond edge. The worst-case message complexity goes up to $4E$, because frond edges carry two information messages and two acknowledgments, while tree edges carry two forwarded tokens and possibly one information and acknowledgment pair. Also, the worst-case time complexity goes up, to $4N - 2$ time units, because tree edges carry two forwarded tokens, and each process may wait at most two time units for acknowledgments to return.

Cidon's depth-first search algorithm improves on Awerbuch's algorithm by abolishing the waiting for acknowledgments. A process p forwards the token without delay and records to which process $forward_p$ it forwarded the token last. In case p receives the token back from a process $q \neq forward_p$, it purges the token and marks the channel pq as frond edge. No further action from p is required, because q will eventually receive the information message from p. Then in turn q marks the channel pq as frond edge, and continues to forward the token to another process (if possible).

Example 4.3 In the following undirected network, with p as initiator, one possible computation of Cidon's depth-first search is depicted.

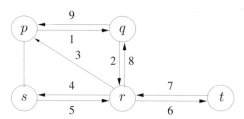

r forwards the token through the frond edge pr before the information message from p reaches r. When the information message from p arrives, r continues to forward the token to s. The information message from p reaches s before the token does, so that s does not send the token to p.

In Cidon's algorithm, frond edges may carry two information messages and two acknowledgments (see exercise 4.2), so the worst-case message complexity is still $4E$. But the worst-case time complexity reduces to $2N - 2$ time units, because at least once per time unit a token is forwarded through a tree edge, and the $N - 1$ tree edges each carry two tokens.

4.2 Tree algorithm

The tree algorithm is a decentralized wave algorithm for undirected, acyclic networks. A process p waits until it has received messages from all its neighbors except one. Then p makes that neighbor its parent and sends a message to it. When p receives a message from its parent, it decides. Always exactly two processes in the network decide, and these two processes consider each other their parent.

Example 4.4 We consider one possible computation of the tree algorithm on the following network.

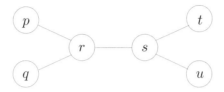

- p and q send a message to r, and make r their parent. Likewise, t and u send a message to s, and make s their parent.
- When the messages from t and u have arrived, s sends a message to r and makes r its parent.
- When the messages from q and s have arrived, r sends a message to p and makes p its parent.
- When p's message has arrived, r decides. Likewise, when r's message has arrived, p decides.

The parent-child relations in the terminal configuration are as follows.

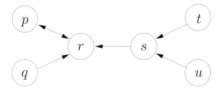

We argue that in each execution of the tree algorithm, exactly two processes decide. As each process sends at most one message, each execution reaches a terminal configuration γ. Suppose, toward a contradiction, that in γ a process p has not sent any message, meaning that it did not receive a message through two of its channels, say qp and rp. Since γ is terminal, q did not send a message to p, which implies it did not receive a message through two of its channels, pq and say sq, and so forth. Continuing this argument, we would establish a cycle of processes that did not receive a message through two of their channels. This contradicts the assumption that the network topology is acyclic. So in γ each process has sent a message, meaning that there have been N messages in total. Since processes send a message into the only channel through which they did not yet receive a message, clearly each channel carries at least one message. An acyclic network has $N - 1$ channels, so exactly one channel carries two messages. Only the two processes t and u connected by this channel decide. All events, except for the reception of t's message and the decision at u, are causally before the decision at t; likewise for the decision at u.

The tree algorithm is incorrect for networks that contain a cycle, because in that case the algorithm does not terminate. For instance, consider a ring of three processes. Since each process has two neighbors, it will wait for a message from one of its neighbors. Hence, all three processes wait for input, meaning that no event ever happens.

The tree algorithm takes at most $\frac{D}{2}$ time units to terminate, if $D > 1$.

4.3 Echo algorithm

The echo algorithm is a centralized wave algorithm for undirected networks. It underlies several of the distributed algorithms presented in the following chapters.

The initiator starts by sending a message to all its neighbors. Intuitively, these messages travel in all directions, and bounce back from the corners of the network toward the initiator. This is achieved as follows. When a noninitiator receives a message for the first time, it makes the sender its parent, and sends a message to all neighbors except its parent. When a noninitiator has received messages from all its neighbors, it sends a message to its parent. Finally, when the initiator has received messages from all its neighbors, it decides.

Example 4.5 We consider one possible computation of the echo algorithm on the following network.

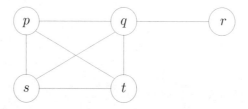

- p sends messages to q, s, and t.
- p's message arrives at q, who makes p its parent and sends messages to r, s, and t.
- q's message arrives at t, who makes q its parent and sends messages to p and s.
- q's message arrives at r, who makes q its parent. Since r has no other neighbors, it sends a message to its parent q straightaway.
- p's message arrives at s, who makes p its parent and sends messages to q and t.
- p's and s's message arrive at t, who sends a message to its parent q.
- r's, s's, and t's message arrive at q, who sends a message to its parent p.

- q's and t's message arrive at s, who sends a message to its parent p.
- q's, s's, and t's message arrive at p, who decides.

The resulting spanning tree is as follows.

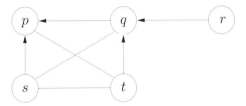

We argue that the echo algorithm is a wave algorithm. Clearly, it constructs a spanning tree that covers the entire network. When a noninitiator joins this tree, at reception of a message from its parent, it sends a message to all its other neighbors. Moreover, the initiator sends a message to all its neighbors. Hence, through each frond edge, one message travels either way. We argue by induction on the size of the network that each noninitiator eventually sends a message to its parent. Consider a leaf p in the spanning tree. Eventually, p will receive a message from all its neighbors (as only the channel to its parent is a tree edge), and send a message to its parent. When this message arrives, we can consider the network without p, in which by induction each noninitiator eventually sends a message to its parent. We conclude that through each channel one message travels either way. So eventually the initiator receives a message from all its neighbors, and decides. All messages are causally before this decision.

In total, the echo algorithm takes $2E$ messages, and it takes at most $2N - 2$ time units to terminate.

Bibliographical notes

Tarry's algorithm originates from [75]. The first distributed depth-first search algorithm was presented in [20]. Awerbuch's algorithm originates from [7], and Cidon's algorithm from [22]. The echo algorithm stems from [18]; the presentation here is based on a slightly optimized version from [70].

Exercises

Exercise 4.1 Give an example of a computation of Awerbuch's algorithm in which an information message and an acknowledgment are communicated through the same tree edge.

Exercise 4.2 Give an example of a computation of Cidon's algorithm in which two information messages and two tokens are communicated through the same channel in the network.

Exercise 4.3 Argue that the tree algorithm takes at most D time units to terminate, in case we take into account the time needed to communicate the decision to all processes.

Exercise 4.4 Consider an undirected network of $N > 3$ processes $p_0, \ldots, p_{N-1}$, where $p_1, \ldots, p_{N-1}$ form a ring and p_0 has a channel to all other processes. (Note that this network has diameter 2.) Give a computation of the echo algorithm on this network, with p_0 as initiator, that takes N time units to complete.

Exercise 4.5 Argue that the echo algorithm takes at most $2N - 2$ time units to terminate.

Exercise 4.6 [76] Suppose you want to use the echo algorithm in a network where duplication of messages may occur. Which modification should be made to the algorithm?

Exercise 4.7 [76] Let each process initially carry a random integer value. Adapt the echo algorithm to compute the sum of these integer values. Explain why your algorithm is correct.

5
Deadlock Detection

A process may wait for other processes to send or be ready to receive some input, or for some resource to become available. A deadlock occurs if a process is doomed to wait forever. This happens if there is a cycle of processes waiting either for each other or for a resource occupied by another process in the cycle. The first type of deadlock is called a *communication deadlock*, while the second type is called a *resource deadlock*.

Deadlock detection is a fundamental problem in distributed computing, which requires determining a permanent cyclic dependency within a running system. For this purpose, the global configuration of the distributed system is regularly examined by individual processes to detect whether a deadlock has occurred. That is, snapshots are taken of the global configuration of the system, and these are examined for cycles. In case a deadlock is detected, the basic algorithm may be rolled back and processes may be restarted in order to remove the detected deadlock. Here we focus on detection of deadlocks and ignore rollback.

5.1 Wait-for graphs

A *wait-for graph* depicts dependencies between processes and resources. A node in a wait-for graph can represent either a process or a resource. Both communication and resource deadlocks can be captured by so-called N-*out-of-*M *requests*, where $N \leq M$. For example, if a process is waiting for one message from a group of M processes, then $N = 1$; or, if a database transaction first has to lock M files, then $N = M$.

A nonblocked node u in a wait-for graph can issue an N-out-of-M request, meaning that it sends a request to M other nodes and becomes blocked until N of these requests have been granted. In the wait-for graph, a directed edge is drawn from u to each of the M nodes to which u issued the N-out-of-M request. Only nonblocked nodes can grant a request. Every time a node v grants u's request, the edge uv can be removed from the wait-for graph. When N requests have been granted, u becomes unblocked and informs the remaining $M - N$ nodes that u's request can be purged; accordingly, the $M - N$ outgoing edges of u are removed from the wait-for graph.

The following example shows how a wait-for graph can be used to model communication deadlocks.

Example 5.1 Suppose process p must wait for a message from process q. In the wait-for graph, p sends a request to q; as a result, an edge pq is created and p becomes blocked. When q sends a message to p, the request from p is granted. Then the edge pq is removed from the wait-for graph, and p becomes unblocked.

The following example shows how a wait-for graph can be used to model resource deadlocks.

Example 5.2 Suppose two different processes p and q want to claim a resource, while at any time only one process can own the resource.

– Nodes u and v, representing p and q, respectively, send a request to node w, representing the resource. As a result, in the wait-for graph, edges uw and vw are created.
– The resource is free, and w sends a grant to say u, so that p can claim the resource. In the wait-for graph, the edge uw is removed.
– The resource must be released by p before q can claim it. Therefore, w sends a request to u, creating an edge wu in the wait-for graph.
– After p releases the resource, u grants the request from w. Then the edge wu is removed from the wait-for graph.
– Now w can grant the request from v, so that q can claim the resource. In the wait-for graph, the edge vw is removed and an edge wv is created.

In wait-for graphs, an M-out-of-M request with $M > 1$ (also called AND request) is drawn with an arc through the M edges, while a 1-out-of-M request (also called OR request) is drawn without an arc. For example, for $M = 3$,

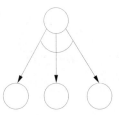 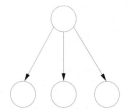

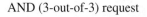

AND (3-out-of-3) request   OR (1-out-of-3) request

The examples in this chapter do not contain any N-out-of-M requests with $1 < N < M$.

5.2 Bracha-Toueg algorithm

To try to detect a deadlock with regard to an ongoing execution of a basic algorithm, first a snapshot can be taken of the corresponding wait-for graph. A process that suspects it is deadlocked, starts a Lai-Yang snapshot to compute the wait-for graph (see section 3.2). To distinguish subsequent snapshots, snapshots (and their control messages) are tagged with a sequence number. Each node u takes a local snapshot to determine the requests it sent or received that were not yet granted or purged, taking into account the grant and purge messages in the snapshot of its incoming edges. Then it computes two sets of nodes:

- Out_u: the nodes u has sent a request to that were not yet granted or purged.
- In_u: the nodes u has received a request from that were not yet granted or purged.

A static analysis on the computed wait-for graph may reveal deadlocks:

- Nonblocked nodes in the wait-for graph can grant requests.
- When a request has been granted, the corresponding edge in the wait-for graph is removed.
- When a node u with an outstanding N-out-of-M request has received N grants, u becomes unblocked. The remaining $M-N$ outgoing edges of u in the wait-for graph are removed.

When no more grants are possible, nodes that are still blocked in the wait-for graph are deadlocked in the snapshot of the basic algorithm.

We consider two examples. Granted requests are drawn as dashed arrows (they are no longer part of the wait-for graph).

Example 5.3 The next wait-for graph contains three 2-out-of-2 requests. Blocked nodes are colored gray.

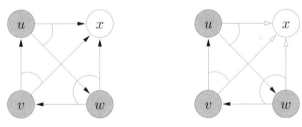

The unblocked node x grants the three incoming requests. After that the three other nodes remain blocked, so no other requests can be granted. Hence, these three nodes are deadlocked.

Example 5.4 The next wait-for graph contains two 2-out-of-2 requests and one 1-out-of-2 request.

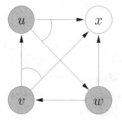 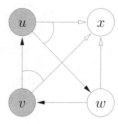

The unblocked node x grants the three incoming requests. As a result node w becomes unblocked, which purges its remaining request to v and grants the incoming request from u. Next, node u becomes unblocked, which grants the last pending request in the graph.

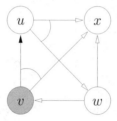 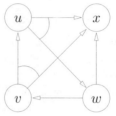

Finally, all nodes have become unblocked, so no nodes are found to be deadlocked.

Let the basic algorithm run on an undirected network, and suppose a wait-for graph has been computed. The Bracha-Toueg deadlock detection algorithm provides a distributed method to perform the static analysis for cleaning out the wait-for graph to try to find deadlocks. The nodes in the wait-for graph start to resolve grants, in the manner described before. Initially, $requests_u$ is the number of grants node u requires in the wait-for graph to become unblocked. When $requests_u$ is or becomes 0, u sends grant messages to all nodes in In_u. When u receives a grant message, $requests_u \leftarrow requests_u - 1$. If after termination of this deadlock detection run $requests > 0$ at the initiator, then it is deadlocked in the basic algorithm.

A key question is how to determine that deadlock detection has terminated. In principle, nodes could apply a termination detection algorithm from chapter 6. However, the Bracha-Toueg algorithm is designed in such a way that termination detection comes for free. We now explain in detail how the nodes choreograph cleaning out the wait-for graph. Initially, $notified_u = false$ and $free_u = false$ at all nodes u; these two variables ensure that u executes at most once the routine $Notify_u$ and $Grant_u$, respectively, given below. The initiator v of deadlock detection starts the resolution of grants throughout the wait-for graph by executing $Notify_v$. It consists of sending a **notify** message into all outgoing edges, and executing $Grant_v$ in case $requests_v = 0$. Noninitiators u that receive a **notify** message for the first time execute $Notify_u$. Moreover, nodes u that are or become unblocked, meaning that $requests_u = 0$, grant all pending requests, by executing $Grant_u$. The pseudocode for the procedure $Notify_u$ is:

$notified_u \leftarrow true$;
send $\langle$**notify**$\rangle$ to all $w \in Out_u$;
if $requests_u = 0$ **then**
    perform procedure $Grant_u$;
end if
await $\langle$**done**$\rangle$ from all $w \in Out_u$;

And the pseudocode for the procedure $Grant_u$ is:

$free_u \leftarrow true$;
send $\langle$**grant**$\rangle$ to all $w \in In_u$;
await $\langle$**ack**$\rangle$ from all $w \in In_u$;

Note that since $Grant_u$ is a subcall of $Notify_u$, waiting for **ack** messages postpones the sending of **done** messages.

If a node u receives a **notify** message from a neighbor v, it does the following:

if $notified_u = false$ **then**
    perform procedure $Notify_u$;
end if
send $\langle$**done**$\rangle$ to v;

If a node u receives a **grant** message from a neighbor v, it does the following:

if $requests_u > 0$ **then**
    $requests_u \leftarrow requests_u - 1$;
    if $requests_u = 0$ **then**
        perform procedure $Grant_u$;
    end if
end if
send $\langle$**ack**$\rangle$ to v;

Note that if u receives a **notify** message and $notified_u = true$ (meaning that u already executed $Notify_u$), or a **grant** message and the assignment $requests_u \leftarrow requests_u - 1$ does not set $requests_u$ from 1 to 0 (meaning that u does not become unblocked by the **grant** message), then u immediately sends back a **done** or **ack** message, respectively.

While a node is awaiting **done** or **ack** messages, it can process incoming **notify** and **grant** messages. The **done** (and **ack**) messages are used for termination detection. That is, when the initiator v has received a **done** message from all nodes in Out_v, it checks the value of $free_v$. If it is still $false$, v concludes that it is deadlocked.

Example 5.5 Suppose the following wait-for graph, consisting of one 2-out-of-2 request and two 1-out-of-1 requests, has been computed in a snapshot. Initially, $requests_u = 2$, $requests_v = requests_w = 1$, and $requests_x = 0$.

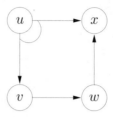

We consider one possible computation of the Bracha-Toueg algorithm.

- Initiator u starts by sending a **notify** to v and x, and must now await a **done** from both v and x before it can examine $requests_u$ to see whether it is deadlocked.

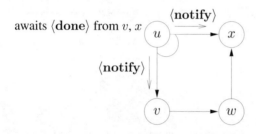

- The **notify** from u is received at v, who sends a **notify** to w and must await a **done** from w before it can send a **done** back to u. Concurrently, the **notify** from u is received at x, who sends a **grant** to u and w, because $requests_x = 0$, and must await an **ack** from both u and w before it can send a **done** back to u.

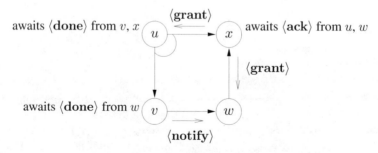

- The **notify** from v is received at w, who sends a **notify** to x and must await a **done** from x before it can send a **done** to v. Concurrently, the **grant** from x is received at u, who sends an **ack** back to x immediately, because the **grant** decreases $requests_u$ from 2 to 1. Next, the **grant** from x is received at w, who sends a **grant** to v, because $requests_w$ decreases from 1 to 0, and must await an **ack** from v before it can send an **ack** back to x.

5.2 Bracha-Toueg algorithm

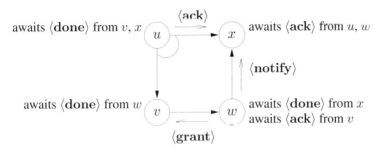

- The **notify** from w is received at x, who sends a **done** back to w immediately. Next, the **ack** from u is received at x, so that x only needs an **ack** from w in order to send a **done** to u. Concurrently, the **grant** from w is received at v, who sends a **grant** to u, because $requests_v$ decreases from 1 to 0, and must await an **ack** from u before it can send an **ack** back to w.

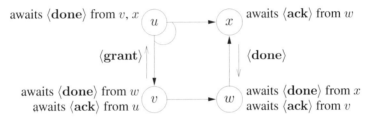

- The **done** from x is received at w, who can now send a **done** to v. Concurrently, the **grant** from v is received at u, who decreases $requests_u$ from 1 to 0 and sends an **ack** back to v immediately, because there are no requests for u to grant.

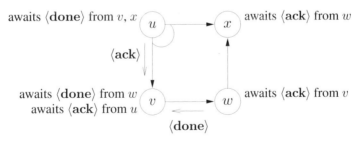

- The **done** from w is received at v, who can now send a **done** to u. Next, the **ack** from u is received at v, who can now send an **ack** to w.

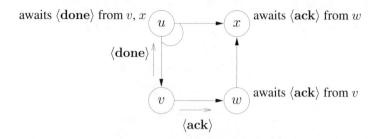

- The **done** from v is received at u, who now only awaits a **done** from x before it can examine $requests_u$ to see whether it is deadlocked. Concurrently, the **ack** from v is received at w, who can now send an **ack** to x.

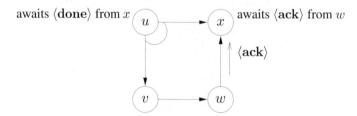

- The **ack** from w is received at x, who can now send a **done** to u.

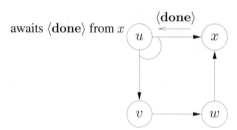

- The **done** from x is received at u, who now examines that $requests_u = 0$, and concludes that it is not deadlocked.

We argue that when the initiator completes its *Notify* call, the Bracha-Toueg algorithm has terminated. The idea is that we can distinguish two types of trees. First, by assuming that each node receiving a **notify** message for the first time makes the sender its parent, we obtain a tree T rooted in the initiator. The **notify/done** messages construct T and travel through (part of) the network similar to the echo algorithm (see section 4.3). Second, by assuming that each node receiving a **grant** message that sets $requests$ to 0 makes the sender its parent, we obtain disjoint trees T_v, each rooted in a node v where from the start $requests_v = 0$. Again, the **grant/ack** messages construct T_v and travel through the network similar to the echo algorithm. A noninitiator v that is the root of a tree T_v only sends a **done** to its parent in T when all **grant**'s sent by nodes in T_v have been acknowledged. This implies that when the initiator completes its *Notify* call, not only all **notify**'s but also all **grant**'s in the network have been acknowledged. So at that moment there are no messages in transit or pending messages.

We argue that the Bracha-Toueg algorithm is deadlock-free. That is, the initiator will eventually complete its *Notify* call. Namely, replying with a **done** (to a **notify**) or **ack** (to a **grant**) is delayed by a node u only if it is executing $Grant_u$ because $requests_u$ is 0 (in case of **done**) or has become 0 by the **grant** (in case of an **ack**), and u is awaiting **ack**'s. We note that there cannot be a cycle of nodes that sent a **grant** to the next node and must wait before sending an **ack** to the previous node in the cycle: such a cycle would always contain a node v of which $requests_v$ was not set to 0 by a **grant** from a node in this cycle. This implies that always some node will be able to respond to a pending **notify** or **grant**.

As we said before, if after resolving the wait-for graph the initiator remains blocked, then it is deadlocked in the snapshot. Namely, the Bracha-Toueg algorithm cleans out the part of the wait-for graph that is reachable from the initiator as much as possible. So if the initiator remains blocked, this means it is part of a cycle of nodes waiting for each other.

In case of a communication deadlock (see example 5.1) the other direction also holds: if the initiator is deadlocked when the snapshot is taken, then it will remain blocked in the wait-for graph. In case of resource deadlock this only holds if resource requests are granted nondeterministically (see exercise 5.6). Namely, as shown in example 5.2, modeling resource deadlock means that removing one edge (in the example, wu) may automatically mean the introduction of another edge (in the example, wv). The Bracha-Toueg approach to resolving edges in wait-for graphs does not take into account this automatic creation of edges.

Bibliographical notes

The Bracha-Toueg algorithm originates from [12].

Exercises

Exercise 5.1 Give one possible computation of the Bracha-Toueg algorithm on the wait-for graph in example 5.5, with v as initiator.

Exercise 5.2 Let node u initiate a deadlock detection run in which the following wait-for graph is computed.

5 Deadlock Detection

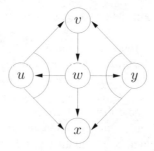

Give one possible computation of the Bracha-Toueg algorithm on this wait-for graph.

Exercise 5.3 Let node u initiate a deadlock detection run in which the wait-for graph from the previous exercise is computed, with as only difference that w is waiting for a 2-out-of-3 (instead of a 1-out-of-3) request. Give one possible computation of the Bracha-Toueg algorithm.

Exercise 5.4 Give a computation on a wait-for graph in which $free_u$ remains $false$ for some noninitiator u after running the Bracha-Toueg algorithm, while u is not deadlocked in the basic algorithm.

Exercise 5.5 Suppose node u sends a request to node v, then purges this request, and next sends another request to v. Let the purge message reach v first, then the second request, and finally the first request. How should v process these three messages?

Exercise 5.6 Suppose that the order in which resource requests are granted is predetermined. Give an example of a snapshot with a resource deadlock that is not discovered by the Bracha-Toueg algorithm.

Show that in case of a nondeterministic selection which resource request is granted, the deadlock in your example may be avoided.

6
Termination Detection

In the previous chapter we looked at deadlocks, in which some processes are doomed to wait for input forever. In the current chapter we turn our attention to the related problem of termination. A distributed algorithm is terminated if all processes are in a terminal state and no (basic) messages are in transit. Termination detection is a fundamental and challenging problem in distributed computing because no process has complete knowledge of the global configuration of the network. Moreover, a terminated process may be reactivated by a message from another process, and absence of messages in the network must be established.

The basic algorithm is the algorithm for which termination is being detected, and the control algorithm is the termination detection algorithm employed for this task. The control algorithm in general consists of two parts: termination detection and announcement. The announcement part, called *Announce*, is straightforward; we therefore focus on the termination detection part. Ideally, termination detection does not require freezing the basic execution.

From the viewpoint of the control algorithm, a simple description of the process states in the basic algorithm suffices. A process is either in an active state if it has not terminated yet, or in a passive state if it has terminated. We are moreover interested in send and receive events, to determine whether there are basic messages under way. As for internal events, we are only interested in those that change a process state from active to passive. A passive process becomes active again upon reception of a basic message. So the abstract view on processes is as follows.

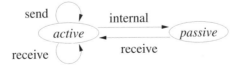

We will consider termination detection techniques based on maintaining trees of active processes (section 6.1), dividing a fixed weight over the active processes and basic messages (section 6.2), waves tagged with logical clock values (section 6.3), and token-based traversal (section 6.4).

6.1 Dijkstra-Scholten algorithm

The Dijkstra-Scholten algorithm is a termination detection algorithm for a centralized basic algorithm on an undirected network. The idea is to build a tree, rooted in the initiator of the basic algorithm, which contains all active processes, and passive ones that have active descendants in the tree. If a basic message from a process p makes a process q active, then q becomes a child of p in the tree. A process can quit the tree only if it is passive and has no children left in the tree. In that case, it informs its parent that it is no longer a child. Termination is detected by the initiator when the tree has disappeared.

To be more precise, initially the tree T consists only of the initiator. Each process p maintains a child counter cc_p that estimates from above its number of children in T. Initially, this counter is zero at all processes. The control algorithm works as follows. When a process p sends a basic message m, it increases cc_p by one, because the receiver q may become active upon reception of m. When the message arrives at q, either q joins T with parent p if q was not yet in T, or otherwise q sends an acknowledgment to p that it is not a new child. Upon reception of an acknowledgment, p decreases cc_p by one. When a process in T is passive and its counter is zero, it quits T. When a noninitiator quits T, it sends an acknowledgment to its parent that it is no longer its child. Finally, when the initiator quits T, it calls *Announce*.

Example 6.1 We consider one possible computation of a basic algorithm supplied with the Dijkstra-Scholten algorithm, on an undirected ring of three processes p, q, r.

- At the start, the initiator p sends basic messages to q and r, and sets cc_p to 2. Upon receipt of these messages, q and r both become active, and join T with parent p.
- q sends a basic message to r, and sets cc_q to 1. Upon receipt of this message, r sends back an acknowledgment, which causes q to decrease cc_q to 0.
- p becomes passive. (Since $cc_p = 2$, it remains in T.)
- r becomes passive. Since $cc_r = 0$, it sends an acknowledgment to its parent p, which causes p to decrease cc_p to 1.
- q sends a basic message to r, and sets cc_q to 1.
- q becomes passive. (Since $cc_q = 1$, it remains in T.)
- Note that all three processes are now passive, but there is still a message traveling from q to r. Upon receipt of this message, r becomes active again, and joins T with parent q.
- r becomes passive. Since $cc_r = 0$, it sends an acknowledgment to its parent q, which causes q to decrease cc_q to 0.
- Since q is passive and $cc_q = 0$, it sends an acknowledgment to its parent p, which causes p to decrease cc_p to 0.
- Since p is passive and $cc_p = 0$, it calls *Announce*.

When all processes have become passive and all basic messages have been acknowledged, clearly the tree T will eventually disappear, and the initiator will call

Announce. Conversely, since active processes and processes that sent a basic message that did not yet reach its destination are guaranteed to be in T, the initiator only calls *Announce* when the basic algorithm has terminated.

The Shavit-Francez algorithm generalizes the Dijkstra-Scholten algorithm to decentralized basic algorithms. The idea is to maintain not one tree, but a forest of (disjoint) trees, one for each initiator. Initially, each initiator constitutes a tree in the forest. A process can only join a tree if it is not yet in a tree in the forest. For the rest, the algorithm proceeds exactly as the Dijkstra-Scholten algorithm. The only distinction is that when an initiator detects that its tree has disappeared, it cannot immediately call *Announce*. Instead, the initiator starts a wave, tagged with its ID, in which only processes that are not in a tree participate, and the decide event calls *Announce*. If such a wave does not complete, this is not a problem, because then another initiator of which the tree has not yet disappeared will start a subsequent wave. And the last tree to disappear is guaranteed to start a wave that will complete.

Example 6.2 We consider one possible computation of a basic algorithm supplied with the Shavit-Francez algorithm, on an undirected ring of three processes p, q, r.

- At the start, the initiators p and q both send a basic message to r, and set cc_p and cc_q to 1. Next, p and q become passive.
- Upon receipt of the basic message from p, r becomes active and makes p its parent. Next, r receives the basic message from q, and sends back an acknowledgment, which causes q to decrease cc_q to 0.
- Since q became passive as the root of a tree, and $cc_q = 0$, it starts a wave. This wave does not complete, because p and r refuse to participate.
- r sends a basic message to q, and sets cc_r to 1. Next, r becomes passive.
- Upon receipt of the basic message from r, q becomes active, and makes r its parent. Next, q becomes passive, and sends an acknowledgment to its parent r, which causes r to decrease cc_r to 0.
- Since r is passive and $cc_r = 0$, it sends an acknowledgment to its parent p, which causes p to decrease cc_p to 0.
- Since p became passive as the root of a tree, and $cc_p = 0$, it starts a wave. This wave completes, so that p calls *Announce*.

6.2 Weight-throwing algorithm

In weight-throwing termination detection, for a centralized basic algorithm on a directed network, the initiator is given a certain amount of weight. During a computation, this weight is divided over active processes and basic messages in transit. Every time a basic message is sent, the sender transfers some (but not all) of its weight to the message. And every time a basic message is received, the receiver adds the weight of the message to its own weight. When a noninitiator becomes passive, it returns its weight to the initiator (possibly via some other processes, in case there is no direct channel to the initiator). When the initiator is passive and has regained its original weight, it calls *Announce*.

Example 6.3 We consider one possible computation of a basic algorithm supplied with the weight-throwing algorithm on an undirected ring of three processes p, q, r.

- At the start, the initiator p has weight 12. It sends basic messages to q and r, with weight 6 and 3, respectively, and reduces its own weight to 3. Upon receipt of these messages, q and r become active, with weight 6 and 3.
- q sends a basic message to r, with weight 3, and reduces its own weight to 3. Upon receipt of this message, r increases its weight to 6.
- p becomes passive. (Since it has weight less than 12, it does not yet call *Announce*.)
- r becomes passive, and sends a control message to p, returning its weight 6. Upon receipt of this message, p increases its weight to 9.
- q sends a basic message to r, with weight 1.5, and reduces its own weight to 1.5.
- q becomes passive, and sends a control message to p, returning its weight 1.5. At receipt of this message, p increases its weight to 10.5.
- Note that all three processes are now passive, but there is still a message traveling from q to r. Upon receipt of this message, r becomes active again, with weight 1.5.
- r becomes passive again. It sends a control message to p, returning its weight 1.5. At receipt of this message, p increases its weight to 12. Since p is passive, it calls *Announce*.

When all processes have become passive and there are no basic messages in transit, clearly all weight will eventually be returned to the initiator, who will then call *Announce*. Conversely, since all active processes and basic messages carry some weight, it is guaranteed that the initiator detects termination only when all processes are passive and there are no basic messages in transit.

The Achilles heel of this simple and effective termination detection scheme is *underflow*: the weight at a process can become too small to be divided further. Two solutions have been proposed for this problem.

The first solution is that a process p where underflow occurs gives itself extra weight. If p is a noninitiator, it must send a control message to the initiator that more weight has been introduced in the system, for else the initiator could call *Announce* prematurely. To avoid race conditions, p must wait for an acknowledgment from the initiator before it can continue sending basic messages. Otherwise, the initiator could regain its original weight before the control message from p has reached it.

The second solution is that p starts a weight-throwing termination detection subcall. Then p only returns its weight to the initiator when it has become passive and its subcall has terminated. The weights originating from the initiator and from p must be maintained separately.

6.3 Rana's algorithm

Rana's algorithm detects termination for a decentralized basic algorithm on an undirected network. It exploits waves that carry a clock value provided by a logical clock (see chapter 2). Each basic message is acknowledged, so that a process can determine whether all the basic messages it sent have reached their destination.

To understand Rana's algorithm, it is helpful to first consider an incorrect termination detection algorithm, which uses waves without clock values. Let a process become *quiet* if (1) it is passive, and (2) all the basic messages it sent have been acknowledged. Then it starts a wave, tagged with its ID. Only quiet processes take part in this wave. If a wave completes, its initiator calls *Announce*. Note that there can be multiple concurrent waves; each process must keep track of its state in each of these waves.

The problem with this termination detection algorithm is that a process p that was not yet visited by a wave may make a quiet process q that already took part in the wave active again. After that p may become quiet, and take part in the wave. Then the wave can complete while q is active.

To avoid this scenario, a logical clock provides each event with a time stamp. The time stamp of a process is the highest time stamp of its events so far (initially it is zero). As we said, each basic message is acknowledged, and a process becomes quiet if (1) it is passive, and (2) all the basic messages it sent have been acknowledged. Then it starts a wave, tagged with its ID *and its time stamp t*. Only quiet processes *that have been quiet from some logical time $\leq t$ onward* take part in this wave. If a wave completes, its initiator calls *Announce*.

Actually, Rana's algorithm does not require a full-blown logical clock. It suffices if only the control messages (acknowledgments and wave messages) are taken into account. That is, a wave tagged with time stamp t puts the clock of each recipient to t (if its value is not $\geq t$ already), and each acknowledgment is tagged with the time stamp t' of the sender and puts the clock of the receiver to $t' + 1$ (if its value is not $\geq t' + 1$ already).

Example 6.4 We consider one possible computation of a basic algorithm supplied with Rana's algorithm, using logical time stamps, on an undirected ring of three processes p, q, r.

– Initially, p, q, and r all have logical time 0, and only p is active. It sends basic messages m_1 to q and m_2 to r. The corresponding receive events of these messages make q and r active. Next, they send an acknowledgment $\langle a_1, 0 \rangle$ and $\langle a_2, 0 \rangle$ to p, respectively.
– p and q become passive. Moreover, p receives both acknowledgments, setting its time to 1. Next, p and q both start a wave, tagged with 1 and 0, respectively. The wave of p first visits q, setting its time to 1; q takes part in the wave, because it is quiet from time 0 onward. The wave of q first visits r, which refuses to take part in the wave, because it is active.
– r sends a basic message m_3 to q. Upon receipt of this message, q becomes active and sends back an acknowledgment $\langle a_3, 1 \rangle$. When r receives this acknowledgment, its clock value becomes 2.
– q and r become passive. Next, r refuses to take part in p's wave, because r is quiet from time 2 onward, while the wave is tagged with 1.

– q and r both start a wave, tagged with 1 and 2, respectively. The wave of r completes, and r calls *Announce*.

We argue that Rana's algorithm is a correct termination detection algorithm. When the basic algorithm has terminated, Rana's algorithm will eventually call *Announce*. Namely, each process eventually becomes quiet, when all the basic message it sent have been acknowledged; and when a process becomes quiet, it starts a wave. Suppose a wave, tagged with some time stamp t, does not complete. Then some process does not take part in the wave, so (by the wave) it is not quiet at some time $> t$. When that process becomes quiet, it starts another wave, tagged with some $t' > t$. This implies that when all processes have become quiet, eventually some wave, with the largest time stamp among all waves, is guaranteed to complete.

Conversely, when Rana's algorithm calls *Announce*, the basic algorithm has terminated. Namely, let a wave complete. Suppose, toward a contradiction, that at that moment the basic algorithm has not terminated. Then some process is active, or some basic message is in transit. Since only quiet processes take part in a wave, such a situation can arise only if a quiet process p was first visited by the wave, and then made active again by a basic message m from a process q that was not yet visited by the wave. Note that q can take part in the wave only after it has received an acknowledgment for m from p. Let the wave be tagged with time stamp t. When p takes part in the wave, its logical time becomes at least t. So the acknowledgment from p to q sets the logical time of q to a value greater than t. However, this means that q is not quiet from a logical time $\leq t$, so it cannot take part in the wave. This contradicts the fact that the wave completes. So at the moment the wave completes, the basic algorithm must have terminated.

6.4 Safra's algorithm

Safra's algorithm is a traversal-based termination detection algorithm. A token visits every process in the network, and only passive processes can forward the token. Although Safra's algorithm is centralized, the basic algorithm can be decentralized. The network can be directed. Note that a traversal of the entire network is always feasible, owing to the fact that networks are assumed to be strongly connected.

There are two complications. First, it must be determined whether there are basic messages in transit. In case of a directed network, there is no simple acknowledgment scheme for basic messages. The second complication is that a traversal of passive processes does not guarantee termination. Namely, a traversal-based algorithm can give rise to an execution similar to the counterexample to the flawed termination detection algorithm presented at the start of section 6.3. An active process p may make a passive process that was already visited by the token active again, after which p becomes passive and forwards the token.

To cope with these complications, in Safra's algorithm every process maintains a counter of type integer; initially it is zero. At each outgoing or incoming basic message, the counter is increased or decreased, respectively. Each round trip, the token carries the sum of the counters of the processes it has traversed.

At any time, the sum of all counters in the network is nonnegative, and it is zero if and only if no basic message is in transit. Still, the token may compute a negative sum for a round trip, if a passive process that already forwarded the token receives a basic message, becomes active, and sends basic messages that are received by a process before this same token arrives.

This scenario is dealt with by coloring processes black after receiving a basic message. Initially, all processes are white. When the initiator of the control algorithm becomes passive, it sends a white token, carrying integer value 0, and the initiator becomes white. When a process receives the token, it adds its counter value to the integer value of the token. A noninitiator must wait until it is passive, and then forwards the token. A white noninitiator leaves the color of the token unchanged. A black noninitiator colors the token black, while the process itself becomes white. Eventually, the token returns to the initiator. If the token and the initiator are white, and the integer value of the token is zero, then the initiator calls *Announce*. Otherwise, the initiator waits until it is passive, sends a white token carrying integer value 0 again, and becomes white.

Example 6.5 We consider one possible computation of a basic algorithm supplied with Safra's algorithm on the following directed network.

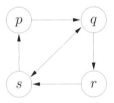

Initially, the token is at the initiator p, only s is active, all processes are white with counter 0, and there are no messages in transit. First, s sends a basic message m to q, setting the counter of s to 1. Now s becomes passive. The token travels around the network, and returns to p white with sum 1. Next, the token travels on from p via q to r, white with sum 0. The message m travels to q and back to s, making them active and black, with counter 0. Now s becomes passive, and the token travels from r via s to p, black with sum 0. Note that s becomes white. Finally, q becomes passive, and after two more round trips of the token (one round trip is needed to color q white), p calls *Announce*.

When all processes have become passive, the token will eventually color them all white. And when there are no messages in transit, the counters of the processes sum up to zero. So in that case the token will return to the initiator colored white and with integer value zero, after which the initiator calls *Announce*. Conversely, if the token returns to the initiator colored white, all processes have been passive and did not receive any messages since the completion of the previous round trip of the token. If, moreover, the token has integer value zero, this implies that no messages are in transit. Hence, the basic algorithm has terminated.

An optimization of Safra's algorithm does away with black tokens. Instead, when a black process p holds the token, it purges the token. As soon as p is passive, it becomes white and sends a fresh token, carrying the counter value of p, and tagged with the p's ID. Suppose the token completes the round trip, meaning that it reaches p, tagged with p. As soon as p is passive, it checks whether p is white and the token's integer value is zero. If so, p calls *Announce*. Otherwise, p purges the token, becomes white, and sends a fresh token, as explained earlier.

Bibliographical notes

The Dijkstra-Scholten algorithm originates from [26], and the Shavit-Francez algorithm from [72]. Weight throwing was proposed in [54]. Rana's algorithm stems from [66]. Safra's algorithm was presented in [25].

Exercises

Exercise 6.1 [76] How much time does the Dijkstra-Scholten algorithm need at most to call *Announce* after the basic algorithm has terminated?

Exercise 6.2 Give a computation of the Shavit-Francez algorithm with two initiators, in which one of the initiators becomes active again after it has become passive, and both initiators concurrently call *Announce*.

Exercise 6.3 Consider weight-throwing termination detection, where in case of underflow at a process p, it gives itself extra weight, and informs the initiator. Give an example to show that if p would not wait for an acknowledgment from the initiator, then the initiator could prematurely detect termination.

Exercise 6.4 Consider the following computation of a decentralized basic algorithm on an undirected ring of size three, with processes p, q and r, where p and q are the initiators. First, p sends a message to q and r and becomes passive, while q sends a message to r. When q receives p's message, it also becomes passive. After reception of the messages from first p and then q, r sends a message to both p and q and becomes passive. After reception of the message from r, p and q send a message to each other, and after reception of these messages become passive.

Add the following termination detection algorithms on top of the basic algorithm, and in each case extend the computation with control messages, to explain how termination is detected.

(a) The Shavit-Francez algorithm.
(b) Rana's algorithm.
(c) Safra's algorithm, with p as initiator of this control algorithm.

Exercise 6.5 Suppose that Rana's algorithm is adapted as follows: only quiet processes that have been quiet from some logical time $< t$ (instead of $\leq t$) onward can take part in a wave tagged with time stamp t. Give an example of a finite computation for which termination would not be detected.

Exercise 6.6 Give an example to show that in Safra's algorithm, coloring sending processes black (instead of receiving ones) is incorrect.

Exercise 6.7 In Safra's algorithm, certain messages do not need to color the receiver black. Only messages that are sent after a token visits the sender and that are received before this same token visits the receiver have to be taken into account. Propose an optimization of Safra's algorithm based on this observation.

Exercise 6.8 [76] Safra's algorithm can be viewed as a snapshot algorithm. Every tour of the token, each process takes a local snapshot when it handles the token. In the constructed snapshot all processes are passive, because the token is handled only by passive processes. Explain how the token's message integer color and value (when the token arrives back at the initiator) capture the consistency and channel states of the snapshot. In particular, argue that the following two claims are true.

1. If the token is white, the snapshot is consistent.
2. If moreover the token's integer value is zero, all channels are empty.

7
Garbage Collection

Each process is provided with memory to store, for example, its local state. An *object* in memory can carry references to other objects, possibly in the memory of other processes. A reference to a local object, which is located at the same process, is called a *pointer*, to distinguish it from a *reference* to a remote object, which is located at another process. An object needs to be kept in memory only if it is accessible by navigating from a *root object*. An object is *garbage* if it cannot be accessed from any root object.

Garbage collection aims to automatically detect and reclaim inaccessible memory objects, in order to free up memory space. The two main techniques for garbage collection are reference counting and tracing. Reference counting, which counts the number of references to an object, is discussed in section 7.1. Tracing, which marks all objects reachable from the root objects, is discussed in section 7.3.

7.1 Reference counting

Reference counting is based on keeping track of the number of references to an object; if it drops to zero, and there are no pointers to the object, the object is garbage.

An advantage of reference counting is that it can be easily performed at runtime. A disadvantage is that cyclic garbage, that is, a cycle of references between garbage objects, is not detected. A separate technique must be added to try and detect such cycles. For instance, a nonroot object that is suspected to be part of cyclic garbage may be virtually deleted. That is, a separate set of reference counts is used to propagate the effects of this trial deletion. If the trial count of the trial-deleted object drops to zero, then it confirms that the object is garbage. In that case, it can be physically deleted.

The owner of an object O, that is, the process where O is located, can easily count the (local) pointers to O. But the challenge is to keep track of the number of (remote) O-references. We distinguish three operations in which processes build or delete a reference to an object O:

48   7 Garbage Collection

- *Creation*: the owner of O sends an O-pointer to another process.
- *Duplication*: a process that is not the owner of O sends an O-reference to another process.
- *Deletion*: an O-reference is deleted, because it has become obsolete.

Reference counting must take into account messages that duplicate a reference. Otherwise, an object could be reclaimed prematurely, if there are no pointers and references to it, but a message is carrying a duplicated reference to this object. One solution is that a process wanting to duplicate a reference must first inform the object owner; the reference is duplicated only after the receipt of the owner's acknowledgment. The drawback of this approach is high synchronization delays. We now discuss two different approaches to avoid such delays.

Indirect reference counting

One method to avoid having to inform the object owner when a reference is duplicated is to maintain a tree for each object, with the object at the root, and the references to this object as the other nodes in the tree. Each reference keeps track where it was duplicated or created from, that is, it stores its parent in the tree. Objects and references are provided with a counter, estimating from above how many children they have in the tree: the counter at an object keeps track how many references to the object have been created, while the counter at a reference keeps track how many times the reference has been duplicated.

When a process receives a reference to an object but already holds a reference to or owns this object, it sends back a decrement to decrease the counter at the sender. A deleted reference can be restored, in case a duplication or creation of this reference is received before its counter has become zero.

When a duplicated (or created) reference has been deleted, and its counter is zero, a decrement message is sent to the process where it was duplicated from (or to the object owner). When the counter of the object becomes zero, and there are no pointers to it, the object can be reclaimed.

Example 7.1 We consider one possible computation with indirect reference counting, on an undirected ring of three processes p, q, r. Let p hold one pointer to the object O.

- p sends O-references to q and r, and sets its counter of created O-references to 2. Upon receipt of these messages, q and r build an O-reference.
- q sends an O-reference to r, and increases its counter of duplicated O-references to 1. Upon receipt of this message, r sends back a decrement message to q, because it already holds an O-reference. Upon receipt of this message, q decreases its counter back to 0.
- p deletes its O-pointer. (Since its counter is 2, O cannot yet be reclaimed by the garbage collector.)
- r deletes its O-reference. Since its counter is 0, r sends a decrement message to p, which causes p to decrease its counter to 1.

- q sends an O reference to r, and increases its counter to 1.
- q deletes its O-reference. (Since its counter is 1, q does not yet send a decrement message to p.)
- Note that there is no pointer or reference to O, but there is still an O-reference traveling from q to r. Upon receipt of this message, r builds an O-reference.
- r deletes its O-reference. Since its counter is 0, r sends a decrement message to q, which causes q to decrease its counter to 0.
- Since q holds no O-reference and its counter is 0, it sends a decrement message to p, which causes p to decrease its counter to 0.
- Since p holds no O-pointer and its counter is 0, O can be reclaimed by the garbage collector.

Weighted reference counting

Another method to avoid having to inform the object owner when a reference is duplicated is to provide each object with a total weight. References are provided with a part of the weight of the object to which they refer. Each object maintains a partial weight that was not yet handed out to references to the object. Initially, the partial weight of an object equals its total weight.

When a reference is created, the partial weight of the object is divided over the object and the reference. That is, the object owner gives some weight to the message responsible for creating this reference, and it deducts this weight from the partial weight of the object. When the message arrives at its destination, either the reference is created with the weight of the message, if the process does not yet hold a reference to this object, or the weight of the message is added to this reference otherwise. Likewise, when a reference is duplicated, the weight of the reference is divided over itself and the copy (except when the reference happens to be duplicated to the object owner, in which case the weight is subtracted from the total weight of the object). When a reference is deleted, the object owner is notified, and the weight of the deleted reference is subtracted from the total weight of the object. When the total weight of the object becomes equal to its partial weight, and there are no pointers to the object, it can be reclaimed.

Example 7.2 We consider one possible computation with weighted reference counting, on an undirected ring of three processes p, q, r. Let p hold one pointer to the object O, which has total and partial weight 12.

- p sends O-references to q and r, with weight 6 and 3, respectively, and reduces the partial weight of O to 3. Upon receipt of these messages, q and r build an O-reference, with weight 6 and 3.
- q sends an O-reference to r, with weight 3, and reduces the weight of its O-reference to 3. Upon receipt of this message, r increases the weight of its O-reference to 6.
- p deletes its O-pointer. (Since the partial weight of O is less than its total weight, O cannot yet be reclaimed by the garbage collector.)

- r deletes its O-reference, and sends a control message to p with weight 6. Upon receipt of this message, p decreases the total weight of O to 6.
- q sends an O-reference to r, with weight 1.5, and decreases the weight of its O-reference to 1.5.
- q deletes its O-reference, and sends a control message to p with weight 1.5. Upon receipt of this message, p decreases the total weight of O to 4.5.
- Note that there is no pointer or reference to O, but there is still an O-reference traveling from q to r. Upon receipt of this message, r builds an O-reference, with weight 1.5.
- r deletes its O-reference, and sends a control message to p with weight 1.5. Upon receipt of this message, p decreases the total weight of O to 3. Since the partial and total weight of O are now equal, and p holds no O-pointer, O can be reclaimed by the garbage collector.

Just as with weight-throwing termination detection, a drawback of weighted reference counting is the possibility of underflow: when the weight of a reference becomes too small to be divided further, no more duplication is possible. There are two possible solutions:

1. The reference increases its weight and tells the object owner to increase its total weight. An acknowledgment from the object owner to the reference is needed before it can be duplicated, to avoid race conditions.
2. The process at which the underflow occurs creates an artificial object, with a reference to the original object. Duplicated references are then to the artificial object, so that references to the original object become indirect.

7.2 Garbage collection implies termination detection

At first sight, garbage collection has little in common with termination detection discussed in the previous chapter. On the other hand, the garbage collection algorithms in the previous section may have reminded you of some of the termination detection algorithms discussed before. This is not a coincidence. It turns out that garbage collection algorithms can be transformed into (existing and new) termination detection algorithms. This works as follows.

Given a basic algorithm. Let each process p host one artificial root object O_p. There is also a special nonroot object Z. Initially, only initiators p hold a reference from O_p to Z. Each basic message carries a duplication of the Z-reference. When a process becomes passive, it deletes its Z-reference. When a process becomes active, it immediately duplicates a Z-reference, owing to the fact that all basic messages carry a Z-reference.

The basic algorithm is terminated if and only if Z is garbage. Namely, if all processes are passive and there are no messages in transit, then clearly there is no Z-reference. And vice versa, if there is an active process or a message in transit, it holds (a duplication of) the Z-reference.

This transformation turns indirect reference counting into Dijkstra-Scholten termination detection (see exercise 7.6), and weighted reference counting into a slight variation of weight-throwing termination detection (see exercise 7.7). Note that examples 7.1 and 7.2 are basically identical to examples 6.1 and 6.3, respectively, but in the context of garbage collection instead of termination detection.

7.3 Tracing

Tracing (or mark-scan) garbage collection consists of two phases. The first phase consists of a traversal of all accessible objects, starting from the root objects; the accessible objects are marked. In the second phase, all unmarked objects are reclaimed.

An advantage of this approach, compared to reference counting, is that it detects all garbage, including cyclic garbage. A disadvantage is that it tends to require freezing the basic execution. In spite of this drawback, tracing has become much more widely used than reference counting, since it has become the method of choice for garbage collection within Java. A key to this success has been the division of objects into two generations.

There are two standard ways to perform the second phase of tracing, in which unmarked objects are reclaimed.

- *Mark-copy*: copy all marked objects to contiguous empty memory space.
- *Mark-compact*: compact all marked objects in the current memory space.

Copying is significantly faster than compaction, because marked objects are copied without changing the memory structure. However, in the long run copying leads to a fragmentation of the memory space.

In practice, most objects either can be reclaimed shortly after their creation, or stay accessible for a very long time. This observation is exploited by generational garbage collection, in which objects are divided into two generations. Garbage in the young generation is collected frequently using mark-copy, while garbage in the old generation is collected sporadically using mark-compact. A newly created object starts in the young generation. If it stays accessible for a certain amount of time (or for a certain number of garbage collection runs), it is moved from the young to the old generation.

Bibliographical notes

The technique to detect cyclic garbage mentioned at the start of this chapter originates from [79]. Indirect reference counting was put forward in [64], and weighted reference counting was proposed independently in [10] and [80]. The derivation of termination detection algorithms from garbage collection algorithms is due to [77]. Generational garbage collection stems from [49].

Exercises

Exercise 7.1 Give an example of cyclic garbage where trial deletion of one object does not help to detect garbage.

Exercise 7.2 Consider the following computation of a basic algorithm on an undirected ring of size three, with processes p, q, and r, where p owns an object O. Initially, there is one O-pointer. First, p sends a message to q and r, both containing a created O-reference. Next, p deletes the O-pointer. At arrival of the message from p, q and r create an O-reference. Now q and r send a message to each other, both containing a duplicated O-reference, and delete their O-reference. At arrival of these messages, q and r create an O-reference again. Finally, q and r both delete their O-reference.

Explain for each of the following two garbage collection algorithms how it is detected that O has become garbage.

(a) Indirect reference counting.
(b) Weighted reference counting.

Exercise 7.3 Argue the correctness of indirect as well as weighted reference counting.

Exercise 7.4 In weighted reference counting, why is underflow much more likely to happen than overflow of a reference counter?

Exercise 7.5 Consider solution 1 for dealing with underflow in weighted reference counting. Give an example to show that if the process where the weight is increased would not wait for an acknowledgment from the object owner, then the object owner could prematurely mark the object as garbage.

Exercise 7.6 Show, using the technique from section 7.2, that indirect reference counting gives rise to Dijkstra-Scholten termination detection.

Exercise 7.7 Show, using the technique from section 7.2, that weighted reference counting gives rise to a variation of weight-throwing termination detection, in which the initiator cannot reuse weight that was returned to it. Also take into account solution 1 in case of underflow.

8
Routing

When a process wants to send a message to another process in the network that is not a direct neighbor, the message needs to be routed through the network. Especially for the Internet, effective routing algorithms are of vital importance. Each process q maintains a routing table, which stores for each destination $p \neq q$ the distance of q to p as well as a neighbor r of q: each message with destination p that arrives at q is passed on to r. We assume that each channel c is provided with a positive weight $weight(c)$, and will discuss algorithms that route messages via shortest paths, meaning that the sum of the weights of the traversed channels is minimal.

8.1 Chandy-Misra algorithm

The Chandy-Misra algorithm is a centralized routing algorithm (also called single-source shortest path algorithm) for undirected networks. It computes a sink tree consisting of shortest paths to the initiator.

Each process p maintains values $dist_p$ and $parent_p$, where $dist_p$ is the length of the shortest known path from p to the initiator, and $parent_p$ the process after p on this path. Initially, the variable $dist$ at the initiator has value 0, $dist_p = \infty$ (that is, infinity) for each noninitiator p, and $parent_p = \bot$ (that is, undefined) for all processes p.

The algorithm starts with messages $\langle \mathbf{dist}, 0 \rangle$, which the initiator sends to all its neighbors, informing them that the initiator knows a path to itself of distance 0.

When a process p receives a message $\langle \mathbf{dist}, d \rangle$ from a neighbor q, it checks whether $d + weight(pq) < dist_p$. If yes, p has found a shorter path to the initiator via q, so it changes $dist_p$ into $d + weight(pq)$ and $parent_p$ into q, and communicates the improved estimate to all neighbors except q in the form of a message $\langle \mathbf{dist}, dist_p \rangle$. If no, p simply purges the incoming message from q.

A termination detection algorithm has to be used on the side. For instance, one could employ the Dijkstra-Scholten algorithm (see section 6.1).

8 Routing

Example 8.1 We consider the longest possible computation of the Chandy-Misra algorithm on the following network, with initiator p.

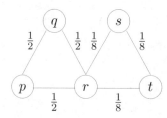

Initially, $dist_p = 0$ and $dist_q = dist_r = dist_s = dist_t = \infty$, while $parent = \bot$ at all five processes.

- p sends $\langle \mathbf{dist}, 0 \rangle$ to q and r.
- When p's message arrives at q, $dist_q \leftarrow \frac{1}{2}$ and $parent_q \leftarrow p$, and q sends $\langle \mathbf{dist}, \frac{1}{2} \rangle$ to r.
- When q's message arrives at r, $dist_r \leftarrow 1$ and $parent_r \leftarrow q$, and r sends $\langle \mathbf{dist}, 1 \rangle$ to p, s and t.
- p purges r's message.
- When r's message arrives at s, $dist_s \leftarrow \frac{9}{8}$ and $parent_s \leftarrow r$, and s sends $\langle \mathbf{dist}, \frac{9}{8} \rangle$ to t.
- When s's message arrives at t, $dist_t \leftarrow \frac{5}{4}$ and $parent_t \leftarrow s$, and t sends $\langle \mathbf{dist}, \frac{5}{4} \rangle$ to r.
- r purges t's message.
- When r's message arrives at t, $dist_t \leftarrow \frac{9}{8}$ and $parent_t \leftarrow r$, and t sends $\langle \mathbf{dist}, \frac{9}{8} \rangle$ to s.
- s purges t's message.
- When p's message (finally) arrives at r, $dist_r \leftarrow \frac{1}{2}$ and $parent_r \leftarrow p$, and r sends $\langle \mathbf{dist}, \frac{1}{2} \rangle$ to q, s and t.
- q purges r's message.
- When r's message arrives at s, $dist_s \leftarrow \frac{5}{8}$ and $parent_s \leftarrow r$, and s sends $\langle \mathbf{dist}, \frac{5}{8} \rangle$ to t.
- When s's message arrives at t, $dist_t \leftarrow \frac{3}{4}$ and $parent_t \leftarrow s$, and t sends $\langle \mathbf{dist}, \frac{3}{4} \rangle$ to r.
- r purges t's message.
- When r's message arrives at t, $dist_t \leftarrow \frac{5}{8}$ and $parent_t \leftarrow r$, and t sends $\langle \mathbf{dist}, \frac{5}{8} \rangle$ to s.
- s purges t's message.

We argue that the Chandy-Misra algorithm computes shortest paths toward the initiator. A safety property of the algorithm is that any process p with $dist_p < \infty$ has a shortest path to the initiator with weight at most $dist_p$. Namely, this property holds initially, and is an invariant: if p receives a message $\langle \mathbf{dist}, d \rangle$ from a neighbor q, then there is a path from p via q to the initiator with weight at most $d + weight(pq)$; so (even) if p changes $dist_p$ into $d + weight(pq)$, the property is preserved. We now reason that for each process p, $dist_p$ will eventually attain the weight of a shortest path from p to the initiator, by induction on the number of channels in such a path. The base case, where p is the initiator, is trivial, because then $dist_p$ is 0 from the start. In the inductive case, let a shortest path from p to the initiator start with the channel pq. By induction, eventually $dist_q$ will attain the weight of a shortest path from q to the initiator; this path cannot go via p, because channels carry positive weights. So q will send $\langle \mathbf{dist}, dist_q \rangle$ to p, and at reception of this message, $dist_p$ will equal the weight of a shortest path from p to the initiator. Finally, if p is a noninitiator, then a shortest path from p to the initiator goes via $parent_p$, because $parent_p$ is updated at each improvement of $dist_p$.

The worst-case message complexity of the Chandy-Misra algorithm is exponential, since there can be exponentially many different cycle-free paths from a process to the initiator, which may be discovered in decreasing order of weight (see exercise 8.3). In case of *minimum-hop paths* in unweighted networks (in other words, each channel has weight 1), the worst-case message complexity of computing shortest paths to all processes in the network drops down to $O(N^2 E)$. Namely, for each process, the algorithm requires at most $O(NE)$ messages to compute all shortest paths to this process: the longest cycle-free path has at most length $N - 1$, so each process sends at most $N - 1$ messages to its neighbors. In case of minimum-hop paths, the sink tree forms a breadth-first search tree.

8.2 Merlin-Segall algorithm

The Merlin-Segall algorithm is a centralized algorithm to compute all shortest paths to the initiator. The underlying idea is to bring structure to the Chandy-Misra algorithm by letting it proceed in rounds. In each round, distance messages à la Chandy-Misra flow up and down the sink tree similar to the echo algorithm, and distance values are updated. At the end of each round, the sink tree is restructured.

Initially, after round 0, the variable $dist$ at the initiator has value 0, $dist_p = \infty$ for each noninitiator p, and the $parent_p$ values form a sink tree with the initiator as root. Such a sink tree can be built by means of a centralized wave algorithm from chapter 4.

Each round > 0 is started by the initiator, which sends the message $\langle \mathbf{dist}, 0 \rangle$ to its neighbors, to inform them that the initiator has a shortest path to itself of length 0.

Let a noninitiator p receive a message $\langle \mathbf{dist}, d \rangle$ from a neighbor q.

- If $d + weight(pq) < dist_p$, then $dist_p \leftarrow d + weight(pq)$ (and p stores q as future value for $parent_p$).
- If $q = parent_p$, then p sends $\langle \mathbf{dist}, dist_p \rangle$ to its neighbors except q.

When p has received a message from all its neighbors in the current round, it sends $\langle \mathbf{dist}, dist_p \rangle$ to $parent_p$, and moves to the next round. If p updated $dist_p$ in the last round, then p updates $parent_p$ to the neighbor whose message is responsible for the current value of $dist_p$. The initiator starts a new round after it has received a message from all its neighbors in the current round.

After round $n \geq 0$, for each process p with a shortest path to the initiator that consists of $\leq n$ channels, $dist_p$ and $parent_p$ have achieved their ultimate value. This is easy to see by induction on n. The base case $n = 0$ is trivial, because at the initiator the variables $dist$ and $parent$ have value 0 and $\perp$ from the start. Now consider the inductive case: a noninitiator p with a shortest path of $\leq n + 1$ channels to the initiator. Let pq be the first channel in this path. Then process q has a shortest path of $\leq n$ channels to the initiator. By the induction hypothesis, after round n, $dist_q$ has obtained its ultimate value. So in round $n + 1$, p receives the message $\langle \mathbf{dist}, dist_q \rangle$ from q. Therefore, $dist_p$ and $parent_p$ have achieved their ultimate values at the end of round $n + 1$. Since shortest paths consist of at most $N - 1$ channels, the Merlin-Segall algorithm can terminate after round $N - 1$.

Example 8.2 We consider one possible computation of the Merlin-Segall algorithm on the following undirected network. The original sink tree, after round 0, consists of edges qr, rp, and sp.

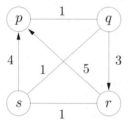

The computation determines the correct sink tree toward the initiator p only at the end of round 3, because (1) there is a shortest path of length three, (2) we start with a sink tree that has nothing in common with the correct sink tree, and (3) every round we let messages in the opposite direction of the sink tree travel very fast, so that processes send messages to their neighbors early on.

The five pictures below show one possible progression of round 1. Process names and channel weights are omitted from these pictures. Messages that are depicted with a solid arrow head are toward a parent. In the first picture, p has sent out messages $\langle \mathbf{dist}, 0 \rangle$. In the second picture, r and s have received this message from their parent p, computed distances 5 and 4, and sent $\langle \mathbf{dist}, 5 \rangle$ and $\langle \mathbf{dist}, 4 \rangle$, respectively, to their other neighbors. In the third picture, q has received $\langle \mathbf{dist}, 5 \rangle$ from its parent r, computed distance 8, and sent $\langle \mathbf{dist}, 8 \rangle$ to its other neighbors. In the fourth picture, s has received $\langle \mathbf{dist}, 8 \rangle$ from q and $\langle \mathbf{dist}, 5 \rangle$ from r, sent $\langle \mathbf{dist}, 4 \rangle$ to its parent p, and made p its parent (again); moreover, q has received $\langle \mathbf{dist}, 0 \rangle$ from p and $\langle \mathbf{dist}, 4 \rangle$ from s, computed an improved distance 1, sent $\langle \mathbf{dist}, 1 \rangle$ to its parent r, and made p its new parent. In the fifth picture, r has received $\langle \mathbf{dist}, 1 \rangle$ from q and $\langle \mathbf{dist}, 4 \rangle$ from s, computed an improved distance 4, sent $\langle \mathbf{dist}, 4 \rangle$ to its parent p, and made q its new parent. When the three messages traveling toward p have reached their destination, round 2 is started.

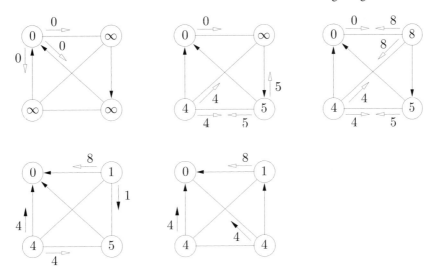

The depictions of the other two rounds are given without further explanations, as they are similar to round 1. The five pictures below show one possible progression of round 2.

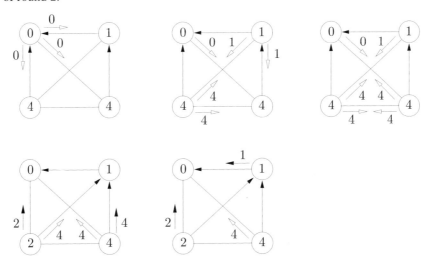

Finally, the five pictures below show one possible progression of round 3.

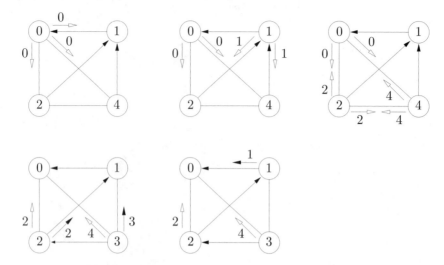

Now the computation has terminated. In the terminal configuration, the correct shortest paths toward p have been computed, leading from r to s to q to p.

The message complexity of the Merlin-Segall algorithm is $\Theta(N^2 E)$. Namely, for each root, the algorithm requires $(N-1)2E$ messages: in $N-1$ rounds, two messages travel through each channel.

The Merlin-Segall algorithm can be adapted to make it robust against topology changes. When a channel fails or becomes operational, the adjacent processes send a special control message toward the initiator via the sink tree. If the failed channel happens to be a tree edge, then the remaining tree is extended to a complete sink tree toward the initiator again. If the special control message meets a failed tree edge, it is discarded. This is no problem, because the other side of this tree edge already sends a control message toward the initiator. When the initiator receives this control message, it starts a new set of N rounds, with a higher number. This number is attached to the messages in this run of the algorithm.

8.3 Toueg's algorithm

Toueg's algorithm is a decentralized algorithm that generalizes the well-known Floyd-Warshall algorithm to a distributed setting. It is an all-pairs shortest path algorithm, meaning that it computes a shortest path between any pair of processes. The idea behind the Floyd-Warshall algorithm is to compute, for each set S of processes, a distance function $d^S(p, q)$, denoting the length of a shortest path between p and q with all *intermediate* processes in S. The following equations hold:

$$d^S(p,p) = 0,$$
$$d^{\emptyset}(p,q) = weight(pq) \text{ if } p \neq q \text{ and there is a channel } pq.$$
$$d^{\emptyset}(p,q) = \infty \text{ if } p \neq q \text{ and there is no channel } pq.$$
$$d^{S \cup \{r\}}(p,q) = \min\{d^S(p,r) + d^S(r,q), d^S(p,q)\} \text{ for each } r \notin S.$$

The first equation is obvious. For the second and third equations, note that if $S = \emptyset$, then a path between two distinct processes p and q with all intermediate processes in S can only consist of a channel between p and q. The fourth equation expresses that a shortest path between p and q with all intermediate processes in $S \cup \{r\}$ either visits r or does not; in the first case this path has length $d^S(p,r) + d^S(r,q)$, and in the second case it has length $d^S(p,q)$.

The Floyd-Warshall algorithm starts with $S = \emptyset$, in which case the first three equations completely define d^S. As long as S does not contain all processes, a so-called pivot $r \notin S$ is selected, and $d^{S \cup \{r\}}$ is computed from d^S using the fourth equation; then r is added to S. Finally, note that if S contains all processes, then d^S is the standard distance function.

Transferring this algorithm to a distributed setting gives rise to two complications. First, all processes must uniformly select the pivots in the same order. Therefore, we make the (strong) assumption that each process knows from the start the IDs of all processes in the network. Second, in each pivot round, the pivot r must broadcast its routing table, because a process p may need to know $d^S(r,q)$ in order to compute $d^{S \cup \{r\}}(p,q)$.

In Toueg's algorithm, each process p starts with $S_p = \emptyset$, and maintains values $dist_p(q)$ and $parent_p(q)$ for each process q, where $dist_p(q)$ is the length of the shortest known path from p to q, and $parent_p(q)$ the process after p on this path. Initially, $dist_p(p) = 0$ and $parent_p(p) = \bot$, while for each $q \neq p$, either $dist_p(q) = weight(pq)$ and $parent_p(q) = q$ if there is a channel pq, or $dist_p(q) = \infty$ and $parent_p(q) = \bot$ otherwise.

In each successive round, the same pivot r is selected by all processes, and added to all sets S_p. The pivot r broadcasts its values $dist_r(q)$ for all processes q. If $parent_p(r) = \bot$ for a process $p \neq r$ in this pivot round, then $dist_p(r) = \infty$, so $dist_p(r) + dist_r(q) \geq dist_p(q)$ for all processes q. Therefore, processes that are not in the sink tree toward r do not need the routing table of r. Hence, this sink tree can be used in the opposite direction to broadcast $dist_r$. To facilitate this use of r's sink tree, in the r-pivot round, each process p sends $\langle \mathbf{request}, r \rangle$ to $parent_p(r)$ if it is not $\bot$, to let it pass on the values $dist_r(q)$ to p. Next, p acts as follows.

- If p is not in the sink tree of r, then p immediately completes the r-pivot round.
- Suppose p is in the sink tree of r (that is, $parent_p(r) \neq \bot$ or $p = r$). If $p \neq r$, then p waits until it has received the values $dist_r(q)$ from $parent_p(r)$. It forwards these values to the neighbors that send $\langle \mathbf{request}, r \rangle$ to p. Moreover, p checks for each process q whether $dist_p(r) + dist_r(q) < dist_p(q)$, and if so, performs $dist_p(q) \leftarrow dist_p(r) + dist_r(q)$ and $parent_p(q) \leftarrow parent_p(r)$.

After completing the r-pivot round, p performs $S_p \leftarrow S_p \cup \{r\}$. Finally, p either proceeds to the next pivot round, if S_p does not contain all processes, or terminates otherwise.

Example 8.3 We give a computation of Toueg's algorithm on the following network, with pivot order $p\ q\ r\ s$.

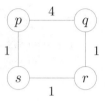

Initially, $dist_t(t) = 0$ for all four processes t, $dist_t(u) = weight(tu)$ if there is a channel tu, and all other $dist$ values are ∞. And $parent_t(u) = u$ if t is a direct neighbor of u, and all other $parent$ values are $\perp$.

In the p-pivot round, q and s both send $\langle \textbf{request}, p \rangle$ to p. So the distance values of p are sent to q and s, but not to r, which is not yet in the sink tree of p. As a result, q and s discover a path to each other via p, so that $dist_q(s)$ and $dist_s(q)$ are set to 5, and $parent_q(s)$ and $parent_s(q)$ to p.

In the q-pivot round, p, r, and s send $\langle \textbf{request}, q \rangle$ to q, q, and p, respectively. So the distance values of q are sent to p, r, and s. As a result, p and r discover a path to each other via q, so that $dist_p(r)$ and $dist_r(p)$ are set to 5, and $parent_p(r)$ and $parent_r(p)$ to q.

In the r-pivot round, p, q, and s send $\langle \textbf{request}, r \rangle$ to q, r, and r, respectively. So the distance values of r are sent to p, q, and s. As a result, q and s discover a shorter path to each other via r, so that $dist_q(s)$ and $dist_s(q)$ are set to 2, and $parent_q(s)$ and $parent_s(q)$ to r.

In the s-pivot round, p, q, and r send $\langle \textbf{request}, x \rangle$ to s, r, and s, respectively. So the distance values of s are sent to p, q, and r. As a result, p and r discover a shorter path to each other via s, so that $dist_p(r)$ and $dist_r(p)$ are set to 2, and $parent_p(r)$ and $parent_r(p)$ to s. Moreover, p and q discover a shorter path to each other via s, so that $dist_p(q)$ and $dist_q(p)$ are set to 3, $parent_p(q)$ to s, and $parent_q(p)$ to r.

The worst-case message complexity of Toueg's algorithm is $O(NE)$: there are N pivot rounds, and each round takes $O(E)$ messages.

By adding messages to inform neighbors that no distance values for the current round need to be forwarded (so negative counterparts of **request** messages), it can be avoided that processes need to store distance values of pivots from past rounds indefinitely.

A drawback of Toueg's algorithm (next to uniform selection of pivots) is that all distance values of a pivot are sent through the sink tree of the pivot, which gives rise to a high bit complexity. This overhead can be reduced as follows. When a process p in the sink tree of the pivot r receives the distance values of r, it first performs for each process q the check whether $dist_p(r) + dist_r(q) < dist_p(q)$. Now p only needs to forward those values $dist_r(q)$ for which this check yields a positive result (see exercise 8.9).

8.4 Frederickson's algorithm

We now discuss a centralized algorithm to compute a breadth-first search tree toward the initiator, in an undirected (unweighted) network. We first consider a simple version of this algorithm, in which the processes at distance n from the initiator are discovered in round n.

Initially (after round 0), the variable $dist$ at the initiator has value 0, $dist_p = \infty$ for each noninitiator p, and $parent_p = \bot$ for all processes p. After each round $n \geq 0$, the breadth-first search tree has been constructed up to depth n: for each process p at a distance $k \leq n$ from the initiator, $dist_p = k$, and p knows which neighbors are at distance $k-1$; and if p is a noninitiator, then it has a parent in the sink tree toward the initiator.

We explain what happens in round $n+1$. It can be depicted as follows:

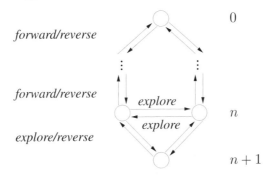

At the start of the round, messages $\langle \textbf{forward}, n \rangle$ travel down the tree, from the initiator to processes at depth n. When a process p at depth n receives this message, it sends $\langle \textbf{explore}, n+1 \rangle$ to its neighbors that are not at depth $n-1$. When such a neighbor q receives this message, it acts as follows, depending on whether $dist_q$ is ∞, $n+1$, or n:

- If $dist_q = \infty$, then $dist_q \leftarrow n+1$, $parent_q \leftarrow p$, and q sends back $\langle \textbf{reverse}, true \rangle$, informing p that q is a child of p.
- If $dist_q = n+1$, then q stores that p is at depth n and sends back $\langle \textbf{reverse}, false \rangle$, informing p that q is not a child of p.
- If $dist_q = n$, then q interprets $\langle \textbf{explore}, n+1 \rangle$ as a negative reply to the message $\langle \textbf{explore}, n+1 \rangle$ that q sent (or will send) to p.

A process p at depth n waits until all messages $\langle \textbf{explore}, n+1 \rangle$ have been answered with a $\langle \textbf{reverse}, \_ \rangle$ or $\langle \textbf{explore}, n+1 \rangle$. Likewise, a noninitiator p at a depth $< n$ waits until all messages $\langle \textbf{forward}, n \rangle$ have been answered with a $\langle \textbf{reverse}, \_ \rangle$. In both cases p sends $\langle \textbf{reverse}, b \rangle$ to its parent, where $b = true$ only if new processes were added to its subtree.

The initiator waits until all messages $\langle \textbf{forward}, n \rangle$ (or, in case of round 1, $\langle \textbf{explore}, 1 \rangle$) have been answered with a $\langle \textbf{reverse}, \_ \rangle$. If no new processes were added in round $n+1$, then the initiator terminates, and it may inform all other processes that the breadth-first search has terminated. Otherwise, the initiator continues with round $n+2$; processes in the tree only send a **forward** to children that reported new processes in round $n+1$.

The worst-case message complexity of this breadth-first search algorithm is $O(N^2)$. Namely, there are at most $N+1$ rounds, and in each round tree edges carry at most one **forward** and one replying **reverse**, adding up to at most $2(N-1)N$ messages. And in total, channels carry one **explore** and one replying **reverse** or **explore**, adding up to $2E$ messages. The worst-case time complexity is also $O(N^2)$: round n is completed in at most $2n$ time units, for $n = 1, \ldots, N$, and $2(1 + 2 + \cdots + N) = N(N+1)$.

The idea behind Frederickson's algorithm is that in the breadth-first search algorithm described earlier, **forward** messages need to travel up and down the tree often, as each round only discovers processes that are one level deeper than the ones discovered in the previous round. Efficiency can be gained by exploring several levels in one round. However, **explore** messages then give a performance penalty, because they may travel through the same channel multiple times in one round. Notably, if we abolished **forward** messages and used only **explore** messages to discover all processes in one round, we would be back at the Chandy-Misra algorithm, which we have seen is not efficient. Therefore, the number of levels explored in one round is included as a parameter ℓ. At the end, an optimal value for ℓ will be determined.

Initially (after round 0), the variable $dist$ at the initiator has value 0, $dist_p = \infty$ for each noninitiator p, and $parent_p = \bot$ for all processes p. After each round $n \geq 0$, the breadth-first search tree has been constructed up to depth ℓn: for each process p at a distance $k \leq \ell n$ from the initiator, $dist_p = k$, and p knows which neighbors are at distance $k-1$; and if p is a noninitiator, then it has a parent in the sink tree toward the initiator.

At the start of round $n+1$, messages $\langle \textbf{forward}, \ell n \rangle$ travel down the tree, from the initiator to processes at depth ℓn. When a process at depth ℓn receives this message, it sends $\langle \textbf{explore}, \ell n + 1 \rangle$ to its neighbors that are not at depth $\ell n - 1$. The parameter in this message is (an overapproximation of) the depth of the receiving process; this value is increased by one every time the message is forwarded. When this parameter becomes divisible by ℓ, the ℓ levels for the current round have been explored.

Compared to the simple breadth-first search algorithm discussed before, there are two complications. First, a process q may receive a **forward** from a neighbor p that is not its parent. This can happen if in the previous round p temporarily was q's parent, but q later selected another parent with a shorter path to the initiator, and p sent the **forward** to q before being informed that q is no longer its child (see exercise 8.13). Such a **forward** can simply be purged by q. Second, a process may send multiple **explore**s into a channel, if its distance value is improved several times in one round. Therefore, **reverse**s in reply to **explore**s are supplied with a distance parameter, so that a process can distinguish to which **explore** an incoming **reverse** is a reply.

Let a process q receive a message $\langle \textbf{explore}, k \rangle$ from a neighbor p. We consider two cases.

- $k < dist_q$.
  Then $dist_q \leftarrow k$ and $parent_q \leftarrow p$.
  * If k is not divisible by ℓ, then q sends $\langle \textbf{explore}, k+1 \rangle$ to its neighbors except p. Next, q waits until it has received $\langle \textbf{reverse}, k+1, \_ \rangle$ or $\langle \textbf{explore}, j \rangle$ with $j \in \{k, k+1, k+2\}$ from all these neighbors. Then q sends $\langle \textbf{reverse}, k, true \rangle$ to p. Only neighbors that reply with $\langle \textbf{reverse}, k+1, true \rangle$ are children of q in the tree. (Unless q also receives a message $\langle \textbf{explore}, k \rangle$ from such a neighbor, in which case the sender is not a child of q.)

    If, later, q receives a message $\langle \textbf{explore}, k' \rangle$ with $k' < k$, then q changes its distance to k', makes the sender its parent, sends messages $\langle \textbf{explore}, k'+1 \rangle$, and waits for replies to these messages before sending $\langle \textbf{reverse}, k', true \rangle$ to its new parent.
  * If k is divisible by ℓ, then q sends $\langle \textbf{reverse}, k, true \rangle$ to p immediately.
- $k \geq dist_q$.
  * If k is not divisible by ℓ, then q does not send a reply to p. In this case q sent $\langle \textbf{explore}, dist_q + 1 \rangle$ into this channel, which already serves as a negative acknowledgment to the current incoming message.
  * If k is divisible by ℓ, then q sends $\langle \textbf{reverse}, k, false \rangle$ to p.

A process p at depth ℓn waits until all messages $\langle \textbf{explore}, \ell n + 1 \rangle$ have been answered with a **reverse** or **explore**. Likewise, a noninitiator p at a depth $< \ell n$ waits until all messages $\langle \textbf{forward}, \ell n \rangle$ have been answered with a **reverse**. In both cases p sends $\langle \textbf{reverse}, b \rangle$ to its parent, where $b = true$ only if new processes were added to its subtree.

The initiator waits until all messages $\langle \textbf{forward}, \ell n \rangle$ (or, in case of round 1, $\langle \textbf{explore}, 1 \rangle$) have been answered with a **reverse**. If no new processes were added in round $n + 1$, then the initiator terminates and may inform all other processes that the breadth-first search has terminated. Otherwise, the initiator continues with round $n + 2$; processes in the tree only send a **forward** to children that reported new processes in round $n + 1$.

Example 8.4 We consider one possible computation of Frederickson's algorithm on the following network, with p as initiator, and $\ell = 3$.

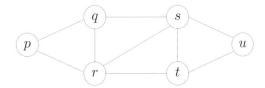

After round 0, $dist_p = 0$, and the distance value of all other processes is ∞; nobody has a parent.

- Round 1 is started by p, who sends $\langle \textbf{explore}, 1 \rangle$ to q and r.
- p's **explore** arrives at q: $dist_q \leftarrow 1$, $parent_q \leftarrow p$, and q sends $\langle \textbf{explore}, 2 \rangle$ to r and s.
- q's **explore** arrives at r: $dist_r \leftarrow 2$, $parent_r \leftarrow q$, and r sends $\langle \textbf{explore}, 3 \rangle$ to p, s and t.
- p purges r's **explore**.
- r's **explore** arrives at s: $dist_s \leftarrow 3$, $parent_s \leftarrow r$, and s sends $\langle \textbf{reverse}, 3, true \rangle$ in reply.
- r's **explore** arrives at t: $dist_t \leftarrow 3$, $parent_t \leftarrow r$, and t sends $\langle \textbf{reverse}, 3, true \rangle$ in reply.
- p's **explore** arrives at r: $dist_r \leftarrow 1$, $parent_r \leftarrow p$, and r sends $\langle \textbf{explore}, 2 \rangle$ to q, s and t.
- r purges the **reverses** from s and t.
- q's **explore** arrives at s: $dist_s \leftarrow 2$, $parent_s \leftarrow q$, and s sends $\langle \textbf{explore}, 3 \rangle$ to r, t, and u.
- r's **explore** arrives at t: $dist_t \leftarrow 2$, and t sends $\langle \textbf{explore}, 3 \rangle$ to s and u.
- s's **explore** arrives at u: $dist_u \leftarrow 3$, $parent_u \leftarrow s$, and u sends back $\langle \textbf{reverse}, 3, true \rangle$.
- t's **explore** arrives at u, who sends back $\langle \textbf{reverse}, 3, false \rangle$.
- r's and t's **explore** and u's **reverse** arrive at s, who sends $\langle \textbf{reverse}, 2, true \rangle$ to q.
- s's **explore** and u's **reverse** arrive at t, who sends $\langle \textbf{reverse}, 2, true \rangle$ to r.
- r's **explore** and s's **reverse** arrive at q, who sends $\langle \textbf{reverse}, 1, true \rangle$ to p.
- s's **explore** and t's **reverse** arrive at r, who sends $\langle \textbf{reverse}, 1, true \rangle$ to p.
- q's and r's **reverse** arrive at p, who starts round 2; no further processes are discovered, after which the computation terminates.

The resulting spanning tree is as follows.

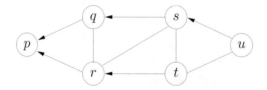

The worst-case message complexity of Frederickson's algorithm, where ℓ levels are explored in each round, is $O(\lceil \frac{N}{\ell} \rceil N + \ell E)$. Namely, there are at most $\lceil \frac{N}{\ell} \rceil + 1$ rounds, and in each round, tree edges carry at most one **forward** and one replying **reverse**, adding up to at most $2 \lceil \frac{N}{\ell} \rceil (N-1)$ messages. And in total, channels carry at most 2ℓ **explore**s and 2ℓ replying **reverse**s, and frond edges carry at most one spurious **forward**, adding up to (fewer than) $(4\ell + 1)E$ messages.

The worst-case time complexity of Frederickson's algorithm is $O(\ell \lceil \frac{N}{\ell} \rceil^2)$: round n is completed in at most $2\ell n$ time units, for $n = 0, \ldots, \lceil \frac{N}{\ell} \rceil$, and $2\ell(1 + 2 + \cdots + \lceil \frac{N}{\ell} \rceil) = \ell \lceil \frac{N}{\ell} \rceil (\lceil \frac{N}{\ell} \rceil + 1)$.

If we take $\ell = \lceil \frac{N}{\sqrt{E}} \rceil$, then both the worst-case message and time complexity are $O(N\sqrt{E})$. So computing a breadth-first search tree toward each process in the network takes $O(N^2 \sqrt{E})$ messages and time in the worst case.

8.5 Packet switching

Consider a network in which routing tables have been computed, so that all processes know how data packets should be forwarded through the network to their destinations. On their way, these packets are stored at a buffer slot of a process, until that process is certain the packet has been stored safely in the buffer of the next process on the packet's route. When a packet reaches its destination it is consumed, that is, removed from the network.

Even with cycle-free routing tables, a store-and-forward deadlock may occur, when a group of packets are all waiting for the use of a buffer slot occupied by a packet in the group. A controller avoids such deadlocks, by prescribing whether a new packet can be generated at a process, or an existing packet can be forwarded to the next process, and possibly in which buffer slot it is put. To avoid a trivial deadlock-free controller that disallows any generation of packets, it is required that generation of a new packet at a process with an empty buffer should always be allowed.

As we said, a process can eliminate a packet from its buffer only when it is sure the packet has arrived safely at the next process. For simplicity, we assume synchronous communication, which basically means that a process can send a packet only when the receiver is ready to receive it. That is, we abstract away from the communication overhead imposed by fruitless attempts to forward a packet.

Destination and hops-so-far controllers

Consider a directed network of processes $p_0, \ldots, p_{N-1}$, and let T_i be the sink tree (with respect to the routing tables) with root p_i for $i = 0, \ldots, N-1$. We discuss two controllers based on these sink trees.

In the destination controller, each process carries N buffer slots, numbered from 0 to $N-1$. The ith buffer slots at the processes are used to mimic the sink tree T_i.

- When a packet with destination p_i is generated at a process q, it is placed in the ith buffer slot of q.
- If qr is an edge in T_i, then a packet in the ith buffer slot of q can be forwarded to the ith buffer slot of r.

The destination controller is deadlock-free. This follows from the fact that, for each i, since T_i is acyclic, packets in the ith buffer slot of any process can always travel to their destination.

Let K be the length of a longest path in any T_i. In the hops-so-far controller, each process carries $K + 1$ buffer slots, numbered from 0 to K.

- When a packet is generated at a process q, it is placed in the 0th buffer slot of q.
- If qr is an edge in some T_i, then for any $j < K$, a packet in the jth buffer slot of q can be forwarded to the $(j + 1)$th buffer slot of r.

We argue that the hops-so-far controller is deadlock-free. It is easy to see, by induction on j, that no packet can get stuck at a $(K - j)$th buffer slot of any process, for $j = 0, \ldots, K$. The base case $j = 0$ is trivial, because a packet in a Kth buffer slot is guaranteed to be at its destination, and so can be consumed. Now consider the inductive case: a packet in a $(K - (j + 1))$th buffer slot. By induction, packets in a $(K - j)$th buffer slot can be forwarded to their destination and consumed. Hence, a packet in a $(K - (j + 1))$th buffer slot can either be consumed or forwarded to a $(K - j)$th buffer slot and from there to its destination where it is consumed.

Acyclic orientation cover controller

An acyclic orientation of an undirected network G is a directed, acyclic network, obtained by directing all the edges of G. Acyclic orientations $G_0, \ldots, G_{n-1}$ of G form an acyclic orientation cover of a set $\mathcal{P}$ of paths in G if each path in $\mathcal{P}$ is the concatenation of paths $P_0, \ldots, P_{n-1}$ in $G_0, \ldots, G_{n-1}$, respectively.

Example 8.5 For each undirected ring there exists a cover, consisting of three acyclic orientations, of the collection of minimum-hop paths. For instance, in case of a ring of size six:

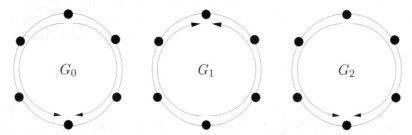

Given an undirected network G, and an acyclic orientation cover $G_0, \ldots, G_{n-1}$ of a set $\mathcal{P}$ of paths in G. In the acyclic orientation cover controller, each process has n buffer slots, numbered from 0 to $n - 1$.

- A packet generated at a process q is placed in the 0th buffer slot of q.
- Let qr be an edge in G_i. For any i, a packet in the ith buffer slot of q can be forwarded to the ith buffer slot of r. Moreover, if $i < n - 1$, then a packet in the ith buffer slot of r can be forwarded to the $(i + 1)$th buffer slot of q.

If all packets are routed via paths in $\mathcal{P}$, then the acyclic orientation cover controller is deadlock-free. Namely, consider a reachable configuration γ. Forward and consume packets until a configuration δ is reached where no forwarding or consumption is possible anymore. We argue by induction on j that in δ each $(n-j)$th buffer slot of any process is empty, for $j=1,\ldots,n$. In the base case $j=1$, consider a packet that is being routed via a concatenation of paths $P_0,\ldots,P_{n-1}$ in $G_0,\ldots,G_{n-1}$. It is not hard to see that when this packet is in a kth buffer slot, it is being routed via a P_ℓ with $\ell \geq k$. This implies that any packet in an $(n-1)$th buffer slot is being routed via G_{n-1}. Since G_{n-1} is acyclic, packets in an $(n-1)$th buffer slot can travel to their destination. Now consider the inductive case: a packet in an $(n-(j+1))$th buffer slot. By induction, in δ all $(n-j)$th buffer slots are empty. Hence, packets in $(n-(j+1))$th buffer slots can be consumed, forwarded via $G_{n-(j+1)}$ since it is acyclic, or forwarded to an $(n-j)$th buffer slot since these are empty. To conclude, in δ all buffer slots are empty.

Example 8.6 For each undirected ring there exists a deadlock-free controller that uses three buffer slots per process and allows packets to travel via minimum-hop paths. This follows from the fact that, according to example 8.5, undirected rings have a cover of the collection of minimum-hop paths that consists of three acyclic orientations. So the resulting acyclic orientation cover controller requires three buffer slots per process.

8.6 Routing on the Internet

The routing approaches discussed so far were not designed to cope with large-sized and dynamic networks. Link-state routing is a pragmatic routing algorithm that has been geared to the Internet.

Each process periodically (and after a network change) sends a *link-state packet* to its neighbors, reporting the channels between the process and its direct neighbors, as well as their weights (typically based on latency or bandwidth). Moreover, it attaches a sequence number to these link-state packets, which is increased every time it broadcasts link-state packets to its neighbors. The link-state packets are flooded through the network, and all processes store their content, so that they obtain a local view of the entire network. Processes also store the sequence numbers of link-state packets on which their local view is based, to avoid that new information is overwritten by old information. With its local view, a process can locally compute shortest paths using a uniprocessor algorithm (mostly Dijkstra's algorithm).

The crash failure and subsequent recovery of a process are eventually detected, and taken into account in the link-state packets broadcast, by its neighbors. When a process recovers from a crash, its sequence number restarts at zero, so that the link-state packets it broadcasts after the crash might be ignored by the other processes for a long time. Therefore, link-state packets carry a *time-to-live field*, defining the moment in time after which the packet becomes stale and may be discarded. To reduce the overhead of flooding, each time a link-state packet is forwarded, its time-to-live field is decreased; when it becomes zero, the packet is discarded.

Link-state routing deals well with dynamicity, but does not scale up to the size of the Internet, because it uses flooding. Therefore, the Internet is divided into so-called autonomous systems, each of which uses link-state routing (notably by means of the OSPF Protocol). Routing between autonomous systems is performed with the Border Gateway Protocol, in which peer routers exchange reachability information, meaning that a router informs its neighbors about updates in its routing table, either because it noticed a topology change, or as a result of an update in the routing table of one of its neighbors. Thus each router maintains an up-to-date routing table based on autonomous system connectivity. When a router connects to the network for the first time, other routers provide it with their entire routing table.

To control congestion in the network, in the Transmission Control Protocol (TCP), processes maintain a congestion window for each of its channels. Packets are acknowledged by the receiver, and the congestion window of a channel provides an upper bound on the number of unacknowledged packets a process is allowed to have sent into this channel. The congestion window grows linearly with each received acknowledgment, up to some threshold. The congestion window may effectively double in size during every round trip time (that is, the time between sending a packet and receiving the corresponding acknowledgment), if all packets are being acknowledged. The congestion window is reset to the initial size (in TCP Tahoe) or halved (in TCP Reno) with each lost data packet.

Bibliographical notes

The Chandy-Misra algorithm originates from [17], the Merlin-Segall algorithm from [60], Toueg's algorithm from [78], and Frederickson's algorithm from [34] (where the algorithm is only sketched). The destination and hops-so-far controllers were proposed in [59] and the acyclic orientation cover controller in [76]. The mechanisms underlying link-state routing were put forward in [56], and a first version of link-state routing was used in ARPANET [57]. Congestion windows can be traced back to [40].

Exercises

Exercise 8.1 Explain in detail how the Dijkstra-Scholten algorithm detects termination in the Chandy-Misra algorithm.

Exercise 8.2 Adapt the Dijkstra-Scholten algorithm so that termination is detected in the Chandy-Misra algorithm without building two distinct sink trees (that is, no separate sink tree is needed for detecting termination).

Exercise 8.3 Let n range over the natural numbers. Generalize example 8.1 to a network with $2n + 1$ processes and $3n$ weighted channels, for which the number of messages sent by the Chandy-Misra algorithm in the worst case grows exponentially (in n). Explain why this is the case.

Exercise 8.4 Run the Merlin-Segall algorithm on the following undirected weighted network, to compute all shortest paths toward process t. Give a computation that takes four rounds before the correct sink tree has been computed.

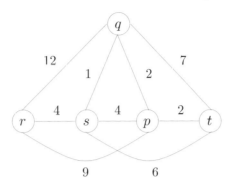

Exercise 8.5 Suppose that in the Merlin-Segall algorithm a process q would update $parent_q$ each time it updates $dist_q$. Explain why the worst-case message complexity would become exponential.

Exercise 8.6 Run Toueg's algorithm on the network in exercise 8.4. Take as pivot order: $p\ q\ r\ s\ t$.

Exercise 8.7 Argue that Toueg's algorithm is an all-pairs shortest path algorithm.

Exercise 8.8 Analyze the space complexity of Toueg's algorithm.

Exercise 8.9 In Toueg's algorithm, when a process $p \neq r$ in the sink tree of the pivot r receives the distance values of r, let p first perform for each process q the check whether $dist_p(r) + dist_r(q) < dist_p(q)$. Explain why p needs only to forward those values $dist_r(q)$ for which this check yields a positive result.

Exercise 8.10 Suppose that channels can carry negative weights. Explain how the output of Toueg's algorithm can be used to detect the presence of a negative-weight cycle of at least two channels.

Exercise 8.11 Apply Frederickson's algorithm with $\ell = 1$ (the "simple" algorithm) to the following undirected network, to find a breadth-first search tree rooted in p. Do the same with $\ell = 2$.

Exercise 8.12 In Frederickson's algorithm, consider a process at k hops from the initiator, with $k \neq \ell n$ for any n. Argue that this process is guaranteed to receive a message $\langle \textbf{reverse}, k+1, \_ \rangle$ or $\langle \textbf{explore}, j \rangle$ with $j \in \{k, k+1, k+2\}$ from all its neighbors.

Exercise 8.13 Give a computation of Frederickson's algorithm on an undirected ring of size three and with $\ell = 2$, to show that a **forward** can be sent to a process that is not a child of the sender.

Exercise 8.14 Argue that Frederickson's algorithm establishes a breadth-first search tree toward the initiator.

Exercise 8.15 Analyze the message and time complexity of Frederickson's breadth-first search algorithm, taking into account the network diameter D.

Exercise 8.16 Develop a distributed version of Dijkstra's celebrated single-source shortest path algorithm for undirected weighted networks. Discuss the worst-case message and time complexity of your algorithm.

Exercise 8.17 [76] Show that there does not exist a deadlock-free controller that uses only one buffer slot per process and allows each process to send packets to at least one other process.

Exercise 8.18 [76] Show that the destination controller is not deadlock-free if packet routing is as follows:

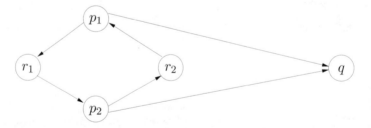

In this picture, packets from p_1 to q are routed via the path $p_1 \, r_1 \, p_2 \cdots q$, and packets from p_2 to q are routed via the path $p_2 \, r_2 \, p_1 \cdots q$.

Exercise 8.19 Argue that the acyclic orientation cover of a ring of size six in example 8.5 covers all shortest paths in this ring.

Exercise 8.20 Give an acyclic orientation cover G_0, G_1 of a set of paths in the following undirected network that contains for each pair of processes p, q a minimum-hop path from p to q.

Describe in detail how the buffer slots are linked in the corresponding acyclic orientation cover controller.

Exercise 8.21 Given the undirected cube, prove that there is an acyclic orientation cover G_0, G_1 such that between every two processes in the cube there is a minimum-hop path that is the concatenation of paths in G_0 and G_1.

Exercise 8.22 Show that for any acyclic undirected network there exists a deadlock-free controller that uses only two buffer slots at each process.

Exercise 8.23 Give an example to show that a *cyclic* orientation cover controller (in which the orientations G_i are allowed to contain cycles) is not always deadlock-free.

Exercise 8.24 Why does the link-state algorithm become less efficient if processes broadcast their entire routing table instead of only their channels and weights?

Exercise 8.25 Argue why a congestion window may effectively double in size during every round trip time.

9
Election

In an election algorithm, the processes in the network elect one process among them as their leader. The aim is usually to let the leader act as the organizer of some distributed task, as the root of a spanning tree of the network, or as the initiator of a centralized algorithm. Each computation must start in a configuration in which the processes are unaware which process will serve as the leader and must terminate in a configuration where exactly one process is the leader.

Election algorithms are decentralized: the initiators can be any nonempty set of processes. We require that all processes have the same local algorithm. This disallows the trivial solution where exactly one process has the algorithm "I am the leader." Process IDs are unique and from a totally ordered set. In chapter 10 we will see that unique IDs are essential to construct election algorithms that always terminate.

9.1 Election in rings

We first consider three election algorithms for ring topologies. In each of these algorithms, the initiators determine among themselves which one has the highest ID. This initiator becomes the leader. Initially, the initiators are active, while all noninitiators are passive. Passive processes are out of the race to become the leader and simply pass on messages.

Chang-Roberts algorithm

The Chang-Roberts algorithm targets a directed ring. Since networks are assumed to be strongly connected, a directed ring is oriented either in a clockwise or in a counterclockwise fashion.

Initially, the initiators send a message to the next process in the ring, tagged with their ID. When an active process p receives a message tagged with q, there are three cases.

- $q < p$: then p purges the message.
- $q > p$: then p becomes passive, and passes on the message.

- $q = p$: then p becomes the leader.

The idea behind the Chang-Roberts algorithm is that only the message with the highest ID will complete the round trip, because every other message is stopped at the latest when it arrives at the initiator with the highest ID (by the first case). Moreover, initiators that do not have the highest ID are made passive at the latest when they receive the message with the highest ID (by the second case). When an initiator receives back its own message, it knows it is the leader (by the third case).

Example 9.1 In the ring below, all processes are initiators. If the ring is directed counterclockwise, then it takes $\frac{1}{2}N(N+1)$ messages to elect process $N-1$ as the leader. Namely, each message is stopped at process $N-1$, so the message from process i travels $i+1$ hops for $i = 0,\ldots,N-1$; and $1+2+\cdots+N = \frac{1}{2}N(N+1)$.

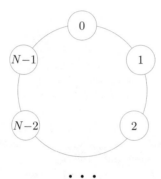

If the ring is directed clockwise, then it takes only $2N-1$ messages to elect process $N-1$ as the leader. Namely, each message is stopped after one hop, except for the message from process $N-1$, which travels N hops.

The preceding example shows that the worst-case message complexity of the Chang-Roberts algorithm is $O(N^2)$. It can be shown, however, that the average-case message complexity is $O(N \log N)$.

Franklin's algorithm

Franklin's algorithm, which requires an undirected ring, improves upon the worst-case message complexity of the Chang-Roberts algorithm. In an election round, each active process p compares its own ID with the IDs of its nearest active neighbors on both sides. If p's ID is the largest of the three IDs, then p proceeds to the next election round. If one of the other IDs is larger than p's ID, then p becomes passive. And if p receives its own ID from either side, then it becomes the leader, because there are no other active processes left in the ring.

To be more precise, at the start of an election round, each active process sends its ID to its neighbors on either side. When an active process p has received messages tagged with q and r from either side, there are three cases:

- $\max\{q,r\} < p$: then p enters another election round by sending its ID in both directions again.
- $\max\{q,r\} > p$: then p becomes passive.
- $\max\{q,r\} = p$: then p becomes the leader.

Since a message can overtake another message from the previous round, processes need to keep track of the parity of their current round number and must attach this parity to the message containing their ID; see the pseudocode of the Dolev-Klawe-Rodeh algorithm in the appendix.

Example 9.2 On the undirected version of the ring in example 9.1, Franklin's algorithm terminates in two rounds. In the first round, only process $N-1$ remains active. In the second round, process $N-1$ finds that it is the leader.

Example 9.3 We run Franklin's algorithm on the following ring, in which all processes are initiators.

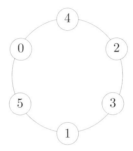

- Processes 3, 4, and 5 progress to the second election round, because their IDs are larger than their (active) neighbors. Processes 0, 1, and 2 become passive in the first round.
- Only process 5 progresses to the third round, because in the second round it finds that its ID is larger than its nearest active neighbors 3 and 4. Process 3 and 4 become passive in the second round, because their nearest active neighbor 5 has a larger ID.
- Finally, in the third round, process 5 finds that it is the leader, because the two messages it sends in either direction complete the round trip.

The worst-case message complexity of Franklin's algorithm is $O(N \log N)$. Namely, in each round with two or more active processes, at least half of the active processes become passive, because for each pair of nearest active neighbors at least one becomes passive. In the final round, the remaining active process becomes the leader. So there are at most $\lfloor \log_2 N \rfloor + 1$ rounds. And each round takes $2N$ messages (two messages per channel).

Dolev-Klawe-Rodeh algorithm

The Dolev-Klawe-Rodeh algorithm transposes the idea behind Franklin's algorithm to a directed ring. In that setting, messages cannot travel in both directions, so that an active process cannot easily compare its own ID p with the IDs q and r of its nearest active neighbors. This is resolved by performing this comparison not at p, but at its next (in the direction of the ring) active neighbor r. That is, the IDs p and q are collected at r. If p is larger than q and r, then r remains active, and progresses to the next election round, in which it assumes the ID p. If p is smaller than q or r, then r becomes passive. And if p equals q and r, then r becomes the leader. If we really want the initiator with the largest ID to become the leader, then in the last case, r could send a special leader message tagged with its last ID around the ring, to inform the initiator that started the election with this ID that it is the leader.

To be more precise, at the start of an election round, each active process sends its ID to its next neighbor, with a 0 attached. When an active process r receives this message $\langle \mathbf{id}, p, 0 \rangle$, it stores the ID p and passes on the message with a 1 attached. And when r receives a message $\langle \mathbf{id}, q, 1 \rangle$, it stores the ID q. Now there are three cases:

- $\max\{q, r\} < p$: then r enters another round with the new ID p by sending $\langle \mathbf{id}, p, 0 \rangle$.
- $\max\{q, r\} > p$: then r becomes passive.
- $\max\{q, r\} = p$: then r becomes the leader (or sends a special leader message tagged with r).

Since a message can overtake another message from the previous round, processes need to keep track of the parity of their current round number and must attach this parity to the message containing their ID; see the pseudocode in the appendix.

Example 9.4 Just as Franklin's algorithm, the Dolev-Klawe-Rodeh algorithm takes just two rounds to terminate on the undirected version of the ring in example 9.1.

This example shows that an active process r that collects IDs p and q in an election round, must really act as if it is the middle process p. If r proceeded to the next round if its own ID were the largest, then it is easy to see that the message complexity of the Dolev-Klawe-Rodeh algorithm on the ring in example 9.1 would become $O(N^2)$.

Example 9.5 We run the Dolev-Klawe-Rodeh algorithm on the ring in example 9.3, oriented in the clockwise direction.

- Processes 0, 1, and 2 progress to the second election round, because they act as processes 5, 3, and 4, respectively. For instance, process 0 collects the IDs 5 (with a 0 attached) and 1 (with a 1 attached); concludes that 5 is the largest ID of 0, 5, and 1; and progresses to the second round with the ID 5. Likewise for processes 1 and 2. Processes 3, 4, and 5 become passive in the first round, because they act as processes 2, 0, and 1, respectively.
- Only process 2 (which assumed the ID 4 for the second round) progresses to the third round, because in the second round it collects the IDs 5 (with a 0 attached) and 3 (with a 1 attached), and concludes that 5 is the largest ID of 4, 5, and 3. Process 0 (which assumed the ID 5) and 1 (which assumed the ID 3) become passive in the second round.

- Finally, in the third round, process 2 (which assumed the ID 5 for the third round) finds that it is the leader, because it receives back its own ID, first with a 0 attached and next with a 1 attached. Alternatively, process 2 can announce to the other processes that 5 is the largest ID in the ring, after which the process that carried the ID 5 at the start of the election becomes the leader.

The worst-case message complexity of the Dolev-Klawe-Rodeh algorithm is the same as of Franklin's algorithm: $O(N \log N)$. Namely, there are at most $\lfloor \log_2 N \rfloor + 1$ rounds, and each round takes $2N$ messages.

It can be shown that $\Omega(N \log N)$ is a lower bound on the average-case message complexity of any election algorithm for rings.

9.2 Tree election algorithm

The tree algorithm from section 4.2 can be used as the basis for an election algorithm in acyclic undirected networks. The idea is that each process p collects IDs from its children, computes the maximum of these IDs and its own ID, and passes on this maximum to its parent. Later, p receives the overall maximum of the IDs in the network from its parent, which p passes on to its children.

In election algorithms the initiators can be any nonempty set of processes, while the tree algorithm starts from all the leaves in the network. Therefore, the tree election algorithm is booted by a wake-up phase, driven by the initiators, which send a wake-up message to all their neighbors. These wake-up messages are then flooded through the network; that is, noninitiators send a wake-up message to their neighbors after they have received a first wake-up message. A process wakes up when it has received wake-up messages from all its neighbors.

The local algorithm at an awake process p is as follows:

- p waits until it has received IDs from all its neighbors except one, which becomes its parent.
- p computes the largest ID $\max_p$ among the received IDs and its own ID.
- p sends a parent message to its parent, tagged with $\max_p$.
- If p receives a parent message from its parent, tagged with q, then it computes $\max'_p$, being the maximum of $\max_p$ and q.
- Next, p sends an information message to all neighbors except its parent, tagged with $\max'_p$.

Each node that receives the information message, tagged with the largest ID in the network, forwards it to its children. Thus the information message is forwarded through the entire network, and eventually the process with the largest ID becomes the leader.

The only tricky part of the algorithm is that if p receives a parent message, tagged with an ID q, from its parent r, then p must compare the ID q with the maximum $\max_p$ it computed before. The reason is that p and r computed the maximum among all IDs in disjoint parts of the network, which together cover the entire network.

Example 9.6 We consider one possible computation of the tree election algorithm on the network below. The wake-up phase is omitted. Messages that are depicted with a solid arrow head are toward a parent.

In the first picture, the leaves 2, 4, 5, and 6 have selected their only neighbor as their parent and sent their ID to their parent. In the second picture, process 1 has received the messages from 2 and 4, calculated the maximum 4, made its remaining neighbor 3 its parent, and sent the maximum to its parent.

In the third picture, process 3 has received the messages from 1 and 6, calculated the maximum 6, made its remaining neighbor 5 its parent, and sent the maximum to its parent. In the fourth picture, processes 3 and 5 have received each other's message, and calculated the maximum 6, concluding that 6 must become the leader; process 3 has moreover sent 6 to its two children.

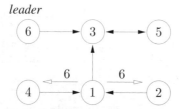

In the fifth picture, processes 1 and 6 have received the message from 3; process 6 has become the leader, while process 1 has sent 6 to its two children. When these two messages have arrived, the algorithm has terminated.

Just as the tree algorithm, the tree election algorithm takes $2N - 2$ messages: two messages per channel. And the wake-up phase also takes $2N - 2$ messages.

9.3 Echo algorithm with extinction

We now discuss an election algorithm for undirected networks that works for any topology. The idea is to let each initiator start a run of the echo algorithm from section 4.3, tagged with its ID. Only the wave started by the initiator with the largest ID completes, after which this initiator becomes the leader. Noninitiators join the first wave that hits them.

At any time, each process takes part in at most one wave. Suppose a process p that is participating in a wave tagged with q is hit by a wave tagged with r.

- If $q < r$, then p makes the sender its parent, changes to the wave tagged with r (it abandons all the wave messages it received earlier), and treats the incoming message accordingly.
- If $q > r$, then p continues with the wave tagged with q (it purges the incoming message).
- If $q = r$, then p treats the incoming message according to the echo algorithm of the wave tagged with q.

If the wave tagged with p completes, by executing a decide event at p, then p becomes the leader.

Waves of initiators that do not have the largest ID among all initiators are guaranteed not to complete (that is, are extinguished), because the initiator with the largest ID will refuse to take part in these waves. Conversely, the wave of the initiator with the largest ID is guaranteed to complete, because each process will eventually switch to this wave.

Example 9.7 We consider a computation of the echo algorithm with extinction on an undirected ring of three processes $0, 1, 2$, which are all initiators.

- The three processes all start a wave, and send a wave message to their two neighbors, tagged with their ID.
- The wave messages from 0, tagged with 0, are purged by 1 and 2.
- 0 receives the wave message from 1, tagged with 1. As a result, 0 changes to 1's wave, makes 1 its parent, and sends a wave message to 2, tagged with 1.
- The wave messages tagged with 1 from 0 and 1 are purged by 2.
- 0 and 1 receive the wave message from 2, tagged with 2. As a result, they change to 2's wave, make 2 their parent, and send a wave message to each other, tagged with 2.
- 0 and 1 receive each other's wave message, tagged with 2. Next, they send a wave message tagged with 2 to their parent 2.
- 2 receives the wave messages from 0 and 1, tagged with 2. As a result, 2's wave decides, and 2 becomes the leader.

The worst-case message complexity of this echo algorithm with extinction is $O(NE)$: there are at most N waves, and each wave uses at most $2E$ messages.

9.4 Minimum spanning trees

We now turn our attention to a topic that at first sight has little to do with election: minimum spanning trees. However, the distributed algorithm for constructing a minimum spanning tree that is discussed in this section will turn out to yield an efficient election algorithm.

Given is an undirected network, in which the channels carry positive weights. A *minimum* spanning tree is a spanning tree of the network for which the sum of the weights of its channels is minimal. They can be employed, for example, to minimize the cost of broadcasting messages through the network.

For convenience we assume that different channels in the network always have different weights; this guarantees that the minimum spanning tree is unique. Alternatively, we could allow different channels to have the same weight, and impose a total order on channels with the same weight, using the IDs of the end points of a channel.

The Gallager-Humblet-Spira algorithm is a distributed version of Kruskal's famous algorithm for computing minimum spanning trees in a uniprocessor setting. We first briefly discuss Kruskal's algorithm, which uses the notion of a *fragment*, being any connected subgraph of the minimum spanning tree. A channel in the network is said to be an *outgoing edge* for a fragment if exactly one of the processes connected by the channel is in the fragment. Kruskal's algorithm is based on the observation that the lowest-weight outgoing edge c of a fragment F is always in the minimum spanning tree. Otherwise, the minimum spanning tree extended with c would contain a cycle, which would include c and another outgoing edge d of F. Replacing d by c in the minimum spanning tree would give another spanning tree of the network, and the sum of the weights of its channels would be smaller than for the minimum spanning tree. This is a contradiction.

In Kruskal's algorithm, initially each process in the network forms a separate fragment. In each step, two different (disjoint) fragments are joined into one fragment via a channel between these fragments that is the lowest-weight outgoing edge for at least one of the two fragments. The algorithm terminates when only one fragment remains.

In a distributed setting, it becomes complicated for a process to decide whether its channels are outgoing edges or not. For each of its channels, it has to communicate with the process at the other side to find out whether it is in the same fragment. And if one of its channels turns out to be an outgoing edge, the process has to work together with the other processes in its fragment to determine whether it is the least-weight outgoing edge for the fragment. And when finally the least-weight outgoing edge for the fragment has been detected, the fragment at the other side of the channel has to be asked to join together, so that the two fragments become one.

In the Gallager-Humblet-Spira algorithm, each fragment carries a *name*, which is a nonnegative real number, and a *level*, which is a natural number. Processes keep track of the name and level of their fragment. Each fragment has a unique name, except initially, when each process starts as a fragment with name and level 0. The level of a fragment is the maximum number of joins any process in the fragment has experienced. When two fragments join, there are two scenarios. If the two joining fragments have different levels, the one with the lowest level copies the name and level of the other fragment (in which case the processes in the other fragment do not experience the join). If they have the same level, the new name of the joint fragment is the weight of the so-called *core edge* via which they are joined, and the level is increased by one.

The core edge of a fragment, that is, the last channel via which two subfragments were joined at the same level, plays a key role in the algorithm. It is the central computing unit of the fragment, to which the processes in the fragment report the lowest-weight outgoing edge they are aware of, and from where the join via the lowest-weight outgoing edge of the fragment is initiated. Each process has a parent, toward the core edge of its fragment (except initially, when fragments consist of a single process). The end points of a core edge are called the *core nodes*; they have each other as parent.

Processes are in one of the following three states:

- *sleep*: this is a special state for noninitiators, so that this algorithm for computing minimum spanning trees can be easily turned in an election algorithm, where we must allow for any nonempty set of initiators. A process that is asleep wakes up as soon as it receives any message.
- *find*: the process is looking for its lowest-weight outgoing edge, and/or waiting for its children to report the lowest-weight outgoing edge they are aware of.
- *found*: the process has reported the lowest-weight outgoing edge it is aware of to its parent, and is waiting either for an instruction from the core edge that a join should be performed via that channel, or for a message informing that a join has been completed elsewhere in the fragment.

Moreover, processes maintain a status for each of their channels:

- *basic edge*: it is undecided whether the channel is part of the minimum spanning tree.
- *branch edge*: the channel is part of the minimum spanning tree.
- *rejected*: the channel is not part of the minimum spanning tree.

Each initiator, and each noninitiator after it has woken up, sets its lowest-weight channel to *branch*, its other channels to *basic*, and its state to *found*. It sends the message $\langle\textbf{connect}, 0\rangle$ into the branch edge, to inform the fragment at the other side that it wants to join via this channel, and that its fragment has level 0.

Let two fragments, one with name fn and level ℓ, and the other with name fn' and level ℓ', be joined via channel pq, where p is in the first and q in the second fragment. Let $\ell \leq \ell'$. As explained before, there are two possible scenarios.

- If $\ell < \ell'$, then in the past p sent $\langle\textbf{connect}, \ell\rangle$ to q, and now q sends the message $\langle\textbf{initiate}, fn', \ell', \frac{find}{found}\rangle$ to p. We write $\frac{find}{found}$ to express that this parameter can be either *find* or *found*, depending on the state q is in.
- If $\ell = \ell'$, then in the past p and q sent $\langle\textbf{connect}, \ell\rangle$ to each other, and now they send $\langle\textbf{initiate}, \text{weight of } pq, \ell+1, find\rangle$ to each other.

At the reception of a message $\langle \mathbf{initiate}, fn, \ell, \frac{find}{found} \rangle$, a process stores fn and ℓ as the name and level of its fragment, assumes the state *find* or *found* depending on the last parameter in the message, and adopts the sender as its parent. It passes on the message through its other branch edges.

In the first scenario, q is in the fragment with the higher level, so that its **initiate** message imposes the name and level of its fragment onto p. Moreover, p makes q its parent, toward the core edge of q's fragment. By forwarding the **initiate** message through its other branch edges, p ensures that all other processes in its fragment update the name and level of their fragment, and select a new parent toward the core edge of q's fragment.

In the second scenario, both fragments have the same level, so that the joint fragment gets a new name, level and core edge. The new name is the weight of the channel pq, the new level is the old level plus one, and the new core edge is pq. Since all processes in both fragments must be informed, p and q send an **initiate** message with the new name and level to each other. As this message is forwarded through the branch edges, the processes in the joint fragment select a new parent toward the core edge pq. The parameter *find* in the **initiate** message makes sure that these processes moreover start looking for the lowest-weight outgoing edge of the joint fragment.

When a process p receives a message $\langle \mathbf{initiate}, fn, \ell, find \rangle$, it starts checking in increasing order of weight whether one of its basic edges pq is outgoing, by sending $\langle \mathbf{test}, fn, \ell \rangle$ to q and waiting for an answer from q. A basic edge pq that was found to be outgoing before has to be tested again, as in the meantime the fragments of p and q may have joined. At reception of the **test** message, q acts as follows.

- If ℓ is greater than the level of q's fragment, then q postpones processing the incoming **test** message, until the level of q's fragment has reached or surpassed ℓ. The reason for this postponement is that p and q might actually be in the same fragment, in which case the message $\langle \mathbf{initiate}, fn, \ell, find \rangle$ is on its way to q.
- If ℓ is not greater than the level of q's fragment, then q checks whether the name of q's fragment is fn. If so, then q replies with a **reject** message to p (except if q is awaiting a reply to a **test** message to p, because then p and q can interpret each other's message $\langle \mathbf{test}, fn, \ell \rangle$ as a **reject**). As a result, p and q will both set the status of the channel pq to *rejected*. If not, then q replies with an **accept** message to p.

When a basic edge is accepted or there are no basic edges left, p stops the search for its lowest-weight outgoing basic edge.

Moreover, p waits for **report** messages through its branch edges, except the one to its parent. Then p sets its state to *found*, and computes the minimum λ_p of these reports and the weight of its lowest-weight outgoing basic edge (or ∞, if no such edge was found). If $\lambda_p < \infty$, then p stores the branch edge through which it received λ_p, or its outgoing basic edge of weight λ_p. Finally, p sends $\langle \mathbf{report}, \lambda_p \rangle$ to its parent.

Only the core nodes receive a **report** message from their parent. If the minimum reported value is ∞, then the core nodes terminate, because then the minimum spanning tree has been computed. If the minimum reported value μ is smaller than

∞, then the core node that received μ first sends a **changeroot** message via branch edges toward the process p that originally reported its channel pq with weight μ as its lowest-weight outgoing basic edge. Here it is used that processes stored their branch edge that reported μ. From then on, the core edge becomes a regular (tree) edge. When p receives the **changeroot** message, it sets the channel pq to *branch*, and sends $\langle$**connect**, $\ell\rangle$ into it, where ℓ is the level of p's fragment.

Let a process q receive a message $\langle$**connect**, $\ell\rangle$ from a neighbor p. We note that the level of q's fragment is at least ℓ: either $\ell = 0$, or q earlier sent **accept** to p, which it could only do if its fragment had a level of at least ℓ, and fragment levels never decrease over time. Now q acts as follows:

- As long as q's fragment has level ℓ and qp is not a branch edge, q postpones processing the **connect** message from p. The reason for this postponement is that q's fragment might be in the process of joining a fragment with a level $\geq \ell$, in which case p's fragment should subsume the name and level of that joint fragment, instead of joining q's fragment at an equal level.
- When the level ℓ' of q's fragment is or becomes greater than ℓ, q sets the channel qp to *branch* and sends $\langle$**initiate**, $fn', \ell', \frac{find}{found}\rangle$ to p, where fn' is the name of q's fragment, and *find* or *found* depends on the state of q.
- When q's fragment has level ℓ and qp is or becomes a branch edge (in which case q sent $\langle$**connect**, $\ell\rangle$ to p), q sends $\langle$**initiate**, weight of qp, $\ell + 1$, $find\rangle$ to p (and vice versa).

In the last case, pq becomes the core edge of the joint fragment.

This completes the description of the Gallager-Humblet-Spira algorithm; we are back at the situation where two fragments are joined at a different or the same level, by means of one or two **initiate** messages, respectively, which was explained before.

Example 9.8 We consider one possible computation of the Gallager-Humblet-Spira algorithm on the following network, in which all processes are initiators.

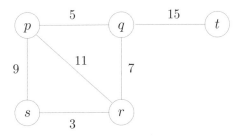

- p and q send $\langle$**connect**, $0\rangle$ to each other, after which they both make the channel pq a branch edge. Since these fragments join at the same level 0, p and q send $\langle$**initiate**, $5, 1, find\rangle$ to each other. Next, p and q send $\langle$**test**, $5, 1\rangle$ to s and r, respectively.

- t sends $\langle \textbf{connect}, 0 \rangle$ to q, after which it makes the channel tq a branch edge. Since the fragment of q is at level 1, q replies with $\langle \textbf{initiate}, 5, 1, \textit{find} \rangle$. Then t sends $\langle \textbf{report}, \infty \rangle$ to its new parent q, as t has no channels except tq.
- r and s send $\langle \textbf{connect}, 0 \rangle$ to each other, after which they both make the channel rs a branch edge. Since these fragments join at the same level 0, r and s send $\langle \textbf{initiate}, 3, 1, \textit{find} \rangle$ to each other. Next, r and s send $\langle \textbf{test}, 3, 1 \rangle$ to q and p, respectively.
- Since the fragments of r and s are at the same level as the fragments of q and p, but have a different name, r and s reply to the **test** message from q and p, respectively, with an **accept** message. As a result, p sends $\langle \textbf{report}, 9 \rangle$ to its parent q, while q sends $\langle \textbf{report}, 7 \rangle$ to its parent p. Because 7 is smaller than 9, q sends $\langle \textbf{connect}, 1 \rangle$ to r.
- Since the fragments of p and q are at the same level as the fragments of s and r, but have a different name, p and q can reply to the **test** message from s and r, respectively, with an **accept** message. As a result, r sends $\langle \textbf{report}, 7 \rangle$ to its parent s, while s sends $\langle \textbf{report}, 9 \rangle$ to its parent r. As 7 is smaller than 9, r sends $\langle \textbf{connect}, 1 \rangle$ to q.
- By the crossing $\langle \textbf{connect}, 1 \rangle$ messages between q and r, the channel between these processes becomes a branch edge as well as the core edge of the new fragment, which has level 2. Messages $\langle \textbf{initiate}, 7, 2, \textit{find} \rangle$ are forwarded through the branch edges. The channels pr and ps are tested (in this order) from either side, both times leading to a reject. Finally, all processes report ∞, and the algorithm terminates.

So the minimum spanning tree consists of the channels pq, qr, qt, and rs.

We argue that the Gallager-Humblet-Spira algorithm is deadlock-free. There are two potential causes for deadlock, because a process q may postpone an incoming message. The first case is if q receives a message $\langle \textbf{test}, \textit{fn}, \ell \rangle$ while ℓ is greater than the level of q's fragment. This postponement does not lead to a deadlock, because there is always a fragment of minimal level, and **test** messages originating from this fragment will be answered promptly. The second case is if q receives a message $\langle \textbf{connect}, \ell \rangle$ while the level of q's fragment equals ℓ and qp is not a branch edge. This postponement also does not lead to a deadlock, because different edges have different weights, so there cannot be a cycle of fragments waiting for a reply to a postponed **connect** message.

The worst-case message complexity of the Gallager-Humblet-Spira algorithm is $O(E + N \log N)$. The summand E is the accumulation of all messages for rejecting channels: each channel outside the minimum spanning tree is rejected by a **test**-**reject** or **test**-**test** pair. This adds up to $2(E - (N - 1))$ messages in total. Furthermore, each process experiences at most $\lfloor \log_2 N \rfloor$ joins, because each time this happens the level at the process increases, and a fragment at a level ℓ contains at least 2^ℓ processes (see exercise 9.6). Each time a process experiences a join, it receives an **initiate** message, and may send the following four messages: one **test** that triggers an **accept** message, a **report**, and a **changeroot** or **connect**. Including the **accept**, these are five messages every time a process experiences a join, adding up to at most $5N \lfloor \log_2 N \rfloor$ messages in total. Thus we have covered all messages in the algorithm.

Finally, as promised at the start of this section, we return to election. By two extra messages at the very end of the Gallager-Humblet-Spira algorithm, the core node with the largest ID can become the leader. This yields an election algorithm for undirected networks.

The lower bound of $\Omega(N \log N)$ for rings mentioned before implies a lower bound of $\Omega(E + N \log N)$ on the average-case message complexity of any election algorithm for general networks. So the message complexity of the Gallager-Humblet-Spira algorithm is optimal.

Bibliographical notes

The Chang-Roberts algorithm originates from [19], and Franklin's algorithm from [33]. The Dolev-Klawe-Rodeh algorithm was proposed independently in [27] and in [63]. The lower bound of $\Omega(N \log N)$ on the average-case message complexity of election algorithms for rings was proved in [61]. The Gallager-Humblet-Spira algorithm stems from [35].

Exercises

Exercise 9.1 [76] Consider the Chang-Roberts algorithm on a directed ring of size N, under the assumption that every process is an initiator. For which distribution of IDs over the ring is the message complexity minimal, respectively maximal, and exactly how many messages are exchanged in these cases? Argue why no distribution of IDs gives rise to fewer or more messages.

Exercise 9.2 [76] Give an initial configuration of a directed ring of size N, with every process an initiator, for which the Dolev-Klawe-Rodeh algorithm requires only two rounds. Also give an initial configuration for which the algorithm requires $\lfloor \log N \rfloor + 1$ rounds.

Exercise 9.3 Give a computation of the tree election algorithm on the network from example 9.6 in which eventually the processes 1 and 4 have each other as parent.

Exercise 9.4 Consider the tree election algorithm.

(a) [76] Show that for undirected networks with a diameter $D > 1$, the time complexity of this algorithm (including the wake-up phase) is at most $2D$.
(b) For $D = 2$, give an example where this algorithm takes four time units to terminate.
(c) Give an example to show that if $D = 1$, this algorithm may take three time units to terminate.

Exercise 9.5 Perform the Gallager-Humblet-Spira algorithm on the following undirected network:

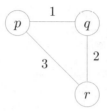

Give one possible computation to determine the minimum spanning tree.

Exercise 9.6 Argue that in the Gallager-Humblet-Spira algorithm, any fragment at a level ℓ always contains at least 2^ℓ processes.

Exercise 9.7 Argue that the Gallager-Humblet-Spira algorithm correctly computes the minimum spanning tree.

Exercise 9.8 Suppose, at some point in the Gallager-Humblet-Spira algorithm, a process reported a lowest-weight outgoing basic edge, and next receives a message $\langle \text{initiate}, \mathit{fn}, \ell, \mathit{find} \rangle$. Explain by means of a scenario why it must test again whether this basic edge is outgoing.

Exercise 9.9 Suppose that, at some point in the Gallager-Humblet-Spira algorithm, a process p receives a message $\langle \text{test}, \mathit{fn}, \ell \rangle$ through channel pq, where p's fragment has a different name than fn and at least level ℓ. Explain why p can send an **accept** message to q, without fear that p and q are in the same fragment.

Exercise 9.10 Consider the following scenario for the Gallager-Humblet-Spira algorithm. In a fragment F with name fn and level ℓ, the core nodes have just determined the lowest-weight outgoing edge of F. Concurrently, another fragment with name fn' and level $\ell' < \ell$ connects to F via a channel qp. Why can we be sure that F has an outgoing edge with a lower weight than pq?

Exercise 9.11 Give an example to show that the Gallager-Humblet-Spira algorithm could get into a deadlock if different channels were allowed to have the same weight. Argue that the deadlock in your example is avoided if a total order is imposed on channels with the same weight.

10
Anonymous Networks

Sometimes the processes in a network are *anonymous*, meaning that they may lack a unique ID. Typically, this is the case if there are no unique hardware IDs (for example, LEGO Mindstorms). Furthermore, when processes do have unique IDs but they cannot reveal their ID to other processes, this is similar to having no unique process IDs at all. For instance, processes may not want to reveal their ID for security concerns, or transmitting/storing IDs may be deemed too expensive, as is the case for the IEEE 1394 serial bus discussed in section 10.7.

In this section we assume that processes (and channels) do not have a unique ID.

10.1 Impossibility of election in anonymous rings

We show that there does not exist an election algorithm that always terminates on any anonymous network. The idea is that if the initial configuration is symmetric (typically, a ring in which all processes are in the same state and all channels are empty), then there is always an infinite execution that cannot escape this symmetry. Apparently, unique process IDs are a crucial ingredient for the election algorithms in chapter 9 to break symmetry.

Note that vice versa, if one leader has been elected, all processes can be given a unique ID using a traversal algorithm (see section 4.1) initiated by the leader.

We recall from chapter 9 that election algorithms are decentralized. The initiators can be any nonempty set of processes, and all processes must have the same local algorithm.

Theorem 10.1 *No election algorithm for anonymous rings always terminates.*

Proof. Suppose we have an election algorithm for (directed or undirected) anonymous rings. We run it on an anonymous ring of size $N > 1$.

A configuration of the algorithm on the ring is *symmetric* if all processes are in the same state and all channels carry the same messages. We make three observations:

- There is a symmetric initial configuration: All processes can be provided with the same initial state, and initially all channels are empty.
- In a symmetric configuration there is not one leader, because all processes are in the same state.
- If γ_0 is a symmetric configuration and $\gamma_0 \to \gamma_1$, then there is a sequence of transitions $\gamma_1 \to \gamma_2 \to \cdots \to \gamma_N$ where γ_N is symmetric. Namely, the transition $\gamma_0 \to \gamma_1$ is caused by an internal, send, or receive event at some process. Since in γ_0 all processes are in the same state and all channels carry the same messages, all other processes in the ring can also perform this event, and the resulting configuration γ_N is symmetric.

These observations together imply that the election algorithm exhibits an infinite execution, which infinitely often visits a symmetric configuration.

We can even construct an infinite execution that is fair; that is, if an event can happen in infinitely many configurations in the execution, then this event is performed infinitely often during the execution. Namely, given the symmetric configuration γ_0 in the third case above, it does not matter which event available in γ_0 is used for the transition $\gamma_0 \to \gamma_1$; we can always build the transition sequence to the symmetric configuration γ_N. This implies that we can make sure no event is ignored infinitely often in the infinite execution. □

10.2 Probabilistic algorithms

In view of the impossibility result in the previous section, we now turn to *probabilistic* algorithms, in which a process may, for example, flip a coin and perform an event based on the outcome of this coin flip. That is, events can happen with a certain probability.

For probabilistic algorithms, we can calculate the probability that an execution from some set of possible executions will occur. Although in the previous section we proved that election algorithms for anonymous rings inevitably contain infinite executions, in the next section we will see that there exists such an algorithm in which the probability that an infinite execution occurs is zero.

Probabilistic algorithms for which all executions terminate in a correct configuration are in general not so interesting (except sometimes from a complexity point of view). Any deterministic version of such an algorithm (for example, let the coin flip always yield heads) produces a correct nonprobabilistic algorithm. We therefore consider two classes of probabilistic algorithms: ones that always terminate but that may terminate incorrectly, and ones that may not terminate but if they do the outcome is always correct.

A probabilistic algorithm is *Las Vegas* if:

- the probability that it terminates is greater than zero, and
- all terminal configurations are correct.

It is *Monte Carlo* if:

- it always terminates, and
- the probability that a terminal configuration is correct is greater than zero.

Note that if the probability that a Las Vegas algorithm terminates is one, there may still be infinite executions. But in this case the probability mass of all infinite executions together is zero. For example, consider an algorithm which consists of flipping a fair coin as long as the result is heads, and which terminates as soon as the result of a coin flip is tails. The algorithm has one infinite execution, in which every time the outcome of the coin flip is heads. But the probability that this execution occurs is zero.

10.3 Itai-Rodeh election algorithm for rings

The Itai-Rodeh election algorithm targets anonymous directed rings. Although in section 10.1 it was shown that there is no terminating election algorithm for this setting, the Itai-Rodeh election algorithm will achieve the next best thing: a Las Vegas algorithm that terminates with probability one.

We adapt the Chang-Roberts algorithm from section 9.1. Each initiator again sends out its ID, and messages with the largest ID are the only one completing their round trip. However, since we are working with an anonymous ring, processes do not have a unique ID. Therefore, each initiator randomly selects an ID. The complication then, of course, is that different processes may select the same ID, in which case the election can be inconclusive.

The Itai-Rodeh election algorithm therefore progresses in rounds. If in a round one active process selects a larger ID than any other active process, then it becomes the leader. If, on the other hand, multiple active processes select the largest ID in that round, then there will be a next round, in which only the active processes that selected the largest ID may participate. At the start of every round, active processes randomly select a new ID. Active processes keep track of round numbers, so that they can ignore messages from earlier rounds; we will see that this is essential, as else the algorithm could terminate in a configuration where all processes have become passive.

Since different processes may select the same ID, a process cannot readily recognize its own message when it completes the round trip. Therefore, each message is supplied with a hop count, which keeps track of how many processes have been visited so far. A message arrives at its source if and only if its hop count is N. Hence, it is required that processes know the ring size; in section 10.5 we will see that this requirement is crucial.

Now the Itai-Rodeh election algorithm is presented in more detail. Initially, initiators are active at the start of election round 0, and noninitiators are passive. At the start of an election round $n \geq 0$, an active process p randomly selects an ID id_p from $\{1, \ldots, N\}$ and sends the message $(n, id_p, 1, \mathit{false})$ into its outgoing channel. The first value is the number of the election round in which this message evolved, the second value the ID of its source, the third value the hop count, and the fourth value a Boolean that is set when an active process different from p with the ID id_p is encountered during the round trip.

Next, p waits for a message (n', i, h, b) to arrive. When this happens, p acts as follows, depending on the parameter values in this message.

- $n' > n$, or $n' = n$ and $i > id_p$:
  p has received a message from a future round, or from the current round with a larger ID. It becomes passive and sends $(n', i, h+1, b)$.
- $n' < n$, or $n' = n$ and $i < id_p$:
  p has received a message from an earlier round, or from the current round with a smaller ID. It purges the message.
- $n' = n$, $i = id_p$ and $h < N$:
  p has received a message from the current round with its own ID, but with a hop count smaller than N. Therefore, p is not the source of this message. It sends $(n, id_p, h+1, true)$.
- $n' = n$, $i = id_p$, $h = N$ and $b = true$:
  p has received back its own message. Since the Boolean was set to $true$ during the round trip, another active process selected the same ID as p in this round. Therefore, p proceeds to round $n+1$.
- $n' = n$, $i = id_p$, $h = N$ and $b = false$:
  p has received back its own message. Since the Boolean is still $false$, all other processes selected a smaller ID in this round and have become passive. Therefore, p becomes the leader.

Passive processes simply pass on messages, increasing their hop count by one.

The Itai-Rodeh election algorithm is a Las Vegas algorithm that terminates with probability one. There are infinite executions, in which active processes keep on selecting the same ID in every election round. However, in each election round with multiple active processes, with a positive probability not all active processes select the same ID. And in that case, not all active processes will make it to the next round. Therefore, with probability one, eventually one process will become the leader.

The following example shows that without round numbers the algorithm would be flawed.

Example 10.1 We consider one possible computation of the Itai-Rodeh election algorithm on an anonymous directed ring of size three. The processes p, q, r are all initiators and know that the ring size is three.

- In round 0, p and q both select ID i, while r selects ID j, with $i > j$. The message sent by q makes r passive, its Boolean is set at p, and it returns to q. Likewise, the Boolean in the message sent by p is set at q, and returns to p. Next, p and q move to the next round.
- In round 1, p and q select IDs k and ℓ, respectively, with $j > k > \ell$. The message sent by r in round 0 is slow; only now it reaches p. If round numbers were omitted, then p and subsequently q would not recognize that r's message is from the previous round, and would become passive. Owing to round numbers,

however, r's message is purged by p, and p and q continue to compete for the leadership. Since $k > \ell$, the message from q is purged at p, while the message from p makes q passive and returns to p with Boolean $true$. So p becomes the leader.

The computation in example 10.1 uses in an essential way that channels are not FIFO. In case of FIFO channels, round numbers can be omitted.

It can be shown that, in case all processes are initiators, the average-case message complexity of the Itai-Rodeh election algorithm is $O(N \log N)$: on average, the N messages travel a logarithmic number of hops before they are purged, and the average number of election rounds is finite. In view of the lower bound of $\Omega(N \log N)$ on the average-case message complexity of election algorithms for rings mentioned in the previous chapter, one cannot hope to do better in a fully asynchronous setting.

Similar to the way the Chang-Roberts algorithm for election in directed rings was turned into a probabilistic version for anonymous directed rings, Franklin's algorithm for undirected rings can be turned into a probabilistic version for anonymous undirected rings. An advantage of the latter probabilistic algorithm, compared to the Itai-Rodeh algorithm, is that round numbers modulo 2, that is, only 0 and 1, suffice.

10.4 Echo algorithm with extinction for anonymous networks

The echo algorithm with extinction from section 9.3 can be adapted to anonymous undirected networks similar to the adaptation of the Chang-Roberts algorithm in the previous section. The resulting election algorithm progresses in rounds; at the start of every round, the active processes randomly select an ID and run the echo algorithm with extinction. Again, round numbers are used to recognize messages from earlier rounds. When a process is hit by a wave with a higher round number than its current wave, or with the same round number but a higher ID, the process becomes passive (if it was not already) and moves to that other wave.

Processes again need to know the network size, to be able to determine at completion of their wave whether it has covered the entire network. Namely, different waves with the same ID in the same round can collide with each other, after which these waves may both complete, but then covered disjoint parts of the network. Therefore, when a process sends a wave message to its parent, it reports the size of its subgraph in this wave, so that in the end the initiator of this wave can determine how many processes participated in its wave. If a wave completes but did not cover the entire network, then the initiator moves to the next election round. If a completed wave covered the entire network, then its initiator becomes the leader.

We now present the echo algorithm with extinction for election in anonymous undirected networks in more detail. Initially, initiators are active at the start of round 0, and noninitiators are passive.

Let process p be active. At the start of an election round $n \geq 0$, p randomly selects an ID $id_p \in \{1, \ldots, N\}$, and starts a wave, tagged with n and id_p. As a third parameter it adds a 0, meaning that this is not a message to its parent. This third parameter is used to report the subtree size in messages to a parent.

A process p, which is in a wave from round n with ID i, waits for a wave message to arrive, tagged with a round number n' and an ID j. When this happens, p acts as follows, depending on the parameter values in this message.

- If $n' > n$, or $n' = n$ and $j > i$, then p makes the sender its parent, changes to the wave in round n' with ID j, and treats the message accordingly.
- If $n' < n$, or $n' = n$ and $j < i$, then p purges the message.
- If $n' = n$ and $j = i$, then p treats the message according to the echo algorithm.

As we said, the echo algorithm is adapted by letting each message sent upward in the constructed tree report the size of its subtree; all other wave messages report 0. When a process decides, meaning that its wave completes, it computes the size of the constructed tree. If this equals the network size N, then the process becomes the leader. Otherwise, it moves to the next election round, in which it randomly selects a new ID from $\{1, \ldots, N\}$, and initiates a new wave.

This election algorithm is a Las Vegas algorithm that terminates with probability one. There are infinite executions, in which active processes keep on selecting the same ID in every election round. However, with a positive probability, in election rounds with multiple active processes, not all active processes select the same ID. And in that case, not all active processes will make it to the next round. Therefore, with probability one, eventually one process will become the leader.

Example 10.2 We consider one possible computation of the echo algorithm with extinction on the anonymous undirected network below. All processes know that the network size is six.

- In round 0, processes p, r, t select ID i and processes q, s, u select ID j, with $i > j$. In the picture below, only the messages carrying ID i are shown; the messages carrying j are all purged at reception. Messages that are depicted with a solid arrow head are toward a parent.

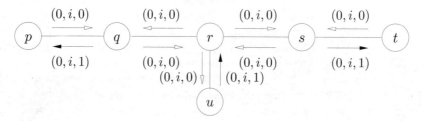

p, r, t start their wave by sending $(0, i, 0)$ to their neighbors. Next, q and s receive the message from p and t, respectively, and send $(0, i, 0)$ to r. When q and s receive $(0, i, 0)$ from r, they interpret this as an answer to their message to r, reporting a subtree of size 0. So q and s report a subtree of size 1 to p and t, respectively. Moreover, u receives $(0, i, 0)$ from r, and reports a subtree of size 1 to r. Finally, p, r, t all compute that their wave covered two processes and move to round 1.

- In round 1, p selects ID k, and r, t select ID ℓ, with $k > \ell$. In the next picture, only the messages carrying ID k are shown.

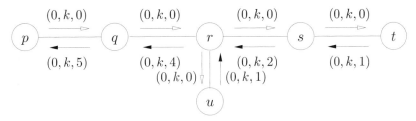

The wave of p completes and reports that it covered six processes. So p becomes the leader.

Note that in round 1 another scenario would be possible, in which the wave of t completes, and t computes that its wave covered two processes, so that it moves to round 2. However, in the computation we consider, the wave of p in round 1 travels faster than the waves of r and t, so that the wave of p completes.

It can be shown that, in case all processes are initiators, the average-case message complexity of the echo algorithm with extinction is $O(E)$: every round takes $2E$ messages, and the average number of election rounds is finite.

10.5 Computing the size of an anonymous ring is impossible

In the previous sections we discussed Las Vegas algorithms for election in anonymous networks, which require that all processes in the network know the network size. We now prove that this assumption is essential. There is no Las Vegas algorithm to compute the size of anonymous rings; every probabilistic algorithm for computing the size of anonymous rings must allow for incorrect outcomes. This implies that there is no Las Vegas algorithm for election in anonymous rings if processes do not know the ring size. Because when there is one leader, network size can be computed using a wave algorithm, initiated by the leader.

Theorem 10.2 *There is no Las Vegas algorithm to compute the size of an anonymous ring.*

Proof. Suppose we have an algorithm for computing the size of a (directed or undirected) anonymous ring of size $N > 2$, with processes $p_0, \ldots, p_{N-1}$. Let C be a computation of the algorithm on this ring that terminates with the correct outcome N. We cut open this ring between p_0 and p_{N-1}, and glue a copy $p'_0, \ldots, p'_{N-1}$ of the ring in between. That is, we consider the following anonymous ring, of size $2N$.

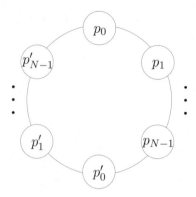

Let the computation C' on this ring consist of replaying C twice; once on the half $p_0, \ldots, p_{N-1}$ and once on the half $p'_0, \ldots, p'_{N-1}$. In C', compared to C, p_0 communicates with p'_{N-1} instead of p_{N-1}, and p_{N-1} communicates with p'_0 instead of p_0. But since p_0 and p'_0 send the same messages in C', and likewise for p_{N-1} and p'_{N-1}, and they do not have unique IDs to tell each other apart, none of these four processes can determine this difference. In C' the processes in the ring of size $2N$ terminate with the incorrect outcome N. □

10.6 Itai-Rodeh ring size algorithm

The Itai-Rodeh ring size algorithm targets anonymous directed rings. In section 10.5 it was shown that it must be a Monte Carlo algorithm, meaning that it must allow for incorrect outcomes. However, in the Itai-Rodeh ring size algorithm the probability of an erroneous outcome can be arbitrarily close to zero, by letting the processes randomly select IDs from a sufficiently large domain.

Each process p maintains an estimate est_p of the ring size; initially $est_p = 2$. During any execution of the algorithm, est_p will never exceed the correct estimate N. The algorithm proceeds in estimate rounds. Every time a process finds that its estimate is too conservative, it moves to another round. That is, a process p initiates an estimate round at the start of the algorithm, and at each update of est_p.

Each round, p randomly selects an ID id_p from $\{1, \ldots, R\}$ and sends the message $(est_p, id_p, 1)$ to its next neighbor. The third value is a hop count, which is increased by one every time the message is forwarded.

Now p waits for a message (est, id, h) to arrive. An invariant of such messages is that always $h \leq est$. When a message arrives, p acts as follows, depending on the parameter values in this message.

- $est < est_p$:
  The estimate of the message is more conservative than p's estimate, so p purges the message.
- $est > est_p$:
  The estimate of the message improves upon p's estimate, so p increases its estimate. We distinguish two cases.

- $h < est$:
  The estimate est may be correct. So p sends $(est, id, h+1)$, to give the message the chance to complete its round trip. Moreover, p performs $est_p \leftarrow est$.
- $h = est$:
  The estimate est is too conservative, because the message traveled est hops but did not complete its round trip. So p performs $est_p \leftarrow est + 1$.

• $est = est_p$:
  The estimate of the message and of p agree. We distinguish two cases.
  - $h < est$:
    p sends $(est, id, h+1)$, to give the message the chance to complete its round trip.
  - $h = est$:
    Once again we distinguish two cases.
    * $id \neq id_p$:
      The estimate est is too conservative, because the message traveled est hops but did not complete its round trip. So p performs $est_p \leftarrow est + 1$.
    * $id = id_p$:
      Possibly p's own message returned. (Or a message originating from a process est hops before p that unfortunately happened to select the same ID as p in this estimate round.) In this case, p purges the message.

When the algorithm terminates, $est_p \leq N$ for all processes p, because processes increase their estimate only when they are certain it is too conservative. Furthermore, est_p converges to the same value at all processes p. For if this were not the case, clearly there would be processes p and q where p is q's predecessor in the ring and p's final estimate is larger than the one of q. But then p's message in its final estimate round would have increased q's estimate to p's estimate.

The Itai-Rodeh ring size algorithm is a Monte Carlo algorithm: it may terminate with an estimate smaller than N. This can happen if in a round with an estimate $est < N$ all processes at distance est from each other happen to select the same ID.

Example 10.3 We consider one possible computation of the Itai-Rodeh ring size algorithm on the following anonymous ring, which is directed in a clockwise fashion.

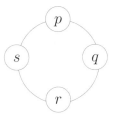

In the initial estimate round with estimate 2, let p and r select ID i, while q and s select ID j. Then p and r send the message $(2, i, 1)$, which is forwarded by q and s, respectively, as $(2, i, 2)$. Likewise, q and s send $(2, j, 1)$, which is forwarded by r

and p, respectively, as $(2, j, 2)$. So all four processes receive a message $(2, k, 2)$ with k equal to their own ID. Hence, the algorithm terminates with the wrong estimate 2.

Example 10.4 We give another computation of the Itai-Rodeh ring size algorithm on the anonymous directed ring from example 10.3, which does converge to the correct estimate. In the initial estimate round, let p select ID i, while q and s select ID j, and r selects ID $k \neq i$. Then p and r send messages $(2, i, 1)$ and $(2, k, 1)$, which are forwarded by q and s, as $(2, i, 2)$ and $(2, k, 2)$, respectively. Since $i \neq k$, these messages make p and r progress to the next estimate round, in which they both select ID j and send $(3, j, 1)$. These messages make q and s progress to the next estimate round, because the estimate of these messages is larger that the estimate of q and s. Let q select ID j and s ID $\ell \neq j$. In this estimate round, the messages $(3, j, 3)$ and $(3, \ell, 3)$ that originate from p and s, respectively, make s and r progress to the next estimate round. The messages from r and s in this last round make p and q progress to the next estimate round too. Finally, all processes terminate with the correct estimate 4.

The probability that the algorithm terminates with an incorrect outcome becomes smaller when the domain $\{1, \ldots, R\}$ from which random IDs are drawn is made larger. This probability tends to zero when R tends to infinity (for a fixed N).

The worst-case message complexity is $O(N^3)$: each process starts at most $N - 1$ estimate rounds, and each round it sends out one message, which takes at most N steps.

10.7 Election in IEEE 1394

The IEEE 1394 serial bus interface standard contains protocols for connecting devices, in order to carry different forms of digital video and audio. Its architecture is scalable, and devices can be added or removed.

We concentrate on the election algorithm in IEEE 1394, which is employed when devices have been added to or removed from the network. Since it is deemed too expensive to store IDs of other processes, no IDs are attached to messages. This means that election is basically performed within an anonymous network. In view of the dynamic nature of the network, processes are not aware of the network size. We have seen in the previous section that no Las Vegas algorithm exists for these types of networks, if cycles can be present. The topology of the undirected network is here assumed to be acyclic, and a variant of the tree election algorithm from section 9.2 is employed. While in the tree election algorithm the process with the largest ID becomes the leader, in IEEE 1394 the leader is selected among the two processes that send a parent request to each other.

All processes in the network are initiators (so no wake-up phase is needed). When a process has one possible parent, it sends a parent request to this neighbor. If the request is accepted, an acknowledgment is sent back. The last two parentless processes may send parent requests to each other simultaneously; this is called root contention.

A process p finds itself in root contention if it receives a parent request instead of an acknowledgment from a neighbor q in reply to its parent request. Then p randomly decides to either immediately send a parent request again, or wait some time for another parent request from q. In the latter case, if p does not receive another parent request from q within the waiting period, then p once again randomly decides to either immediately send a parent request or wait some more time. Root contention is resolved when one of the processes waits while the other sends immediately. Then the process that is waiting becomes the leader.

Example 10.5 We run the IEEE 1394 election protocol on an acyclic undirected network of three processes p, q, r, with channels pq and qr.

- p and r have only one possible parent, so they send a parent request to q.
- q receives the parent request of r and sends an acknowledgment back to r.
- q has only one possible parent left, so it sends a parent request to p. Now p and q are in root contention.
- p and q receive each other's parent requests. Now p (randomly) decides to wait some time, while q decides to send a parent request again immediately.
- p receives the parent request of q and sends back an acknowledgment. Thus p has become the leader.

In practice the election algorithm in IEEE 1394 is sometimes employed on networks that contain a cycle, which leads to a deadlock. For example, if the network is an undirected ring, no process ever sends a parent request, because every process has two possible parents. Therefore, the election algorithm contains a timeout mechanism, so that networks containing a cycle lead to a timeout.

Bibliographical notes

The impossibility results regarding election in and computing the size of an anonymous network date back to [4]. The Itai-Rodeh election and ring size algorithms originate from [39]. A variant of the Itai-Rodeh election algorithm without round numbers in case of FIFO channels was proposed in [32]. A probabilistic version of Franklin's algorithm was presented in [9]. The echo algorithm with extinction for anonymous networks stems from [76]. The IEEE 1394 standard was published in [38].

Exercises

Exercise 10.1 [76] Give a centralized algorithm for assigning unique IDs to processes that terminates after at most $D + 1$ time units.

Exercise 10.2 Assume a Monte Carlo algorithm, and a (deterministic) algorithm to check whether the Monte Carlo algorithm terminated correctly. Give a Las Vegas algorithm that terminates with probability one.

Suppose the Monte Carlo algorithm gives a correct outcome with some probability π. How many applications of this algorithm does it take on average to come to a correct outcome?

Exercise 10.3 Apply the Itai-Rodeh election algorithm to an anonymous directed ring of size three, in which all processes know the network size. Initially, let two processes select the ID i, and one the ID j, with $i > j$. Give one possible computation.

Exercise 10.4 Give a probabilistic version of the Dolev-Klawe-Rodeh algorithm for election in anonymous directed rings of known size. Argue that your algorithm is a Las Vegas algorithm that terminates with probability one.

Exercise 10.5 Apply the echo algorithm with extinction to elect a leader in the following anonymous undirected network. All processes are initiators and know the network size. In election round 0, let p and r select ID i, while q and s select ID j, with $i > j$.

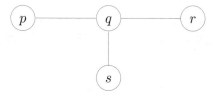

Give a computation in which s becomes the leader in round 1. Explain why, in such a computation, p and r will not both progress to round 1.

Exercise 10.6 Argue that there is no Las Vegas algorithm for election in anonymous rings of unknown size.

Exercise 10.7 Give a Monte Carlo algorithm for election in anonymous networks of unknown size. What is the success probability of your algorithm?

Exercise 10.8 Argue that there does not exist a termination detection algorithm that always correctly detects termination on anonymous rings.

Exercise 10.9 Give an (always correctly terminating) algorithm for computing the size of anonymous acyclic networks.

Exercise 10.10 Apply the Itai-Rodeh ring size algorithm to an anonymous directed ring of size three in the following two cases.

(a) All three processes initially choose the same ID. Show that the algorithm computes ring size two.

(b) Only two processes initially choose the same ID. Show that the algorithm computes ring size three.

Exercise 10.11 Consider an anonymous ring of which the size N is an odd prime number, and channels are FIFO. Determine the probability that the Itai-Rodeh ring size algorithm computes the correct ring size N.

Exercise 10.12 Given a Monte Carlo algorithm to compute the size of anonymous rings, and an $\epsilon > 0$. Argue that there exists an N such that the probability that the algorithm terminates with the correct outcome on an anonymous ring of size N is smaller than ϵ.

Exercise 10.13 In case of root contention in the IEEE 1394 election algorithm, is it optimal for the average-case time complexity to give an equal chance of fifty percent to both sending immediately and waiting for some time?

11
Synchronous Networks

A *synchronous system* is a network in which the processes proceed in lockstep. That is, a synchronous system proceeds in pulses, and in each pulse, each process:

1. sends messages to its neighbors,
2. receives messages from its neighbors, and
3. performs internal events.

Messages that are sent in a pulse must reach their destination before the receiver moves to the next pulse.

A *synchronizer* turns a network with asynchronous communication into a synchronous system. Thus one can develop a distributed algorithm for synchronous systems, which in some cases is easier than developing it for a setting with fully asynchronous communication, and then use a synchronizer to make this algorithm applicable to general networks.

11.1 A simple synchronizer

A synchronizer must make sure that a process only moves to the next pulse when it has received all messages for its current pulse. A simple synchronizer can be implemented as follows. At the start of each pulse, processes are required to send exactly one message to each neighbor. If a process wants to send multiple messages to a neighbor in one pulse, these can be lumped together. If a process does not want to send a message to a neighbor in a pulse, it sends a dummy message. When a process has received a message from all its neighbors in a pulse, it can perform internal events, and move to the next pulse. The simple synchronizer can be initiated by any process, by sending messages to all its neighbors in the first pulse.

Initialization gives a time delay of at most D time units, after which each process will have received a message. If the last process to start a pulse does so at time t, then each process is guaranteed to receive its messages in this pulse no later than time $t + 1$. Hence, the time overhead is at most one time unit per pulse.

The main drawback of the simple synchronizer is a high message overhead: every pulse in the worst case gives rise to $2E$ dummy messages.

11.2 Awerbuch's synchronizer

Awerbuch's synchronizer for undirected networks comprises three classes of synchronizers: α, β, and γ. The α synchronizer has a better time complexity, while the β synchronizer has a better message complexity. The γ synchronizer is a mix of the α and β synchronizers, combining the best of both worlds.

Let a basic algorithm run on the network. A process becomes *safe* in a pulse when it knows that all the basic messages it sent in this pulse have reached their destination. Each basic message is therefore acknowledged, and a process becomes safe in a pulse as soon as all the basic messages it sent in this pulse have been acknowledged. A process can move to the next pulse when all its neighbors have become safe in its current pulse.

We note that often acknowledgments of messages come for free, since they may be part of the underlying transport layer anyhow, as is the case in TCP. Therefore, we take the liberty to ignore them in the analysis of the message overhead of Awerbuch's synchronizer.

α synchronizer

In the α synchronizer, when a process has received acknowledgments for all the basic messages it sent in a pulse, it sends a **safe** message to its neighbors. When a process p has received **safe** messages from all its neighbors in a pulse, it moves to the next pulse. Namely, then all the basic messages sent by p's neighbors in this pulse have reached their destination, so in particular p must have received all basic messages for this pulse.

In every pulse, the α synchronizer requires $2E$ **safe** messages. If the last process to start a pulse does so at time t, then this process is guaranteed to receive acknowledgments for its basic messages in this pulse no later than time $t+2$, so each neighbor will receive a **safe** message no later than time $t+3$. Hence, the time overhead is at most three time units per pulse.

β synchronizer

The β synchronizer reduces the number of required **safe** messages. The key idea is to include an initialization phase, in which a centralized wave algorithm from chapter 4 is employed to build a spanning tree of the network. The **safe** messages travel up the tree to the root. When the root of the tree has received **safe** messages from all its children, all processes have become safe, so that all processes can move to the next pulse. Then **next** messages travel down the tree to start this next pulse.

To be more precise, when a nonroot has in a pulse received acknowledgments for all the basic messages it sent in this pulse as well as **safe** messages from all its children in the tree, it sends a **safe** message to its parent in the tree. When the root of the tree has in a pulse received acknowledgments for all the basic messages it sent as well as **safe** messages from all its children, or when a nonroot receives a **next** message from its parent, it sends a **next** message to its children, and moves to the next pulse.

In comparison to the α synchronizer, where $2E$ **safe** messages per pulse are sent, the β synchronizer uses $N-1$ **safe** and $N-1$ **next** messages, since they are sent only through tree edges. One penalty is the overhead of building a spanning tree to start with. More important, the time overhead of the β synchronizer is more severe than of the α synchronizer. If the last process to start a pulse does so at time t, then this process is guaranteed to receive acknowledgments for its basic messages in this pulse no later than time $t+2$. So if the spanning tree has depth k, the root will receive a **safe** message from its children no later than time $t+k+2$, and each nonroot will receive a **next** message from its parent no later than time $t+2k+2$. Hence, the time overhead is at most $2k+2$ time units per pulse.

γ synchronizer

The γ synchronizer divides the network into clusters, and within each cluster a spanning tree is built. Between each pair of neighboring clusters, that is, distinct clusters that are connected by a channel, one of these connecting channels is selected as a designated channel. Each pulse consists of three phases. First, the β synchronizer is applied in each cluster to determine that all the processes in the cluster have become safe. Next, clusters signal to each other via the designated channels that they contain only safe processes, by means of the α synchronizer. Finally, within each cluster the β synchronizer is used once more, to conclude that all neighboring clusters are safe, so that all processes in the cluster can move to the next pulse.

As we said, each pulse, first the β synchronizer is applied within each cluster. Note that a process must receive acknowledgments for all the basic messages it sent, so also to neighbors outside its cluster, before it can become safe. When the **next** messages of the β synchronizer travel down the tree within a cluster, the processes do not immediately move to the next pulse. Instead, they send **cluster-safe** messages into their designated channels. When a nonroot has received **cluster-safe** messages through all its designated channels as well as from all its children, it sends a **cluster-safe** message to its parent. When a root has received **cluster-safe** messages through all its designated channels as well as from all its children, or when a nonroot receives a **cluster-next** message from its parent, it sends a **cluster-next** message to its children, and moves to the next pulse.

The message overhead of the γ synchronizer is:

- a **safe**, a **next**, a **cluster-safe**, and a **cluster-next** message through each tree edge in any cluster, and
- two **cluster-safe** messages, one either way, through each designated channel.

Let the spanning trees of the clusters have depth at most ℓ. If the last process to start a pulse does so at time t, then this process is guaranteed to receive acknowledgments for its basic messages in this pulse no later than time $t+2$. So each root will receive a **safe** message from its children no later than time $t + \ell + 2$, and each nonroot will receive a **next** message from its parent no later than time $t + 2\ell + 2$. Then **cluster-safe** messages through designated channels will reach their destination no later than time $t + 2\ell + 3$. So each root will receive a **cluster-safe** message from its children (and through its designated channels) no later than time $t + 3\ell + 3$, and each nonroot will receive a **cluster-next** message from its parent no later than time $t + 4\ell + 3$. Hence, the time overhead is at most $4\ell + 3$ time units per pulse.

In conclusion, on one hand we want to have few clusters to minimize the number of designated channels and thus reduce the message overhead. On the other hand, we want the trees in the clusters to have a small depth to minimize the time overhead.

Example 11.1 The network below has been divided into three clusters. The dark processes depict the roots, and the dark lines depict the tree edges and the designated channels.

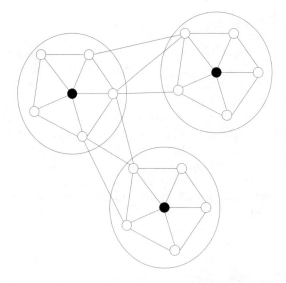

Since there are fifteen tree edges in total, and two designated channels, the message overhead of the γ synchronizer in a pulse consists of sixty messages through the tree edges plus four messages through the designated channels. The trees all have depth one, that is, $\ell = 1$, so the time overhead of the γ synchronizer is at most seven time units per pulse.

Note that because the network has 36 channels, the α synchronizer would give a message overhead of 72 **safe** messages per pulse. Furthermore, since a spanning tree of the entire network has depth at least three, that is, $k = 3$, the β synchronizer may give a time overhead of eight time units per pulse.

11.3 Bounded delay networks with local clocks

This section discusses a synchronizer for *bounded delay networks*, meaning that an upper bound $d_{\max}$ is known on network latency; when a message is sent, it is guaranteed to reach its destination within $d_{\max}$ time units.

Moreover, each process p is supposed to have a local clock C_p. A process can read as well as adjust the value of its local clock. The time domain is $\mathbb{R}_{\geq 0}$, that is, the nonnegative real numbers. We distinguish real time, meaning time progression in the real world, from local clock times, which try to estimate real time. At real time τ, the clock at p returns the value $C_p(\tau)$. The local clocks are started at real time 0: for all processes p, $C_p(0) = 0$.

Each local clock C_p is assumed to have *ρ-bounded drift*, for some $\rho > 1$, compared to real time. That is, if $\tau_2 \geq \tau_1$, then

$$\frac{1}{\rho}(\tau_2 - \tau_1) \leq C_p(\tau_2) - C_p(\tau_1) \leq \rho(\tau_2 - \tau_1).$$

To build a synchronous system, the local clocks should moreover have *precision* δ for some $\delta > 0$. That is, at any time τ and for any pair of processes p, q:

$$|C_p(\tau) - C_q(\tau)| \leq \delta.$$

Consider a bounded delay network, with local clocks that have ρ-bounded drift and precision δ; we assume that upper bounds for ρ and δ are known. The synchronizer is defined as follows: when a process reads the time

$$(i-1)(\rho^2 \delta + \rho d_{\max})$$

at its local clock, it starts pulse i, for any $i \geq 1$.

Theorem 11.1 *The synchronizer for bounded delay networks, with local clocks that have ρ-bounded drift and precision δ, is correct.*

Proof. We must show that any process p is guaranteed to receive all its messages for a pulse $i \geq 1$ before starting pulse $i + 1$. It suffices to prove that for all processes p, q and all τ,

$$C_q^{-1}(\tau) + d_{\max} \leq C_p^{-1}(\tau + \rho^2 \delta + \rho d_{\max})$$

(where $C_r^{-1}(\tau)$ is the first moment in real time that the clock of process r returns the value τ). Because taking $\tau = (i-1)(\rho^2 \delta + \rho d_{\max})$, this implies that q starts pulse i at least $d_{\max}$ time units before p starts pulse $i+1$. Since network latency is assumed to be at most $d_{\max}$, this assures that p receives the messages from q for pulse i in time.

The desired inequality follows immediately from the following two inequalities:

$$C_q^{-1}(\tau) \leq C_p^{-1}(\tau + \rho^2 \delta) \tag{11.1}$$

$$C_p^{-1}(\tau) + v \leq C_p^{-1}(\tau + \rho v) \tag{11.2}$$

(In the first inequality, add a summand $d_{\max}$ at both sides; in the second inequality, replace τ by $\tau + \rho^2 \delta$ and v by $d_{\max}$.) We now set out to prove these two inequalities.

Consider the moment in time that q's clock returns some value $\tau - \delta$, and let real time progress for $\rho\delta$ time units. Since q's clock is ρ-bounded from below, in that period q's clock will progress with at least δ time units, so it will return a clock value of at least τ. This can be depicted as follows:

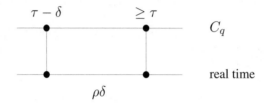

In other words,
$$C_q^{-1}(\tau) \leq C_q^{-1}(\tau - \delta) + \rho\delta.$$

Furthermore, since local clocks have precision δ,
$$C_q^{-1}(\tau - \delta) \leq C_p^{-1}(\tau).$$

Combining these two inequalities, we conclude that for all τ,
$$C_q^{-1}(\tau) \leq C_p^{-1}(\tau) + \rho\delta \tag{11.3}$$

Now consider the moment in time that p's clock returns some value τ, and let real time progress for v time units. Since p's clock is ρ-bounded from above, in that period p's clock will progress with at most ρv time units, so it will return a clock value of at most $\tau + \rho v$. This can be depicted as follows:

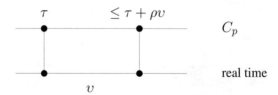

In other words, we have argued that inequality (11.2) holds. Furthermore, inequalities (11.3) and (11.2), with $v = \rho\delta$, together yield inequality (11.1). □

11.4 Election in anonymous rings with bounded expected delay

Bounded *expected* delay networks relax the restriction of bounded network latency to a known upper bound on the expected network latency. This means that arbitrarily long message delays are possible, but very long delays are less probable than short delays. In this setting, for anonymous directed rings in which all processes know the ring size N, a Las Vegas election algorithm exists with an average-case message and time complexity of $O(N)$. This shows that even mild synchrony restrictions can be helpful for the development of efficient distributed algorithms. We recall that without restrictions on the expected network latency, there is a lower bound $O(N \log N)$ for the average-case message complexity of election algorithms on rings.

The election algorithm for anonymous directed rings with bounded expected delay, which we refer to as the resuscitation algorithm, requires that processes have clocks with ρ-bounded drift, for some $\rho > 1$. The algorithm starts, just as in the tree election algorithm, with a wake-up phase, in which each initiator, and each noninitiator when it is woken up, sends a wake-up message to its successor in the ring. After sending this message, the process becomes idle. Each (awake) process can be in four states: idle, active, passive, or leader.

Each process p maintains a counter $np\text{-}hops_p$, which estimates from below the number of hops between p and its first nonpassive predecessor in the ring. Initially, $np\text{-}hops_p = 1$ at all processes p. An idle process p at each clock tick (so every moment its clock progresses one time unit) remains idle with some probability $\pi_p \in \langle 0, 1 \rangle$ and become active with probability $1 - \pi_p$. When p becomes active, it sends a message $\langle \mathbf{np\text{-}hops}, 1 \rangle$, where the argument provides the receiver with a safe value for $np\text{-}hops$.

Let a message $\langle \mathbf{np\text{-}hops}, h \rangle$ arrive at a process q. Then q performs the assignment $np\text{-}hops_q \leftarrow \max\{np\text{-}hops_q, h\}$ and acts as follows, depending on its state.

- In case q is idle or passive, it sends $\langle \mathbf{np\text{-}hops}, np\text{-}hops_q + 1 \rangle$. And if q is idle, then it becomes passive.
- In case q is active, either it becomes idle, if $h < N$, or it becomes the leader, if $h = N$.

When a process q receives a message $\langle \mathbf{np\text{-}hops}, h \rangle$ from its predecessor p, at least the first $h - 1$ predecessors of q in the ring are passive. This can be seen by induction on h: the case $h = 1$ is trivial, and if $h > 1$, then clearly p is passive, and must have received a message $\langle \mathbf{np\text{-}hops}, h - 1 \rangle$ in the past, so by induction the first $h - 2$ predecessors of p in the ring are also passive. Since $np\text{-}hops_q$ stores the maximum of all the messages q has received, at least the first $np\text{-}hops_q - 1$ predecessors of q in the ring are passive.

We discuss the correctness of the resuscitation algorithm. The number of messages in transit always equals the number of active processes in the ring: initially, both numbers are zero; processes that become active send a message; idle and passive processes forward messages; and at arrival of a message, active processes become nonactive and do not forward the message. Since only idle processes can become passive, it follows that at the moment a message arrives, there must be an active process. Active processes do not become passive at the arrival of a message, so there is always a nonpassive process. Furthermore, when a process becomes active, there is a positive probability that the message it sends will complete the round trip, after which the process becomes the leader. And we have argued before that when a process receives $\langle \mathbf{np\text{-}hops}, N \rangle$, all other $N - 1$ processes must have become passive.

To conclude, the resuscitation algorithm is a Las Vegas algorithm that terminates with probability one.

Example 11.2 We consider one possible computation of the resuscitation algorithm on an anonymous directed ring with processes p, q, r. At the first tick of their clocks, all three processes happen to become active and send $\langle \textbf{np-hops}, 1 \rangle$. Next, p and q receive these messages from r and p, respectively, and both become idle. At the next tick of its clock, p becomes active again and sends $\langle \textbf{np-hops}, 1 \rangle$. This message arrives at q, which becomes passive and sends $\langle \textbf{np-hops}, 2 \rangle$. This message arrives at r, which sets $np\text{-}hops_r$ to 2 and becomes idle. Finally, the message $\langle \textbf{np-hops}, 1 \rangle$ that q sent at the start of the computation arrives at r. As a result, r becomes passive and sends $\langle \textbf{np-hops}, 3 \rangle$ (because $np\text{-}hops_r = 2$). When this message arrives at p, it becomes the leader.

The computation in this example shows that it is beneficial for the message complexity that an idle or passive process r, at the arrival of a message $\langle \textbf{np-hops}, h \rangle$, forwards $\langle \textbf{np-hops}, np\text{-}hops_r + 1 \rangle$ instead of $\langle \textbf{np-hops}, h + 1 \rangle$. Otherwise, at the end of the computation in the example, r would not send $\langle \textbf{np-hops}, 3 \rangle$ but $\langle \textbf{np-hops}, 2 \rangle$ to p. Then p would have become idle, instead of the leader.

Key to the favorable average-case message complexity of the resuscitation algorithm mentioned at the start of this section is a smart choice of the probability π_p with which an idle process p remains idle at a clock tick. This choice depends on the number of idle processes in the ring; the more idle processes, the larger π_p should be, to maximize the chance that exactly one idle process becomes active, and its message completes the round trip without any other idle process becoming active in the meantime. Therefore, the initial value of π_p depends on N, and π_p decreases at every increase of $np\text{-}hops_p$:

$$\pi_p = \left(\frac{N-1}{N+1}\right)^{\frac{np\text{-}hops_p}{N}}.$$

We argue that these dynamic values of the π_p yield an average-case message and time complexity of $O(N)$. For simplicity, we assume that local clocks are perfectly synchronized with real time, that messages on average take exactly one time unit to reach their destination, and that the values $np\text{-}hops_p$ at nonpassive processes p always equal the number of hops between p and its first nonpassive predecessor. The forthcoming argumentation is somewhat more involved when clocks have ρ-bounded drift, or $np\text{-}hops_p$ may temporarily be smaller than the number of hops between p and its first nonpassive predecessor.

Consider a clock tick at which all nonpassive processes are idle. By assumption, the values of the parameters $np\text{-}hops_p$ of the nonpassive processes p always add up to N. Therefore, the probability that the idle processes all remain idle at this clock tick, that is, the product of the π_p of the idle processes p, is $\frac{N-1}{N+1}$. So the probability that an idle process becomes active and sends a message at this clock tick is $\frac{2}{N+1}$. By assumption, a round trip of this message on average takes N time units. Therefore, the probability that another idle process becomes active during this round trip is at most $1 - (\frac{N-1}{N+1})^N$, which is at most $\frac{8}{9}$ because $N \geq 2$; so this probability has an upper bound < 1 that is independent of the ring size. In conclusion, on average once every $O(N)$ time units an idle process becomes active, and with an average probability of $O(1)$ the message of this active process completes its round trip. These two observations together imply that the average-case message and time complexity of the resuscitation algorithm are $O(N)$.

Bibliographical notes

Awerbuch's synchronizer originates from [6]. Bounded delay networks were introduced in [21], and a synchronizer for bounded delay networks with local clocks that have bounded drift was presented in [76]. Expected bounded delay networks and the resuscitation algorithm stem from [8].

Exercises

Exercise 11.1 Consider a network of processes $p_0, \ldots, p_{N-1}$ on a line (so with diameter $N-1$). Let p_0 initiate the simple synchronizer. Give an example where at some point p_0 is in pulse $N-1$ while p_{N-2} is in pulse 1.

Exercise 11.2 Give an example to show that with the α synchronizer a process can be two pulses ahead of another process in the network. Argue that with the β synchronizer this can never be the case.

Exercise 11.3 Argue the correctness of the γ synchronizer.

Exercise 11.4 Suppose that performing internal events at the end of a pulse takes time, and that an upper bound ϵ is known for this processing time. Explain how the synchronizer for bounded delay networks, with local clocks that have ρ-bounded drift and precision δ, needs to be adapted. Argue that your adapted synchronizer is correct.

Exercise 11.5 Suppose that the resuscitation algorithm would not start with a wake-up phase, but instead initiators would be idle and noninitiators would be passive at the start. Explain why then, in case of a single initiator, the average-case time complexity would not be $O(N)$.

12
Crash Failures

In practice, processes in a distributed system may crash, meaning that they stop executing unexpectedly. In this chapter we consider how the rest of the system can cope with a crash of one or more processes, if at all possible. The next chapter will consider the more severe type of so-called Byzantine failures, where processes may show behavior that is not in line with the specification of the distributed algorithm that is being executed.

The problem of failures can be alleviated by including redundancy and replication in the system, and letting processes negotiate before a certain action is taken. A typical example is a database management system in which the processes collectively decide whether to commit or abort a transaction.

The challenge we pose to the system is to let its processes agree on a single value, even though some processes may have crashed. The (binary) consensus problem is that the correct processes, that is, the processes that have not crashed (or, in the next chapter, that are not Byzantine), must eventually uniformly decide for either 0 or 1. In a crash consensus algorithm to solve this problem, each process randomly chooses an initial value 0 or 1; so with N processes there are 2^N different initial configurations. In all executions of a crash consensus algorithm, each correct process should perform one decide event, and the following three properties must be satisfied.

- *Termination*: every correct process eventually decides for either 0 or 1.
- *Agreement*: all correct processes decide for the same value.
- *Validity*: if all processes choose the same initial value, then all correct processes decide for this value.

The validity requirement rules out trivial solutions where the processes always decide for 0, or always decide for 1, irrespective of their initial values.

A reachable configuration of a crash consensus algorithm is called *bivalent* if from this configuration one can reach a terminal configuration where consensus has been reached on the value 0, as well as a terminal configuration where consensus has been reached on the value 1. The validity requirement implies that each crash consensus algorithm has a bivalent initial configuration; see exercise 12.1.

A k-crash consensus algorithm, for a $k > 0$, is a crash consensus algorithm that can cope with up to k crashing processes. A basic assumption we make is that the network topology is complete. This guarantees that the network topology always stays strongly connected, even when processes have crashed.

12.1 Impossibility of 1-crash consensus

In this section, we assume that processes cannot observe whether some process has crashed. If a process does not send messages for a very long time, this may simply be because the process or its outgoing channels are very slow. It turns out that in this setting one cannot hope to develop a terminating 1-crash consensus algorithm. It does not matter how large the network is, the prospect of one crashing process suffices to yield infinite executions in which no decision is ever made. The basic idea behind this impossibility result is that a decision for either 0 or 1, in an asynchronous setting, must be enforced by an event at a single process. But what if this process crashes immediately after this event, and in case of a send event, the message travels through the channel for a very long, indefinite amount of time? Then at some moment in time the remaining processes should organize themselves to mimic the decision of the crashed process, but without any input from this crashed process. This is shown to be impossible, if crashes cannot be observed.

Theorem 12.1 *There is no terminating algorithm for 1-crash consensus.*

Proof. Consider any 1-crash consensus algorithm. Let γ be a bivalent configuration. Then $\gamma \to \gamma_0$ and $\gamma \to \gamma_1$, where γ_0 can lead to decision 0 and γ_1 to decision 1. We argue that γ_0 or γ_1 must be bivalent. We distinguish two cases.

- The transitions $\gamma \to \gamma_0$ and $\gamma \to \gamma_1$ correspond to events e_0 and e_1 at different processes p_0 and p_1, respectively. Then in γ_0 the event e_1 at p_1 can still be performed, and likewise in γ_1 the event e_0 at p_0 can still be performed. Performing e_1 at p_1 in γ_0 and performing e_0 at p_0 in γ_1 lead to the same configuration δ, because in both cases the resulting configuration is reached from γ by performing the concurrent events e_0 and e_1 at p_0 and p_1. So there are transitions $\gamma_0 \to \delta$ and $\gamma_1 \to \delta$. Hence, γ_0 or γ_1 is bivalent, if δ can lead to a decision 1 or 0, respectively.
- The transitions $\gamma \to \gamma_0$ and $\gamma \to \gamma_1$ correspond to events at the same process p. In γ, p can crash. Moreover, the messages sent by p can take indefinitely long to reach their destination. Therefore, in γ the processes except p must be b-*potent* for some $b \in \{0, 1\}$. In a configuration, a set S of processes is said to be b-potent if by executing only events at processes in S, some process in S can decide for b. In γ_0 and γ_1 the processes except p are clearly still b-potent. So γ_{1-b} is bivalent.

In conclusion, a bivalent configuration can always make a transition to some bivalent configuration. Since the crash consensus algorithm has a bivalent initial configuration, there is an infinite execution, visiting only bivalent configurations. □

We can even construct an infinite execution that is fair; see exercise 12.3.

12.2 Bracha-Toueg crash consensus algorithm

In chapter 10, to circumvent the impossibility of a terminating election algorithm for anonymous networks, we moved to probabilistic algorithms. Here we follow the same approach. First we discuss another impossibility result: there is no Las Vegas algorithm for crash consensus if half of the processes can crash. Namely, then the network can be divided into two disjoint halves, where in each half the processes do not receive messages from the processes in the other half for a very long time, so that they must act under the assumption that the processes in the other half have crashed. As a result, the two halves may act as independent entities, that can come to different decisions.

Theorem 12.2 *Let $k \geq \frac{N}{2}$. There is no Las Vegas algorithm for k-crash consensus.*

Proof. Suppose, toward a contradiction, that such an algorithm does exist. Divide the processes into two disjoint sets S and T, which both contain at most $\lceil \frac{N}{2} \rceil$ processes.

Since $k \geq \lceil \frac{N}{2} \rceil$, the processes in S must be able to come to a decision by themselves, in case all processes in T have crashed. In other words, S is always 0-potent or 1-potent. Likewise, T is always 0-potent or 1-potent. In each reachable configuration, S and T should be either both 0-potent or both 1-potent. For otherwise they could independently decide for different values, because they are disjoint sets.

Consider a bivalent initial configuration γ. There must be a configuration δ reachable from γ, and a transition $\delta \to \delta'$, with S and T both only b-potent in δ and only $(1-b)$-potent in δ', for some $b \in \{0,1\}$. Since this transition would correspond to a single event, at a process in either S or T, clearly such a transition cannot exist. □

If $k < \frac{N}{2}$, then a Las Vegas algorithm for k-crash consensus does exist. The Bracha-Toueg k-crash consensus algorithm, for $k < \frac{N}{2}$, progresses in rounds. Initially, at the start of round 0, each process randomly chooses a value 0 or 1. The weight of a process, holding value $b \in \{0,1\}$, approximates from below the number of processes that voted b in the previous round. In round 0, each process has weight 1.

In each round $n \geq 0$, each correct, undecided process p sends its value and weight to all processes, and determines a new value and weight, based on the first $N - k$ messages it receives in this round:

- p sends $\langle n, value_p, weight_p \rangle$ to all processes (including itself).
- p waits until $N - k$ messages $\langle n, b, w \rangle$ have arrived. (It purges/stores messages from earlier/future rounds.)
  - If $w > \frac{N}{2}$ for an incoming message $\langle n, b, w \rangle$, then $value_p \leftarrow b$.
    Otherwise, $value_p \leftarrow 0$ if most messages voted 0, or else $value_p \leftarrow 1$.
  - $weight_p$ is changed into the number of incoming votes for $value_p$ in round n.
- If $w > \frac{N}{2}$ for more than k incoming messages $\langle n, b, w \rangle$, then p decides for b.

If p decides for b in round n, it broadcasts $\langle n+1, b, N-k \rangle$ and $\langle n+2, b, N-k \rangle$, and terminates. This suffices because when a process decides, all other correct processes are guaranteed to decide within two rounds; see the proof of theorem 12.3.

In reality, p does not send messages to itself, but can simply include a message it broadcasts in the collection of messages it receives from other processes in the same round. Note that if p waited for more than $N-k$ messages $\langle n,b,w\rangle$ in a round n, then a deadlock could occur, in case k processes have crashed. Note also that if p receives messages $\langle n,b,w\rangle$ and $\langle n,1-b,w'\rangle$, then $w+w'\leq N$, so that w and w' cannot both be greater than $\frac{N}{2}$. Note, finally, that since p waits for $N-k$ messages $\langle n,b,w\rangle$ and can decide only if more than k of those messages have a weight greater than $\frac{N}{2}$, it is essential that $N-k>k$.

Example 12.1 Given a network of three processes p,q,r, and $k=1$. Each round a process requires two incoming messages to determine a new value and weight, and two b-votes with weight 2 to decide for b. We consider one possible computation of the Bracha-Toueg 1-crash consensus algorithm on this network.

- Initially, p and q randomly choose the value 0 and r the value 1, all three with weight 1.
- In round 0, p takes into account the messages from p and r; it sets its value to 1, and its weight to 1. Moreover, q and r both take into account the messages from p and q; they set their value to 0, and their weight to 2.
- In round 1, q takes into account the messages from q and r; since both messages carry weight 2, it decides for 0. Moreover, p and r both take into account the messages from p and r; since the message from r carries weight 2, they set their value to 0, and their weight to 1.

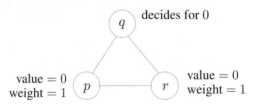

- At the start of round 2, q crashes. So p and r can take into account only the messages from p and r; as a result, they set their value to 0, and their weight to 2.
- In round 3, p and r can again only take into account the messages from p and r; since both messages carry weight 2, they decide for 0.
- p and r send messages with value 0 and weight 2 for two more rounds, and terminate.

Theorem 12.3 *If scheduling of messages is fair, then the Bracha-Toueg k-crash consensus algorithm, for any $k<\frac{N}{2}$, is a Las Vegas algorithm that terminates with probability one.*

Proof. First we prove that processes cannot decide for different values. Then we prove that the algorithm terminates with probability one, under the assumption that scheduling of messages is fair, meaning that each possible order of delivery of the messages in a round occurs with a positive probability.

Suppose a process p decides for a value b at the end of a round n. Then at the start of round n, $value_q = b$ and $weight_q > \frac{N}{2}$ for more than k processes q. Since in every round, each correct, undecided process ignores messages from only k processes, in round n these processes all take into account a message $\langle q, b, w \rangle$ with $w > \frac{N}{2}$. So in round $n+1$, all correct processes vote b. So in round $n+2$, all correct processes vote b with weight $N - k$. Hence, after round $n+2$, all correct processes have decided for b. To conclude, all correct processes decide for the same value.

Due to fair scheduling, in each round there is a positive probability that all processes receive the first $N - k$ messages from the same $N - k$ processes. After such a round n, all correct processes have the same value b. Then after round $n + 1$, all correct processes have the value b with weight $N - k$. And after round $n + 2$, all correct processes have decided for b. In conclusion, the algorithm terminates with probability one. □

12.3 Failure detectors

The impossibility result in theorem 12.1, namely that there is no terminating 1-crash consensus algorithm, assumes that crashes of processes cannot be observed. In the next section we will see that this is a crucial assumption: when crashes can be detected, there does exist a terminating k-crash consensus algorithm, if $k < \frac{N}{2}$. In the current section, we discuss the notion of failure detectors, their properties, and two straightforward implementations with different properties.

As time domain we take $\mathbb{R}_{\geq 0}$. Each execution of a crash consensus algorithm is provided with a failure pattern, consisting of sets $F(\tau)$ that contain the crashed processes at time τ. Crashed processes cannot restart: $\tau_0 \leq \tau_1 \Rightarrow F(\tau_0) \subseteq F(\tau_1)$. It is assumed that processes cannot observe $F(\tau)$.

Processes carry a failure detector, to try to detect crashed processes. With $H(p, \tau)$ we denote the set of processes that are suspected to be crashed by (the failure detector of) process p at time τ. Each execution of a crash consensus algorithm is provided with a failure detector history H. In general, such suspicions may turn out to be false, typically because at a time τ a process p receives a message from a suspected process $q \in H(p, \tau)$. However, we require that failure detectors are always *complete*: from some time onward, every crashed process is suspected by every correct process.

A failure detector is called *strongly accurate* if only crashed processes are ever suspected. In bounded delay networks, a strongly accurate (and complete) failure detector can be implemented as follows. Suppose $d_{\max}$ is a known upper bound on network latency. Let each process broadcast a message **alive** every ν time units. Each process from which no message is received for $\nu + d_{\max}$ time units has crashed. Since crashed processes stop sending **alive** messages, the failure detector is clearly complete. And the bound on network latency ensures that there can never be more than $\nu + d_{\max}$ time units between the arrival at p of subsequent **alive** messages from q, so the failure detector is strongly accurate.

A failure detector is called *eventually strongly accurate* if from some point in time onward, only crashed processes are suspected. Suppose there is an unknown upper bound on network delay. Again, let each process broadcast a message **alive** every ν time units. An eventually strongly accurate (and complete) failure detector can be implemented as follows. Each process p initially guesses as network latency $d_p = 1$. If p does not receive a message from a process q for $\nu + d_p$ time units, then p suspects that q has crashed. This suspicion may be false, in case the value d_p is too conservative. When p receives a message from a suspected process q, then q is no longer suspected by p, and $d_p \leftarrow d_p + 1$. Since crashed processes stop sending **alive** messages, the failure detector is clearly complete. And since network latency is bounded, each process p can only finitely many times receive a message from a suspected process and as a result increase d_p. This guarantees that the failure detector is eventually strongly accurate.

12.4 Consensus with a weakly accurate failure detector

A failure detector is called *weakly accurate* if some correct process is never suspected by any process. In the presence of a weakly accurate failure detector, there is a simple k-crash consensus algorithm for any k.

Let the processes be numbered: $p_0, \ldots, p_{N-1}$. Initially, each process randomly chooses a value 0 or 1. The crash consensus algorithm proceeds in rounds $n = 0, \ldots, N-1$. In a round n, the process p_n acts as the coordinator:

- p_n (if not crashed) broadcasts its value.
- Each process waits:
- either for an incoming message from p_n, in which case it adopts the value of p_n;
- or until it suspects that p_n has crashed.

After round $N - 1$, each correct process decides for its value at that time.

This rotating coordinator algorithm is a k-crash consensus algorithm for any $k < N$. Since the failure detector is weakly accurate, some correct process p_i is never suspected by any process. This implies that after round i, all correct processes have the same value b. Then clearly in the rounds $i + 1, \ldots, N - 1$, all processes keep this value b. Hence, after round $N - 1$, all correct processes decide for b.

12.5 Chandra-Toueg algorithm

With an eventually strongly accurate failure detector, the proof of theorem 12.2, that there is no Las Vegas algorithm for k-crash consensus if $k \geq \frac{N}{2}$, still applies. Namely, it could take a very long, indefinite period of time before the failure detector becomes strongly accurate, and up to that point there can still be false suspicions.

Theorem 12.4 *Let $k \geq \frac{N}{2}$. There is no Las Vegas algorithm for k-crash consensus based on an eventually strongly accurate failure detector.*

Proof. Suppose, toward a contradiction, that such an algorithm does exist. Divide the processes into two disjoint sets S and T, which both contain at most $\lceil \frac{N}{2} \rceil$ processes.

Since $k \geq \lceil \frac{N}{2} \rceil$, the processes in S are able to come to a decision by themselves, as they must be able to cope if all processes in T have crashed. In other words, S is always 0-potent or 1-potent. Likewise, T is always 0-potent or 1-potent. In each reachable configuration, S and T should be either both 0-potent or both 1-potent, for otherwise they could independently decide for different values. *Namely, since the failure detector is only eventually strongly accurate, the processes in S (or T) may suspect for a very long period of time that the processes in T (respectively S) have crashed, and at some point have to come to a decision by themselves.*

Consider a bivalent initial configuration γ. Then there must be a configuration δ reachable from γ, and a transition $\delta \to \delta'$, with S and T both only b-potent in δ and only $(1-b)$-potent in δ', for some $b \in \{0, 1\}$. Since this transition would correspond to a single event, at a process in either S or T, clearly such a transition cannot exist. □

A failure detector is called *eventually weakly accurate* if from some point in time on, some correct process is never suspected by any process. The Chandra-Toueg crash consensus algorithm, which uses an eventually weakly accurate failure detector, is an always correctly terminating k-crash consensus algorithm for any $k < \frac{N}{2}$.

Let the processes be numbered: $p_0, \ldots, p_{N-1}$. Initially, each process randomly chooses a value 0 or 1. The algorithm proceeds in rounds. Each process q records the number of the last round $\textit{last-update}_q$ in which it updated its value; initially, $\textit{last-update}_q = -1$.

Each round $n \geq 0$ is coordinated by the process p_c with $c = n \bmod N$. Round n progresses as follows.

- Every correct, undecided process q (including p_c) sends to p_c the message $\langle \mathbf{vote}, n, \textit{value}_q, \textit{last-update}_q \rangle$.
- p_c (if not crashed and undecided) waits until $N - k$ such messages have arrived, selects one, say $\langle \mathbf{vote}, n, b, \ell \rangle$, with ℓ as large as possible, and broadcasts $\langle \mathbf{value}, n, b \rangle$.
- Every correct, undecided process q (including p_c) waits either:
  - until $\langle \mathbf{value}, n, b \rangle$ arrives; then it performs $\textit{value}_q \leftarrow b$ and $\textit{last-update}_q \leftarrow n$, and sends $\langle \mathbf{ack}, n \rangle$ to p_c;
  - or until it suspects that p_c has crashed; then it sends $\langle \mathbf{nack}, n \rangle$ to p_c.
- p_c waits for $N - k$ acknowledgments. If more than k of them are positive, then p_c decides for b, broadcasts $\langle \mathbf{decide}, b \rangle$, and terminates.

A correct, undecided process that receives $\langle \mathbf{decide}, b \rangle$, decides for b and terminates.

The idea behind the decision criterion for the coordinator in a round n, the reception of more than k positive acknowledgments, is that then more than k processes have adopted the value b of the coordinator and set their $\textit{last-update}$ parameter to n. Since in each round the coordinator ignores messages of only k processes and adopts the value from a message with a maximal $\textit{last-update}$, this guarantees that in future rounds coordinators will always adopt the value b.

Example 12.2 Given a complete network of three processes p_0, p_1, p_2, and $k = 1$. Each round the coordinator waits for two incoming votes, and needs two positive acknowledgments to decide. We consider one possible computation of the Chandra-Toueg 1-crash consensus algorithm on this network.

- Initially, p_0 and p_2 randomly choose the value 1 and p_1 the value 0; $last\text{-}update = -1$ at all three processes.
- In round 0, the coordinator p_0 takes into account the messages from p_0 and p_1, selects the message from p_1 to determine its new value, and broadcasts the value 0. When p_0 and p_1 receive this message, they set their value to 0 and $last\text{-}update$ to 0, and send **ack** to p_0; moreover, p_1 moves to round 1. However, p_2 moves to round 1 without waiting for a message from p_0, because its failure detector falsely suspects that p_0 has crashed; p_2 sends **nack** to p_0, and moves to round 1. The coordinator p_0 receives the **ack**'s of p_0 and p_1, decides for 0, and crashes before it can broadcast a **decide** message.

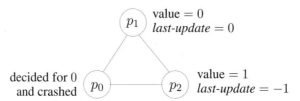

- In round 1, the coordinator p_1 can take into account only the messages from p_1 and p_2. It must select the message from p_1 to determine its new value, because it has the highest $last\text{-}update$. So p_1 broadcasts the value 0. When p_1 receives this message, it sets its value to 0 and $last\text{-}update$ to 1, and sends **ack** to itself. The process p_2 moves to round 2 without waiting for a message from p_1, because its failure detector falsely suspects that p_1 has crashed; p_2 sends **nack** to p_0, and moves to round 2. After p_1 has received the **ack** and **nack** from p_1 and p_2, respectively, it also moves to round 2.

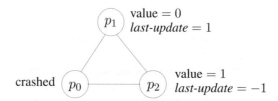

- In round 2, the coordinator p_2 can take into account only the messages from p_1 and p_2. It must select the message from p_1 to determine its new value, because it has the highest $last\text{-}update$. So p_2 broadcasts the value 0. When p_1 and p_2 receive this message, they set their value to 0 and $last\text{-}update$ to 2, and send **ack** to p_2; moreover, p_1 moves to round 3. The coordinator p_2 receives the **ack**'s of p_1 and p_2, decides for 0, and broadcasts $\langle \mathbf{decide}, 0 \rangle$. When p_1 receives this message, it also decides for 0.

Theorem 12.5 *In the presence of an eventually weakly accurate failure detector, the Chandra-Toueg algorithm is an (always correctly terminating) k-crash consensus algorithm for any $k < \frac{N}{2}$.*

Proof. First we prove that processes cannot decide for different values. Then we prove that the algorithm always terminates.

Let round n be the first round in which the coordinator decides for a value, say b. Then the coordinator received more than k **ack**'s in this round, so that:

(1) there are more than k processes q with $last\text{-}update_q \geq n$, and
(2) $last\text{-}update_q \geq n$ implies $value_q = b$.

We argue, by induction on $m - n$, that properties (1) and (2) are preserved in all rounds $m > n$. In round m, since the coordinator ignores votes of only k processes, by (1) it takes into account at least one vote with $last\text{-}update \geq n$ to determine its new value. Hence, by (2), the coordinator of round m sets its value to b, and broadcasts $\langle \textbf{value}, m, b \rangle$. To conclude, from round n onward, processes can decide only for b.

Now we argue that eventually some correct process will decide. Since the failure detector is eventually weakly accurate, from some round onward, some correct process p will never be suspected. So in the next round where p is the coordinator, all correct processes will wait for a **value** message from p. Therefore, p will receive at least $N - k$ **ack**'s, and since $N - k > k$, it will decide. All correct processes will eventually receive the **decide** message of p and will also decide. □

Bibliographical notes

Impossibility of a terminating 1-crash consensus algorithm was proved in [30]. The Bracha-Toueg crash consensus algorithm originates from [11], and the Chandra-Toueg crash consensus algorithm from [15].

Exercises

Exercise 12.1 Prove that any 1-crash consensus algorithm has a bivalent initial configuration.

Exercise 12.2 [76] Give terminating 1-crash consensus algorithms for each of the following restrictions on the chosen values in initial configurations.

(a) An even number of processes choose the value 1.
(b) At least $\lceil \frac{N}{2} + 1 \rceil$ processes choose the same value.

Exercise 12.3 Argue that each algorithm for 1-crash consensus exhibits a *fair* infinite execution.

Exercise 12.4 Give a Monte Carlo algorithm for k-crash consensus for any k.

Exercise 12.5 Consider a complete network of five processes. Apply the Bracha-Toueg 2-crash consensus algorithm, where initially three processes choose the value 0 and two processes the value 1. Give two computations: one where all correct processes decide for 0, and one where all correct processes decide for 1.

Exercise 12.6 [76] Consider the Bracha-Toueg k-crash consensus algorithm, for $k < \frac{N}{2}$.

(a) Let more than $\frac{N+k}{2}$ processes choose the value b in the initial configuration. Prove that then always the correct processes decide for b within three rounds.
(b) Let more than $\frac{N-k}{2}$ processes choose the value b in the initial configuration. Give a computation in which all correct processes decide for b within three rounds.
(c) Let $N - k$ be even. Is a decision for b possible if exactly $\frac{N-k}{2}$ processes choose the value b in the initial configuration?

Exercise 12.7 Give an example to show that if scheduling of messages is not fair, then the Bracha-Toueg crash consensus algorithm may not terminate with probability one.

Exercise 12.8 Give an example, with $N = 3$ and $k = 1$, to show that in the Bracha-Toueg k-crash consensus algorithm, k incoming messages with a weight greater than $\frac{N}{2}$ are not sufficient to decide.

Exercise 12.9 [76] The requirement of strong accuracy for failure detectors is stronger than the requirement that processes that never crash are never suspected. Give an example of a failure pattern and a failure detector history that satisfy the latter property, but that are not allowed in case of a strongly accurate failure detector.

Exercise 12.10 Suppose that the implementation of the eventually strongly accurate failure detection is adapted as follows. When p receives a message from a suspected process q, then it no longer suspects q. If this message arrives $\nu + d_p + \rho$ time units after the previous message from q, with $\rho > 0$, then $d_p \leftarrow d_p + \rho$. Give an example to show that this failure detector need not be eventually strongly accurate.

Exercise 12.11 Consider a complete network of five processes. Apply the Chandra-Toueg 2-crash consensus algorithm, where initially four processes choose the value 0 and one process the value 1. Give a computation where all correct processes decide for 1.

Exercise 12.12 Suppose we adapt the Chandra-Toueg algorithm k-crash consensus for $k < \frac{N}{2}$ as follows. If the coordinator p_c receives *at least* (instead of more than) k acknowledgments **ack**, then p_c decides for its value. Give an example to show that this could lead to inconsistent decisions.

13
Byzantine Failures

In this chapter we consider Byzantine failures, meaning that a process may start to show behavior that is not in line with the specification of the distributed algorithm that is being executed. The class of Byzantine failures includes crash failures. We assume that Byzantine failures can in general not be observed, and that processes are either correct or Byzantine from the start.

Again, the challenge we pose to the system is to let its correct processes, that is, the processes that are not Byzantine, agree on a value 0 or 1. The network topology is still assumed to be complete.

In a (binary) Byzantine consensus algorithm, each correct process randomly chooses an initial value 0 or 1. In all executions of a Byzantine consensus algorithm, each correct process should perform exactly one decide event. The properties termination and agreement mentioned at the start of chapter 12 must be satisfied, together with a slightly strengthened version of validity.

- *Validity*: if all *correct* processes choose the same initial value, then all correct processes decide for this value.

Similar to the case of crash consensus, the validity requirement implies that each Byzantine consensus algorithm has a bivalent initial configuration.

A k-Byzantine consensus algorithm, for a $k > 0$, is a Byzantine consensus algorithm that can cope with up to k Byzantine processes.

13.1 Bracha-Toueg Byzantine consensus algorithm

With Byzantine failures, fewer incorrect processes can be allowed than in the case of crashing processes, if one wants to achieve a Las Vegas consensus algorithm. A k-Byzantine consensus algorithm is possible only if $k < \frac{N}{3}$. The reason is that correct processes must be able to cope with k Byzantine processes, which may not cast a vote. So they can collect votes from at most $N - k$ processes, as else a deadlock could occur. Among these $N - k$ processes, k could be Byzantine. Only if $k < \frac{N}{3}$, it is guaranteed that the (in the worst case) $N - 2k$ votes from correct processes outnumber the k votes from Byzantine processes.

Theorem 13.1 *Let $k > \frac{N}{3}$. There is no Las Vegas algorithm for k-Byzantine consensus.*

Proof. Suppose, toward a contradiction, that such an algorithm does exist. Since $k \geq \lceil \frac{N}{3} \rceil$, the processes can be divided into two sets S and T that both contain $N - k$ processes, while $S \cap T$ contains at most k processes.

Since S contains $N - k$ elements, the processes in S must be able to come to a decision by themselves, in case all processes outside S are Byzantine. In other words, S is always 0-potent or 1-potent. Likewise, T is always 0-potent or 1-potent. In each reachable configuration, S and T should be either both 0-potent or both 1-potent, for else they could independently decide for different values. *Namely, the processes in $S \cap T$ could all be Byzantine, and could therefore be free to participate in an execution leading to a decision for b with the processes in S, while participating in an execution leading to a decision for $1 - b$ with the processes in T.*

Consider a bivalent initial configuration γ. Then there must be a configuration δ reachable from γ, and a transition $\delta \to \delta'$, with S and T both only b-potent in δ and only $(1-b)$-potent in δ', for some $b \in \{0, 1\}$. Since this transition would correspond to a single event, at a process in either S or T, clearly such a transition cannot exist. □

If $k < \frac{N}{3}$, then a Las Vegas algorithm for k-Byzantine consensus does exist. The Bracha-Toueg k-Byzantine consensus algorithm works as follows. The algorithm progresses in rounds. Just as in the Bracha-Toueg crash consensus algorithm, in each round, every correct, undecided process sends its value to all processes, and determines a new value, based on the first $N - k$ messages it receives in this round: the new value is 0 if most messages voted 0, and 1 otherwise. A process p decides for b if in a round it receives more than $\frac{N+k}{2}$ b-votes; note that by assumption $\frac{N+k}{2} < N - k$. Then p broadcasts $\langle \textbf{decide}, b \rangle$ and terminates. The other processes interpret $\langle \textbf{decide}, b \rangle$ as a b-vote by p for all rounds to come. Note that they cannot simply decide for b at the reception of this message, since p might be Byzantine. This completes the informal description of the algorithm, except for a verification phase of votes.

The example below shows that this algorithm would be flawed if in a round two correct processes could accept different votes from a Byzantine process.

Example 13.1 Given a network of four processes p, q, r, s, and $k = 1$. Suppose that q is Byzantine. We consider one possible computation of the Bracha-Toueg 1-Byzantine consensus algorithm. Each round, a correct process waits for three votes, and needs three b-votes to decide for b. Initially, p and s randomly choose the value 1 and r the value 0.

- In round 0, p, r, and s broadcast their value, while q sends a 0-vote to p and r, and a 1-vote to s. Next, p and r take into account a 1-vote by p and 0-votes by q

and r, and set their value to 0. Furthermore, s takes into account 1-votes by p, q, and s, decides for 1, and broadcasts ⟨**decide**, 1⟩.
- In round 1, p and r broadcast their value, while q broadcasts a 0-vote. Next, p and r take into account 0-votes by p, q, and r, and decide for 0. So we have inconsistent decisions.

The cause for the inconsistent decisions in example 13.1 is that in round 0, p and r use a 0-vote from q while s uses a 1-vote from q, which can happen because q is Byzantine. To avoid this mishap, the Bracha-Toueg Byzantine consensus algorithm includes a verification phase of votes. When a process p receives a b-vote from a process q, p does not accept this vote straightaway. Instead, p echoes this vote to all processes, and it accepts a b-vote by q only if it receives an echo of a b-vote by q in this round from more than $\frac{N+k}{2}$ processes. This guarantees that the correct processes in a round never accept different votes from the same process, even if that process is Byzantine.

As we said before, a process decides for b if it accepts more than $\frac{N+k}{2}$ b-votes in a round. Since $\frac{N+k}{2} = \frac{N-k}{2} + k$, each correct processes then will find that more than $\frac{N-k}{2}$ of the first $N-k$ votes it accepts in this round are b-votes. So at the end of this round all correct processes will take on the value b, and hence will continue to do so for all future rounds.

We now give a more precise description of the Bracha-Toueg k-Byzantine consensus algorithm. Initially, each correct process randomly chooses a value 0 or 1. In each round $n \geq 0$, each correct, undecided process p acts as follows:

- p sends ⟨**vote**, n, $value_p$⟩ to all processes (including itself).
- When p receives ⟨**vote**, m, b⟩ from a process q, it sends ⟨**echo**, q, m, b⟩ to all processes (including itself).
- p stores incoming messages ⟨**vote**, m, b⟩ and ⟨**echo**, q, m, b⟩ with $m > n$ for future rounds.
- p counts incoming messages ⟨**echo**, q, n, b⟩ for each pair q, b. When more than $\frac{N+k}{2}$ such messages have arrived, p accepts a b-vote by q.
- The round is completed when p has accepted votes from $N-k$ processes. If most votes are for 0, then $value_p \leftarrow 0$. Otherwise, $value_p \leftarrow 1$.
- If more than $\frac{N+k}{2}$ of the accepted votes are for b, then p decides for b, broadcasts ⟨**decide**, b⟩, and terminates.

The other processes interpret ⟨**decide**, b⟩ as a b-vote by p, and a b-echo by p for each q, for all rounds to come.

Processes keep track whether multiple messages ⟨**vote**, m, _⟩ or ⟨**echo**, q, m, _⟩ arrive via the same channel; the sender must be Byzantine. To avoid miscounts, only the first of these messages is taken into account.

Theorem 13.2 *If scheduling of messages is fair, then the Bracha-Toueg k-Byzantine consensus algorithm, for any $k < \frac{N}{3}$, is a Las Vegas algorithm that terminates with probability one.*

Proof. First we prove that processes cannot decide for different values. Then we prove that the algorithm terminates with probability one, under the assumption that scheduling of messages is fair.

Each round, the correct processes eventually accept $N-k$ votes, since there are at least $N-k$ correct processes which faithfully confirm each other's votes, and by assumption $N-k > \frac{N+k}{2}$.

In a round n, let correct processes p and q accept votes for b and b', respectively, from a process r. Then p and q received more than $\frac{N+k}{2}$ messages $\langle \text{echo}, r, n, b \rangle$ and $\langle \text{echo}, r, n, b' \rangle$, respectively. More than k processes, so at least one correct process, sent such messages to both p and q. This implies that $b = b'$.

Suppose a correct process p decides for b at the end of a round n, meaning that p accepted more than $\frac{N+k}{2}$ b-votes. In every round, each correct process ignores votes from only k processes, and we argued earlier that two correct processes never accept different values from the same process. So since p accepted more than $\frac{N+k}{2}$ b-votes in round n, all correct processes will accept more than $\frac{N+k}{2} - k = \frac{N-k}{2}$ b-votes in round n. Hence, after round n, all correct processes will have the value b. As a consequence, every correct process will vote b in each round $m > n$, because in each round $m \geq n$ it accepts at least $N - 2k > \frac{N-k}{2}$ b-votes. This implies that correct processes cannot decide for different values.

Let S be a set of $N-k$ correct processes. Due to fair scheduling, in each round there is a probability $\rho > 0$ that each process in S accepts $N-k$ votes from the processes in S. With probability ρ^2 this happens in consecutive rounds $n, n+1$. After round n, all processes in S have the same value b. After round $n+1$, all processes in S have decided for b, and broadcast $\langle \text{decide}, b \rangle$. To conclude, the algorithm terminates with probability one. □

Example 13.2 We revisit example 13.1, but now taking into account the verification phase of votes. Given a network of four processes p, q, r, s, and $k = 1$. Suppose that q is Byzantine. We consider one possible computation of the Bracha-Toueg 1-Byzantine consensus algorithm on this network. Each round, a correct process needs three confirming echoes to accept a vote, three accepted votes to complete the round, and three accepted b-votes to decide for b. Initially, p and s randomly choose the value 1 and r the value 0. In the pictures of the consecutive rounds, for every process two accepted votes from other processes and its own value in that round are depicted, which are used to determine the value of that process in the next round.

- In round 0, p and r accept a 1-vote by p and 0-votes by q and r, because they get confirmations for these votes from p, q, r. As a result, they set their value to 0. Furthermore, s accepts 1-votes by p and s, because it gets confirmations for these votes from p, r, s. However, s does not accept a 1-vote by q, because it receives only two confirmations, from q and s. In the end, s accepts a 0-vote by r, for which it gets confirmations from p, r, s, and sets its value to 1.

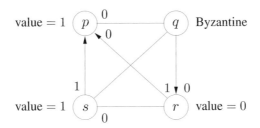

- In round 1, p and r accept 0-votes by p and q, because they get confirmations for these votes from p, q, r. Moreover, r accepts a 0-vote by r, decides for 0, and broadcasts $\langle \mathbf{decide}, 0 \rangle$. On the other hand, p accepts a 1-vote by s, because it gets confirmations for these votes from p, r, s, and sets its value to 0. Once again, s does not accept a 1-vote by q, because it receives only two confirmations, from q and s. Instead, s accepts 0-votes by p and r, and a 1-vote by s, because it gets confirmations for these votes from p, r, s. As a result, s sets its value to 0.

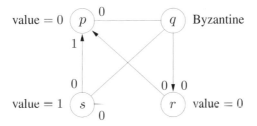

- Now that all correct processes have the value 0, in all future rounds this will remain the case. A decision for 0 by p and s could be postponed indefinitely, if q gets a 1-vote accepted by p and s in successive rounds. However, in order to complete this computation swiftly, we let $\langle \mathbf{decide}, 0 \rangle$ arrive at p and s, and in round 2 we let p and s accept each other's 0-vote, so that they decide for 0.

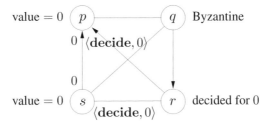

13.2 Mahaney-Schneider synchronizer

In this section we revisit bounded delay networks, in which there is an upper bound $d_{\max}$ on network latency; processes carry a local clock with ρ-bounded drift for some $\rho > 1$ (see section 11.3). It is shown that even in the presence of Byzantine processes, local clocks can be synchronized regularly so that they have a precision $\delta > 0$: at any time τ and for any pair of processes p, q, $|C_p(\tau) - C_q(\tau)| \leq \delta$.

First, it is shown that such a clock synchronization algorithm is possible only if fewer than one-third of the processes are Byzantine.

Theorem 13.3 *Let $k \geq \frac{N}{3}$. There is no k-Byzantine clock synchronization algorithm.*

Proof. Suppose we want to achieve clock synchronization so that the local clocks have precision $\delta > 0$. Consider a network of three processes p, q, r, where r is Byzantine, and let $k = 1$. (The following computation can be easily extended to general N and $k \geq \frac{N}{3}$; see exercise 13.4.)

Let the clock of p run faster than the clock of q. Suppose a synchronization takes place at real time τ, in which r sends $C_p(\tau) + \delta$ to p, and $C_q(\tau) - \delta$ to q. Since r reports a clock value to p that is within δ of p's local clock value, and since p receives only one other clock value (from q), p cannot recognize that r is Byzantine. Likewise, q cannot recognize that r is Byzantine. So p and q have to stay within range δ of the value reported by r, meaning that p cannot decrease and q cannot increase its clock value.

By repeating this scenario at each synchronization round, the clock values of p and q get further and further apart. So eventually, p will have to choose whether its clock stays within range δ of q's or r's clock, without being able to determine which of the two processes is Byzantine. And likewise for q. □

If at most $k < \frac{N}{3}$ processes are Byzantine, then clock synchronization can be achieved. To simplify the forthcoming presentation of Byzantine clock synchronization, we take the bound $d_{\max}$ on network latency to be zero. (In a sense, we assume that $d_{\max}$ is negligible compared to δ.)

In the Mahaney-Schneider k-Byzantine clock synchronization algorithm, processes regularly communicate their clock values to each other, and each process takes the average of all these clock values, whereby clock values that are provably from Byzantine processes are discarded. It is assumed that at the start of a clock synchronization, the local clocks have precision $\delta > 0$. This algorithm achieves that after a clock synchronization, the local clocks have precision $\frac{2}{3}\delta$.

The Mahaney-Schneider synchronizer proceeds in synchronization rounds, in which each correct process:

- collects the clock values of all processes,
- discards those reported values τ for which fewer than $N - k$ processes report a value in the interval $[\tau - \delta, \tau + \delta]$ (they are from Byzantine processes),
- replaces all discarded and nonreceived values by an accepted value, and
- takes the average of these N values as its new clock value.

Theorem 13.4 *The Mahaney-Schneider synchronizer is a k-Byzantine clock synchronization algorithm for any $k < \frac{N}{3}$.*

Proof. First we argue that if in some synchronization round, values a_p and a_q are accepted at correct processes p and q, respectively, then

$$|a_p - a_q| \leq 2\delta.$$

In this synchronization round, at least $N - k$ processes reported a value in $[a_p - \delta, a_p + \delta]$ to p, and at least $N - k$ processes reported a value in $[a_q - \delta, a_q + \delta]$ to q. Since $N - 2k > k$, this implies that at least one correct process r reported a value in $[a_p - \delta, a_p + \delta]$ to p, and in $[a_q - \delta, a_q + \delta]$ to q. Since r reports the same value to p and q, it follows that $|a_p - a_q| \leq 2\delta$.

In some synchronization round, let the correct processes p and q accept from (or assign to) each process r a value a_{pr} and a_{qr}, respectively. Then p and q compute as new clock value $\frac{1}{N}(\sum_{\text{processes } r} a_{pr})$ and $\frac{1}{N}(\sum_{\text{processes } r} a_{qr})$, respectively.

By the argument above, for all processes r, $|a_{pr} - a_{qr}| \leq 2\delta$. And $a_{pr} = a_{qr}$ for all correct processes r. Hence,

$$\left|\frac{1}{N}(\sum_{\text{processes } r} a_{pr}) - \frac{1}{N}(\sum_{\text{processes } r} a_{qr})\right| \leq \frac{1}{N}k2\delta < \frac{2}{3}\delta. \qquad \square$$

In the proof of theorem 13.4 it was shown that after a synchronization round, the clocks at correct processes have a precision smaller than $\frac{2}{3}\delta$. If the local clocks have been synchronized at time τ, then due to ρ-bounded drift of local clocks, if no synchronization takes place in the time interval $[\tau, \tau + R]$:

$$|C_p(\tau + R) - C_q(\tau + R)| < \frac{2}{3}\delta + (\rho - \frac{1}{\rho})R < \frac{2}{3}\delta + \rho R.$$

So to achieve precision δ, a synchronization of local clocks should be performed every $\frac{\delta}{3\rho}$ time units.

13.3 Lamport-Shostak-Pease broadcast algorithm

To cope with crash failures, failure detectors were introduced in section 12.3 to try to detect crashed processes. The two implementations of failure detectors that we discussed were both based on the absence of messages from a crashed process over a certain period of time. Detecting Byzantine processes is much more complicated, since they can keep on sending messages, and in general it is far from easy to determine that a process is performing events that are not in line with the specification of the distributed algorithm that is being executed. Therefore, to cope with Byzantine processes, another strategy is followed: the network must be transformed into a synchronous system.

In this section and the next we consider a variation on the Byzantine consensus problem, called Byzantine broadcast, in the setting of synchronous networks. One process, called the general, randomly chooses an initial value 0 or 1. The other processes, called lieutenants, know who is the general. In each execution of a (binary) Byzantine broadcast algorithm, the requirements termination and agreement must be satisfied, together with a variation on validity.

- *Dependence*: if the general is correct, then it decides for its own initial value.

A k-Byzantine broadcast algorithm can cope with at most k Byzantine processes. It will come as no surprise that for $k \geq \frac{N}{3}$ such an algorithm does not exist, even if we have a synchronous network.

Theorem 13.5 *Let $k \geq \frac{N}{3}$. There is no k-Byzantine broadcast algorithm for synchronous networks.*

Proof. Suppose toward a contradiction that a k-Byzantine broadcast algorithm for synchronous networks does exist. Divide the processes into three disjoint sets S, T, and U, with each at most k elements. Let the general be in S. We consider three different scenarios, which are depicted here.

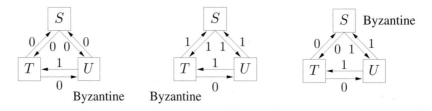

In the first scenario at the left, the processes in U are Byzantine, and the general starts with the value 0. The processes in S and T propagate 0. Moreover, all processes in $S \cup T$ should decide for 0. The Byzantine processes in U, however, propagate 1 to the processes in T.

In the second scenario in the middle, the processes in T are Byzantine, and the general starts with the value 1. The processes in S and U propagate 1. Moreover, all processes in $S \cup U$ should decide for 1. The Byzantine processes in T, however, propagate 0 to the processes in U.

In the third scenario at the right, the processes in S, including the general, are Byzantine. The processes in S propagate 0 to T, and as a result the processes in T do so too. Likewise, the processes in S propagate 1 to U, and as a result the processes in U do so too. Note that the inputs of the processes in T agree with the first scenario, so they all decide for 0. By contrast, the inputs of the processes in U agree with the second scenario, so they all decide for 1. This is a contradiction. □

The Lamport-Shostak-Pease broadcast algorithm for synchronous networks is a k-Byzantine broadcast algorithm for any $k < \frac{N}{3}$. Since the algorithm contains recursive calls to itself, we denote it with $Broadcast_g(N, k)$, where g denotes the general. Let *majority* be a (deterministic) function that maps each multiset (or bag) of elements from $\{0, 1\}$ to either 0 or 1; in a multiset, the same element can occur multiple times. If more than half of the elements in a multiset M are equal to b, then $majority(M) = b$.

The algorithm $Broadcast_g(N, k)$ proceeds in $k + 1$ pulses.

- *Pulse* 1: the general g, if correct, broadcasts its value, and decides for its value.

Each correct lieutenant q acts as follows. If q receives a value b from g, then it sets its value to b; else it sets its value to 0.
- If $k = 0$, then q decides for its value.
- If $k > 0$, then for every lieutenant p, q takes part in $Broadcast_p(N-1, k-1)$, starting in pulse 2.

- *Pulse $k + 1$ (if $k > 0$)*: each correct lieutenant q has, for every lieutenant p, computed a value in $Broadcast_p(N-1, k-1)$; it stores these $N-1$ values in a multiset $Decisions_q$. Finally, q sets its value to $majority(Decisions_q)$, and decides for this value.

Note that if the general is correct, then it can decide immediately, because by the dependence requirement all correct lieutenants are supposed to decide for the general's value. If $k = 0$, then the general is certainly correct, so that the lieutenants can also decide immediately, for the received value. However, if $k > 0$, then the lieutenants must count with the fact that the general may be Byzantine. Therefore, each correct lieutenant p starts a recursive call $Broadcast_p(N-1, k-1)$, reminiscent of the echo principle in the Bracha-Toueg Byzantine consensus algorithm; the general is excluded from this calls. This gives rise to a cascade of recursive calls, because if $k > 1$, then each of these calls may start another $N-2$ recursive calls, and so on.

We informally argue the correctness of the Lamport-Shostak-Pease broadcast algorithm; a more formal proof will be given at the end of this section. In case the general is correct, each recursive call $Broadcast_p(N-1, k-1)$ with p correct is guaranteed to yield the general's value at all correct lieutenants. Since a majority of the lieutenants is correct, by definition of the $majority$ function, all correct lieutenants will decide for the general's value. On the other hand, in case the general is Byzantine, by induction on k, all correct lieutenants are guaranteed to compute the same values in the $N-1$ recursive calls $Broadcast_p(N-1, k-1)$. So due to the deterministic nature of the $majority$ function, in pulse $k+1$ all correct lieutenants will compute and decide for the same value in $Broadcast_g(N, k)$.

We consider two examples of the Lamport-Shostak-Pease broadcast algorithm: one where the general is correct and one where the general is Byzantine.

Example 13.3 Consider a complete network with four processes g, p, q, r, and $k = 1$. Suppose that the general g and lieutenants p, q are correct, while lieutenant r is Byzantine. We consider one possible computation of the Lamport-Shostak-Pease broadcast algorithm $Broadcast_g(4, 1)$ on this network.

In pulse 1, g broadcasts and decides for 1. So after pulse 1, p and q carry the value 1. These lieutenants build, by the three recursive calls $Broadcast_s(3, 0)$ with $s \in \{p, q, r\}$, a multiset $\{1, 1, b\}$, where b can be distinct for p and q, as they may compute different values in $Broadcast_r(3, 0)$. Since the majority of values in these multisets equals 1, both p and q decide for 1.

Example 13.4 Consider a complete network with $N = 7$ and $k = 2$. Suppose that the general g and one lieutenant r are Byzantine. We consider one possible computation of the Lamport-Shostak-Pease broadcast algorithm $Broadcast_g(7, 2)$ on this network.

In pulse 1, the general sends 0 to three correct lieutenants, and 1 to the other two correct lieutenants. The five correct lieutenants all build, by the six recursive calls $Broadcast_s(6,1)$, the same multiset $M = \{0,0,0,1,1,b\}$, for some $b \in \{0,1\}$. Namely, even in $Broadcast_r(6,1)$, all correct lieutenants are guaranteed to compute the same value b. So they all decide for $majority(M)$.

For instance, in $Broadcast_r(6,1)$ the Byzantine lieutenant r could send 0 to two correct lieutenants, and 1 to the other three correct lieutenants. Then the five correct lieutenants all build, by five recursive calls $Broadcast_s(5,0)$, the same multiset $M = \{0,0,1,1,1\}$. So in this case $b = major(\{0,0,1,1,1\}) = 1$.

Theorem 13.6 *The Lamport-Shostak-Pease broadcast algorithm is a k-Byzantine broadcast algorithm for any $k < \frac{N}{3}$.*

Proof. Let f be the number of Byzantine processes in the network. First we prove that if the general g is correct, and $f < \frac{N-k}{2}$, then in $Broadcast_g(N,k)$ all correct processes decide for g's value. This holds even if $f > k$.

We prove this claim by induction on k. The base case $k=0$ is trivial, because g is assumed to be correct, so all correct processes decide for g's value in pulse 1. We now consider the inductive case $k > 0$. Since g is assumed to be correct, in pulse 1, all correct lieutenants set their value to g's value. By assumption, $f < \frac{(N-1)-(k-1)}{2}$, so by induction, for all correct lieutenants q, in $Broadcast_q(N-1,k-1)$ the value of q, that is, g's value is computed. Since a majority of the lieutenants is correct ($f < \frac{N-1}{2}$), in pulse $k+1$, a majority of the values that a correct lieutenant computes in the recursive calls $Broadcast_q(N-1,k-1)$ equal g's value. So in pulse $k+1$, each correct lieutenant computes and decides for g's value.

Now we prove that the Lamport-Shostak-Pease broadcast algorithm is a k-Byzantine broadcast algorithm for any $k < \frac{N}{3}$, again by induction on k. The case where g is correct follows immediately from the statement proved above, together with the fact that $f < \frac{N}{3} < \frac{N-k}{2}$. Therefore, we can assume that g is Byzantine (so $k > 0$). Then at most $k-1$ lieutenants are Byzantine. Since $k-1 < \frac{N-1}{3}$, by induction, all correct lieutenants compute the same value in $Broadcast_p(N-1,k-1)$ for every lieutenant p. Hence, all correct lieutenants compute the same multiset M in pulse $k+1$. So all correct lieutenants decide for the same value $majority(M)$. □

13.4 Lamport-Shostak-Pease authentication algorithm

A public-key cryptographic system consists of a finite message domain $\mathcal{M}$ and, for each process q, functions $S_q, P_q : \mathcal{M} \to \mathcal{M}$ with $S_q(P_q(m)) = P_q(S_q(m)) = m$ for all $m \in \mathcal{M}$. The key S_q is kept secret by q, while P_q is made public. The underlying assumption is that computing S_q from P_q is very expensive. A well-known and widely used public-key cryptographic system is RSA.

If a process p wants to send a secret message m to a process q, then p can send $P_q(m)$ to q. Because only q knows the secret key S_q that is needed to decrypt this message. Furthermore, if p wants to send a signed message m to q, such that other processes cannot fraudulently sign their messages with p's signature, then p can send $\langle m, S_p(m)\rangle$ to q. Because only p can compute $S_p(m)$, and q can obtain p's public key P_p, apply this to the signature $S_p(m)$, and check whether the result equals the message m.

The Lamport-Shostak-Pease authentication algorithm for synchronous systems uses this signature principle of public-key cryptographic systems in such a way that the Byzantine processes cannot lie about the values they have received. It is a correct and terminating k-Byzantine broadcast algorithm for any k. Each process p has a secret key S_p and a public key P_p. We step away from binary Byzantine broadcast: the correct processes must uniformly pick a value from a large domain of possible values. The reason is that on a small domain (in case of binary consensus consisting of only two values), computing S_q from P_q is easy. It is assumed that processes $q \neq p$ cannot guess values $S_p(v)$ without acquiring extra knowledge about S_p.

The Lamport-Shostak-Pease authentication algorithm proceeds in $k+1$ pulses:

- In pulse 1, the general, if correct, broadcasts $\langle value_g, (S_g(value_g), g)\rangle$, and decides for $value_g$.
- If in a pulse $i \leq k+1$ a correct lieutenant q receives a message $\langle v, (\sigma_1, p_1) : \cdots : (\sigma_i, p_i)\rangle$ that is *valid*, meaning that
  - $p_1 = g$,
  - $p_1, \ldots, p_i, q$ are distinct, and
  - $P_{p_k}(\sigma_k) = v$ for all $k = 1, \ldots, i$,

  then q includes v in the set $Values_q$.

  If $i \leq k$, then in pulse $i+1$, q sends to all other lieutenants the message

  $$\langle v, (\sigma_1, p_1) : \cdots : (\sigma_i, p_i) : (S_q(v), q)\rangle.$$

- After pulse $k+1$, each correct lieutenant q decides for v if $Values_q$ is a singleton $\{v\}$, or 0 otherwise. (In the latter case, the general is Byzantine.)

The second part of a message is a list of signatures. If a correct lieutenant q receives a valid message, meaning that the signatories are distinct, include the general and not the receiver, and each signatory p has added the correct signature $S_p(v)$, where v is the value contained in the first part of the message, then q takes v on board as possible value, adds its signature to the list of signatures, and broadcasts the message. A key observation is that each such message in pulse $k+1$ contains a list of $k+1$ signatures, so at least one signature from a correct process. This means that no later than pulse $k+1$, every lieutenant will have received a valid message with this value. As a result, after pulse $k+1$ all correct lieutenants have computed the same set $Values$. So they all decide for the same value. And if the general is correct, then these sets are guaranteed to only contain $value_g$, because then Byzantine processes cannot forge signatures by the general for other values.

Example 13.5 Consider a complete network of four processes g, p, q, r, and let $k = 2$. Suppose that the general g and lieutenant r are Byzantine. We consider one possible computation of the Lamport-Shostak-Pease authentication algorithm.

- In pulse 1, g sends $\langle 0, (S_g(0), g)\rangle$ to p and q, and $\langle 1, (S_g(1), g)\rangle$ to r. Then $Values_p$ and $Values_q$ become $\{0\}$.
- In pulse 2, p and q broadcast $\langle 0, (S_g(0), g) : (S_p(0), p)\rangle$ and $\langle 0, (S_g(0), g) : (S_q(0), q)\rangle$, respectively. And r sends $\langle 1, (S_g(1), g) : (S_r(1), r)\rangle$ to only q. Then $Values_p$ remains $\{0\}$, while $Values_q$ becomes $\{0, 1\}$.
- In pulse 3, q broadcasts $\langle 1, (S_g(1), g) : (S_r(1), r) : (S_q(1), q)\rangle$. Then $Values_p$ becomes $\{0, 1\}$.
- After pulse 3, p and q both decide for 0, because $Values_p$ and $Values_q$ contain two elements.

Theorem 13.7 *The authentication algorithm from Lamport-Shostak-Pease is a k-Byzantine broadcast algorithm for any k.*

Proof. If the general is correct, then Byzantine processes will not get an opportunity to forge a signature for a value different from $value_g$ on behalf of the general. So owing to authentication, correct lieutenants will only add $value_g$ to their set $Values$. Hence, all processes will decide for $value_g$.

Suppose a correct lieutenant q receives a valid message $\langle v, \ell\rangle$ in a pulse $i = 1, \ldots, k + 1$. We distinguish two cases.

- $i \leq k$: then in the next pulse, q broadcasts a message that will make all correct lieutenants add v to their set $Values$.
- $i = k + 1$: since the list ℓ of signatures has length $k + 1$, it contains a correct process p. Then p received a valid message $\langle v, \ell'\rangle$ in a pulse $j \leq k$. In pulse $j + 1$, p has broadcast a message that makes all correct lieutenants add v to their set $Values$.

So after pulse $k + 1$, $Values_q$ is the same for all correct lieutenants q. Hence, after pulse $k + 1$ they all decide for the same value. □

The Dolev-Strong optimization minimizes the number of required messages. This optimization lets each correct lieutenant broadcast at most two messages, with different values. When it has broadcast two different values, all correct lieutenants are certain to compute a set $Values$ with at least two values, so that all correct lieutenants will decide for 0.

Bibliographical notes

The Bracha-Toueg Byzantine consensus algorithm stems from [11]. The Mahaney-Schneider synchronizer originates from [52]. The Lamport-Shostak-Pease broadcast and authentication algorithms were proposed in [47]. The Dolev-Strong optimization is due to [28].

Exercises

Exercise 13.1 Consider a complete network of four processes, in which one process is Byzantine. Apply the Bracha-Toueg 1-Byzantine consensus algorithm, where initially one correct process chooses the value 0 and two correct processes the value 1. Give a computation in which all correct processes decide for 0.

Exercise 13.2 [76] In the Bracha-Toueg k-Byzantine consensus algorithm, suppose that more than $\frac{N+k}{2}$ correct processes initially choose the value b. Explain why the correct processes will eventually decide for b.

Exercise 13.3 Given three correct processes p_0, p_1, p_2 and a Byzantine process q. Let the local clocks of p_0 and p_1 run half as fast as real time, and let the local clock of p_2 run twice as fast as real time. Consider the Mahaney-Schneider synchronizer for some precision $\delta > 0$, whereby it is assumed that $d_{\max} = 0$ (that is, messages are communicated instantaneously).

(a) What is the smallest $\rho > 1$ for which the clocks of p_0, p_1, p_2 are all ρ-bounded?
(b) Suppose that at real time τ, the clocks of p_0 and p_1 are at $\tau - \frac{\delta}{3}$, while the clock at p_2 is at $\tau + \frac{\delta}{3}$. Let p_0, p_1, p_2 synchronize their clocks at real time $\tau + \frac{\delta}{3\rho}$ (with the ρ from part (a)). Show that whatever input q gives at this synchronization point, the clocks of p_0, p_1, p_2 are not more than $\frac{2\delta}{3}$ apart.
(c) Repeat the exercise in part (b), but now leaving out p_0. Show that in this case after synchronization at real time $\tau + \frac{\delta}{3\rho}$, the clocks of p_1 and p_2 can be more than $\frac{2\delta}{3}$ apart.

Exercise 13.4 Argue the impossibility of k-Byzantine clock synchronization for general N and $k \geq \frac{N}{3}$.

Exercise 13.5 The k-Byzantine synchronizer of Lamport and Melliar-Smith differs from the Mahaney-Schneider synchronizer in one aspect: a correct process p accepts a local clock value of another process q if it differs no more than δ from its own clock value, at the moment of synchronization.

Explain why that synchronizer has precision $\frac{3k}{N}\delta$ (versus precision $\frac{2k}{N}\delta$ of the Mahaney-Schneider synchronizer).

Exercise 13.6 Explain how the Mahaney-Schneider synchronizer must be adapted in case $d_{\max} > 0$.

Exercise 13.7 Let $N = 5$ and $k = 1$, and let the general g be Byzantine. Suppose that in pulse 1, g sends the value 1 to two lieutenants, and the value 0 to the other two lieutenants. Give a computation of $Broadcast_g(5, 1)$ (including a definition of the *majority* function) such that all lieutenants decide for 0.

Exercise 13.8 Let $N = 7$ and $k = 2$, and let the general g and one lieutenant be Byzantine. Give a computation of $Broadcast_g(7, 2)$ (and its subcalls) in which all correct lieutenants decide for $majority(\{0, 0, 0, 1, 1, 1\})$.

Exercise 13.9 [76] Determine the worst-case message complexity of the correct processes in $Broadcast_g(N, k)$.

Exercise 13.10 Apply the Lamport-Shostak-Pease authentication algorithm to a complete network of five processes. Let three of the processes be Byzantine. Give a computation in which the two correct processes would decide for different values at the end of pulse 3, but decide for the same value in pulse 4.

Exercise 13.11 Let $k \geq N - 1$. Explain why the Lamport-Shostak-Pease authentication algorithm can then be adapted by letting it already terminate at the end of pulse $N - 1$.

Exercise 13.12 Determine the worst-case message complexity of the correct processes in the Lamport-Shostak-Pease authentication algorithm, taking into account the Dolev-Strong optimization.

14
Mutual Exclusion

Mutual exclusion in distributed systems aims to serialize access to a shared resource, such as updating a database or sending a control signal to an I/O device. Although multiple processes may want to access the resource concurrently, at any moment in time at most one process should be privileged, meaning that it is allowed access. A process that becomes privileged is said to enter its critical section, which is a block of source code where the process needs access to the resource. When a process gives up the privilege, it is said to exit its critical section. Mutual exclusion algorithms are supposed to satisfy the following two properties, in each execution:

- *Mutual exclusion*: in every configuration, at most one process is privileged.
- *Starvation-freeness*: if a process p tries to enter its critical section, and no process remains privileged forever, then p will eventually enter its critical section.

In a message-passing setting, mutual exclusion algorithms are generally based on one of the following three paradigms.

- *A logical clock*: requests for entering a critical section are prioritized by means of logical time stamps.
- *Token passing*: the process holding the token is privileged.
- *Quorums*: to become privileged, a process needs the permission from a quorum of processes. Each pair of quorums should have a nonempty intersection.

We will discuss one mutual exclusion algorithm for each of these categories.

14.1 Ricart-Agrawala algorithm

The Ricart-Agrawala mutual exclusion algorithm uses a logical clock (see chapter 2). For simplicity, we assume that the network topology is complete.

When a process p_i (where i is its ID) wants to enter its critical section, it sends the message $\langle \textbf{request}, ts_i, i \rangle$ to all other processes, with ts_i its logical time stamp. The second argument of this message, the process ID, is meant to break ties between two competing processes that send concurrent requests with the same logical time stamp; then the request from the process with the lowest ID has the highest priority. When another process p_j receives this request, it sends permission to p_i as soon as:

- p_j is not privileged, and
- p_j does not have a pending request with a logical time stamp ts_j where $(ts_j, j) < (ts_i, i)$ (with respect to the lexicographical order).

p_i enters its critical section when it has received permission from all other processes.

Actually, the Ricart-Agrawala algorithm does not require a full-blown logical clock. It suffices if only requests are taken into account. That is, if a process receives a request with time stamp t, then it increases its clock value to $t + 1$.

We consider two examples, both with $N = 2$. Let clocks start at time 1.

Example 14.1 p_1 sends $\langle \textbf{request}, 1, 1 \rangle$ to p_0. At reception of this request, p_0 sends permission to p_1, and sets its clock value to 2. Next, p_0 sends $\langle \textbf{request}, 2, 0 \rangle$ to p_1. When p_1 receives this message, it does not send permission to p_0, because $(1, 1) < (2, 0)$; it sets its clock value to 3. Finally, p_1 receives permission from p_0, and enters its critical section.

Example 14.2 p_1 sends $\langle \textbf{request}, 1, 1 \rangle$ to p_0, and p_0 sends $\langle \textbf{request}, 1, 0 \rangle$ to p_1. When p_0 receives the request from p_1, it does not send permission to p_1, because $(1, 0) < (1, 1)$. When p_1 receives the request from p_0, it does send permission to p_0, because $(1, 0) < (1, 1)$. Both p_0 and p_1 set their clock value to 2. Finally, p_0 receives permission from p_1, and enters its critical section.

We argue that the Ricart-Agrawala algorithm guarantees mutual exclusion. Suppose a process p wants to enter its critical section and sends requests to all other processes. When another process q sends permission to p, q is not privileged; and since q's pending or future request is larger than p's request, q will not get permission from p to enter its critical section until after p has entered and left its critical section. The Ricart-Agrawala algorithm is also starvation-free, because each request will eventually become the smallest request in the network.

A drawback of the Ricart-Agrawala algorithm is the high message overhead, because requests must be sent to all other processes. The Carvalho-Roucairol optimization reduces this message overhead. Suppose a process p entered its critical section before and wants to enter it again. Then p only needs to send requests to processes that p has sent permission to since the last exit from its critical section. Because as long as another process q has not obtained p's permission, q cannot enter its critical section (even when the Carvalho-Roucairol optimization is being applied), because q has previously given permission to p. If such a process q sends a request to p while p is waiting for permissions, and q's request is smaller than p's outstanding request, then p sends both permission and a request to q.

14.2 Raymond's algorithm

Raymond's mutual exclusion algorithm is based on token passing; only the process holding the token may be privileged. It assumes an undirected network, and starts from a spanning tree in this network; the root of this sink tree holds the token.

Each process maintains a FIFO queue, which can contain IDs of its children in the sink tree, and its own ID. Initially, this queue is empty. A process maintains its queue as follows:

- When a nonroot wants to enter its critical section, it adds its ID to its own queue.
- Each time a nonroot gets a new head at its (nonempty) queue, it sends a request for the token to its parent in the sink tree.
- When a process receives a request for the token from a child, it adds the ID of this child at the end of its queue.
- When the root has left its critical section and its queue is or becomes nonempty, it sends the token to the process q at the head of its queue, makes q its parent, and removes q's ID from the head of its queue.

In the special case that the root wants to enter its critical section again and its queue is empty, it can become privileged straightaway.

Let a nonroot p get the token from its parent, and let the ID of the process q be at the head of p's queue.

- If $p \neq q$, then p sends the token to q, and makes q its parent.
- If $p = q$, then p becomes the root; that is, it has no parent and is privileged.

In both cases, p removes q's ID from the head of its queue.

Example 14.3 We consider one possible computation of Raymond's algorithm, on an undirected network of five processes. In every picture, the gray process is the root.

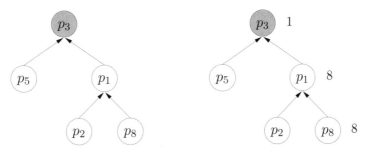

Initially, in the picture at the left, p_3 is the root, and in its critical section. Next, in the picture at the right, the following has happened. Since p_8 wants to enter its critical section, it placed its own ID in its queue. Since this was a new head of its queue, p_8 sent a request for the token to its parent p_1. As a result, p_1 also placed the ID 8 in its queue. Since this was a new head of its queue, p_1 sent a request for the token to its parent p_3. As a result, p_3 placed the ID 1 in its queue.

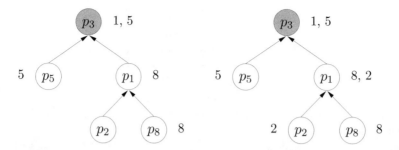

In the picture at the left, p_5 wants to enter its critical section, so it placed its own ID in its queue. Since this was a new head of its queue, p_5 sent a request for the token to its parent p_3. As a result, p_3 also placed the ID 5 in its queue. In the picture at the right, p_2 wants to enter its critical section, so it placed its own ID in its queue. Since this was a new head of its queue, p_2 sent a request for the token to its parent p_1. As a result, p_1 also placed the ID 2 in its queue.

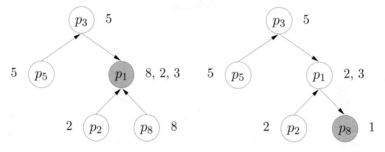

In the picture at the left, p_3 exited its critical section. Since the ID 1 was the head of its queue, it sent the token to p_1, made p_1 its parent, and removed 1 from its queue. Then 5 became the new head of its queue, so p_3 sent a request for the token to its parent p_1. When p_1 received the token, it became the root. Moreover, the request from p_3 made p_1 add the ID 3 to its queue. In the picture at the right, since the ID 8 was the head of its queue, p_1 forwarded the token to p_8, made p_8 its parent, and removed 8 from its queue. Then 2 became the new head of its queue, so p_1 sent a request for the token to its parent p_8. When p_8 received the token, it became the root, removed 8 from its queue, and entered its critical section. Moreover, the request from p_1 made p_8 add the ID 1 to its queue.

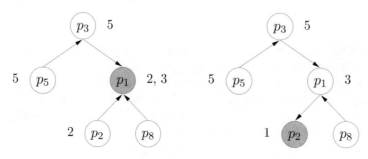

14.2 Raymond's algorithm

In the picture at the left, p_8 exited its critical section. Since the ID 1 was the head of its queue, it sent the token to p_1, made p_1 its parent, and removed 1 from its queue. When p_1 received the token, it became the root. In the picture at the right, since the ID 2 was the head of its queue, p_1 forwarded the token to p_2, made p_2 its parent, and removed 2 from its queue. Then 3 became the new head of its queue, so p_1 sent a request for the token to its parent p_2. When p_2 received the token, it became the root, removed 2 from its queue, and entered its critical section. Moreover, the request from p_1 made p_2 add the ID 1 to its queue.

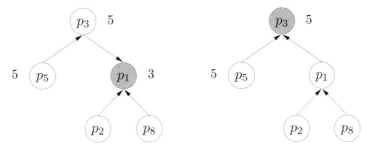

In the picture at the left, p_2 exited its critical section. Since the ID 1 was the head of its queue, it sent the token to p_1, made p_1 its parent, and removed 1 from its queue. When p_1 received the token, it became the root. In the picture at the right, since the ID 3 was the head of its queue, p_1 forwarded the token to p_3, made p_3 its parent, and removed 3 from its queue. When p_3 received the token, it became the root.

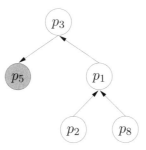

In the final picture, since the ID 5 was the head of its queue, p_3 sent the token to p_5, made p_5 its parent, and removed 5 from its queue. When p_5 received the token, it became the root, removed 5 from its queue, and entered its critical section.

Whenever a process holds the token, it is easy to see that it is the root of the sink tree. Raymond's algorithm clearly provides mutual exclusion, because at all times at most one process holds the token. Raymond's algorithm also provides starvation-freeness, because eventually each request in a queue moves to the head of this queue, and a chain of requests never contains a cycle.

14.3 Agrawal-El Abbadi algorithm

In the Agrawal-El Abbadi mutual exclusion algorithm, a process must obtain permission from a quorum of processes to enter its critical section. The crucial property of quorums is that each pair of quorums has a nonempty intersection. This guarantees mutual exclusion. The key of the Agrawal-El Abbadi algorithm is how quorums are defined. A strong point of this algorithm is that it can cope with processes that are not responsive.

For simplicity, we assume that the network topology is complete and that $N = 2^{k+1} - 1$ for some $k > 0$. The processes are structured in a binary tree of depth k. A quorum consists of all processes on a path in this binary tree from the root to a leaf. If a nonleaf r is unresponsive, then instead of asking permission from p, permission can be asked from all processes on two paths: from each child of r to some leaf. We note that a process may have to ask permission from itself.

To be more precise, a process p that wants to enter its critical section, places the root of the tree in a queue. Then it repeatedly tries to get permission from the process r at the head of its queue. If successful, r is removed from p's queue; in case r is a nonleaf, *one* of the two children of r is appended at the end of p's queue. If a nonleaf r is found to be unresponsive, then r is removed from p's queue, and *both* of its children are appended at the end of the queue, in a fixed order, to avoid deadlocks; for instance, the left child is always placed before the right node. Otherwise, two processes p and q could find that a nonleaf r is unresponsive, after which p and q might obtain permission from the left and right child of r, respectively, leading to a deadlock. If a leaf r is found to be unresponsive, p's attempt to become privileged must be aborted. When p's queue becomes empty, it has received permission from a quorum of processes, so that it can enter its critical section. After exiting its critical section, p informs all processes in the quorum that their permission to p can be withdrawn.

If processes may crash, a complete and strongly accurate failure detector is required, and a process withdraws its permission if it detects that the process to which it has given permission has crashed.

Example 14.4 Let $N = 7$, and suppose the processes are structured in a binary tree as follows.

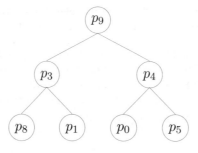

Some possible quorums are:

- $\{p_9,p_3,p_8\}$, $\{p_9,p_3,p_1\}$, $\{p_9,p_4,p_0\}$, and $\{p_9,p_4,p_5\}$.
- If p_9 is not responding: $\{p_3,p_8,p_4,p_0\}$, $\{p_3,p_1,p_4,p_0\}$, $\{p_3,p_8,p_4,p_5\}$, and $\{p_3,p_1,p_4,p_5\}$.
- If p_3 is not responding: $\{p_9,p_8,p_1\}$.
- If p_4 is not responding: $\{p_9,p_0,p_5\}$.

For more possible quorums in this network, see exercise 14.8.

Suppose that two processes p and q concurrently want to enter their critical section; we consider one possible computation, with regard to the binary tree above. First, p obtains permission from p_9, and now it wants to obtain permission from p_4. Next, p_9 crashes, which is observed by q, who now wants to obtain permission from p_3 and p_4. Let q obtain permission from p_3, after which it appends p_8 at the end of its queue. Next, q obtains permission from p_4, after which it appends p_5 at the end of its queue. Next, p_4 crashes, which is observed by p, who now wants to obtain permission from p_0 and p_5. Next, q obtains permission from p_8, and now it wants to obtain permission from p_5. Finally, p obtains permission from both p_0 and p_5, and enters its critical section. It has obtained permission from the quorum $\{p_9,p_0,p_5\}$.

We argue, by induction on the depth of the binary tree, that each pair of quorums Q and Q' have a nonempty intersection. This implies that the Agrawal-El Abbadi algorithm guarantees mutual exclusion. A quorum that includes the root contains a quorum in one of the subtrees below the root, while a quorum without the root contains a quorum in both subtrees below the root. If Q and Q' both contain the root, then we are done, because the root is in their intersection. If they both do not contain the root, then by induction they have elements in common in the two subtrees below the root. Finally, if Q contains the root while Q' does not, then Q contains a quorum in one of the subtrees below the root, and Q' also contains a quorum in this subtree; so by induction, Q and Q' have an element in common in this subtree.

The Agrawal-El Abbadi algorithm is deadlock-free, if all leaves are responsive. This property depends crucially on the strict queue management. Suppose that in case of an unresponsive process, its left child is placed before its right child in the queue of a process that wants to become privileged. Consider the following total order $<$ on processes, based on their position in the binary tree: $p < q$ if either p occurs at smaller depth than q in the binary tree, or p and q occur at the same depth and q is placed more to the right than p in the binary tree. Then a process which has obtained permission from a process r, never needs permission from a process $q < r$ to enter its critical section. This guarantees that in case all leaves are responsive, some process will always become privileged. Starvation may happen if a process infinitely often fails to get permission from a process in the binary tree, but this could be easily resolved.

Bibliographical notes

The Ricart-Agrawala algorithm was presented in [68], and the Carvalho-Roucairol optimization in [14]. Raymond's algorithm originates from [67], and the Agrawal-El Abbadi algorithm from [2].

Exercises

Exercise 14.1 Say for both mutual exclusion and starvation-freeness whether this is a safety or liveness property.

Exercise 14.2 Explain in detail why the Carvalho-Roucairol optimization of the Ricart-Agrawala algorithm is correct.

Exercise 14.3 Show that if processes could apply the Carvalho-Roucairol optimization from the start (instead of after a first entry of their critical section), then the resulting mutual exclusion algorithm would be incorrect.

Exercise 14.4 The logical clock values in the Ricart-Agrawala algorithm are unbounded. Adapt the algorithm such that the range of these values becomes finite (using modulo arithmetic).

Exercise 14.5 Run Raymond's algorithm on the network from example 14.3. Initially, process p_3 holds the token, and all buffers are empty. Give a computation (including all messages) in which first p_8, then p_2, and finally p_5 requests the token, but they receive the token in the opposite order.

Exercise 14.6 Argue that in Raymond's algorithm, each request to enter a critical section gives rise to at most $2D$ messages.

Exercise 14.7 Explain in detail why Raymond's algorithm is starvation-free.

Exercise 14.8 Consider the Agrawal-El Abbadi algorithm, with seven processes structured in a binary tree as in example 14.4. What are the quorums if p_9, p_4 crashed? And if p_9, p_3, p_4 crashed? And if p_9, p_3, p_8 crashed?

Exercise 14.9 In the Agrawal-El Abbadi algorithm, what is the minimum and the maximum size of a quorum (in terms of N)?

Exercise 14.10 Prove that for each pair of quorums Q and Q' in the Agrawal-El Abbadi algorithm, $Q \subseteq Q'$ implies $Q = Q'$.

Exercise 14.11 Adapt the Agrawal-El Abbadi algorithm to make it starvation-free, if all leaves in the binary tree are responsive.

II

Shared Memory

15
Preliminaries

In a shared-memory framework, a number of (hardware) processors communicate with main memory, and with the other processors, over a bus. Processors and main memory are snooping, meaning that they are listening for messages that are broadcast over the bus.

The processes (or threads) are sequential programs that can run on a processor; at any time at most one process is running on each processor. Processes communicate with each other, asynchronously, via variables in main memory, called registers (or fields). We distinguish single-reader registers, which are fields that can be read by only one process, and multi-reader registers, which can be read by all processes. Likewise we distinguish single-writer and multi-writer registers. Unless stated differently, it will be assumed that registers are multi-reader.

An event at a process typically consists of a read or write to a register. *Read-modify-write* operations, however, read a memory location and write a new value into it in one atomic step; this new value may be computed on the basis of the value returned by the read. Atomicity is obtained by keeping a lock on the bus from the moment the value is read until the moment the new value is written. Typical examples of read-modify-write operations are:

- *test-and-set*, which writes $true$ in a Boolean register, and returns the previous value of the register.
- *get-and-increment*, which increases the value of an integer register by one, and returns the previous value of the register.
- *get-and-set(new)*, which writes the value *new* in a register, and returns the previous value of the register.
- *compare-and-set(old, new)*, which checks whether the value of the register equals *old*, and if so, overwrites it with the value *new*; a Boolean value is returned to signal whether the new value was actually written.

We note that a software crash is always a consequence of a hardware instruction (for example, a program counter is set to an incorrect address). Therefore, processes do not crash during a read-modify-write operation; this means that, in the absence of a hardware crash, the lock on the bus is always eventually released.

Mutual exclusion is of the essence in a shared-memory framework, to avoid simultaneous use of, for instance, a block of memory. A common way to achieve this is by means of locks; to become privileged, one must obtain the lock, and at any time at most one process can hold the lock. The three mutual exclusion algorithms presented in chapter 14 basically all use this principle. In a setting with locks, we distinguish two kinds of progress properties for mutual exclusion algorithms, under the assumption that no process holds the lock forever. An algorithm is *livelock-free* if some process trying to get the lock eventually succeeds. It is *starvation-free* if every process trying to get the lock eventually succeeds.

Sometimes we will take into account caches, which are relatively small memory units, local to a processor, to store copies of data from main memory that are frequently used. Access to main memory is slow compared to cache access. Changes to data values are therefore accumulated in the local cache, and written back to main memory when needed: to make place in the cache, when another process wants the value, or at some memory barrier which enforces that writes are performed. When a process takes a cache miss, meaning that it cannot find some data in its cache, the required data is fetched from main memory, or provided by a snooping processor.

We assume that some cache coherence protocol is in place to maintain the consistency of the data in the local caches. In the presence of caches, typically synchronization primitives are needed to avoid that processes read stale values from a cache, but instead fetch fresh values from main memory. Notably, one can impose memory barriers, or declare that for certain variables the writes and reads are always with regard to main memory (for example, in Java such variables are declared volatile). Locks and read-modify-write operations tend to come with automatic synchronization primitives: when a process acquires a lock or performs a read-modify-write operation, it invalidates its working memory, to ensure that fields are reread from main memory; and when it releases the lock, modified fields in its working memory are written back to main memory.

Exercises

Exercise 15.1 Suppose that crashes of processes cannot be observed. Argue that it is impossible to achieve 2-crash consensus for three processes with only *test-and-set*.

Exercise 15.2 Give a k-crash consensus algorithm using *compare-and-set* that works for any k.

16
Mutual Exclusion II

Mutual exclusion, which aims to serialize access to a shared resource (see chapter 14), is of vital importance in a shared-memory setting. Notably, a process may want to lock a block of shared memory, to ensure exclusive access to it.

We assume that mutual exclusion needs to be resolved among N processes $p_0, \ldots, p_{N-1}$. The algorithms in this chapter use *spinning* (also called busy-waiting), meaning that values of registers are read repeatedly, until some condition is met.

16.1 Peterson's algorithm

Mutual exclusion for two processes

Peterson's algorithm provides mutual exclusion for two processes p_0 and p_1. The basic idea is that when a process p_b wants to enter its critical section, it signals its intention to the process p_{1-b} by setting a Boolean flag. Next, p_b repeatedly checks whether p_{1-b}'s flag is set. As soon as this is not the case, p_b enters its critical section. When p_b exits its critical section, it resets its flag.

This simple mutual exclusion algorithm suffers from livelock, if p_0 and p_1 concurrently set their flag. To avoid livelock, Peterson's algorithm exploits a *wait* register. When p_b wants to enter its critical section, not only does it set its flag, but it also sets *wait* to b. If p_b now finds that $wait = 1 - b$, it can enter its critical section, even when the flag of p_{1-b} is set. In the latter case p_0 and p_1 concurrently set their flag, and p_{1-b} wrote to *wait* last, so that it must wait.

To be more precise, Peterson's algorithm uses a multi-writer register *wait* with range $\{0, 1\}$, and single-writer registers $flag[b]$ of type Boolean for $b = 0, 1$; only p_b can write to $flag[b]$. Initially, $flag[b] = false$. When p_b wants to enter its critical section, it first sets $flag[b]$ to $true$ and then *wait* to b. Next, it spins on $flag[1-b]$ and *wait* until $flag[1-b] = false$ or $wait = 1 - b$, and then enters its critical section. When p_b exits its critical section, it sets $flag[b]$ to $false$.

Example 16.1 We consider one possible execution of Peterson's algorithm. Initially, $flag[b] = false$ for $b = 0, 1$.

- p_1 wants to enter its critical section, sets $flag[1]$ to $true$ and $wait$ to 1.
- p_0 wants to enter its critical section and sets $flag[0]$ to $true$.
- Since $flag[0] = true$ and $wait = 1$, p_1 does not yet enter its critical section.
- p_0 sets $wait$ to 0. Since $flag[1] = true$ and $wait = 0$, p_0 does not yet enter its critical section.
- Since $wait = 0$, p_1 enters its critical section.
- p_1 exits its critical section and sets $flag[1]$ to $false$.
- p_1 wants to enter its critical section, sets $flag[1]$ to $true$ and $wait$ to 1. Since $flag[0] = true$ and $wait = 1$, p_1 does not yet enter its critical section.
- Since $wait = 1$, p_0 enters its critical section.

We argue that Peterson's algorithm provides mutual exclusion. Suppose p_b is in its critical section (so it performed $flag[b] \leftarrow true$ and $wait \leftarrow b$), and p_{1-b} tries to enter its critical section. There are two possibilities:

1. Before entering its critical section, p_b read $flag[1-b] = false$. Then p_{1-b} must set $flag[1-b]$ to $true$ and $wait$ to $1-b$ before it can enter its critical section.
2. Before entering its critical section, p_b read $wait = 1-b$.

In both cases, $wait$ has the value $1-b$ by the time p_{1-b} starts spinning on $flag[b]$ and $wait$. Since, moreover, $flag[b] = true$, p_{1-b} can enter its critical section only after p_b has set $flag[b]$ to $false$ or $wait$ to b. Hence, p_{1-b} must wait until p_b is no longer in its critical section.

Peterson's algorithm is starvation-free. Let p_{1-b} try to enter its critical section. Then it sets $flag[1-b]$ to $true$ and $wait$ to $1-b$. Now p_b could only starve p_{1-b} by repeatedly trying to entering its critical section, because p_{1-b} should continuously read $flag[b] = true$. However, before (re)entering, p_b sets $wait$ to b, after which p_{1-b} can enter its critical section.

Mutual exclusion for more than two processes

To obtain a mutual exclusion algorithm for $N > 2$ processes, we build a *tournament tree*, being a binary tree of depth $k > 0$ in which each node represents an application of Peterson's algorithm for two processes. Initially, at most two processes are assigned to each of the 2^k leaves of the tournament tree; for simplicity, we assume that $N = 2^{k+1}$. A process that wants to enter its critical section performs Peterson's algorithm at its leaf. When a process becomes privileged at a nonroot, it proceeds to the parent of this node in the tournament tree. There it runs Peterson's algorithm again, where it may have to compete with the winner of the competition of the subtree below the other side of this node. A process that becomes privileged at the root in the tournament tree enters its critical section.

To be more precise, nodes in the tournament tree are numbered as follows: the root carries number 0, and given a node with the number n, its left and right child carry the number $2n+1$ and $2n+2$, respectively. To each node n we associate three multi-writer registers: $wait_n$ with range $\{0,1\}$, and $flag_n[b]$ of type Boolean for $b = 0, 1$. Initially, $flag_n[b] = false$. Each node has two sides, 0 and 1, and a process p_i that wants to enter its critical section is assigned to the leaf $(2^k - 1) + \lfloor i/2 \rfloor$, at

16.1 Peterson's algorithm

the side $i \bmod 2$. A process at side b of a node n performs the following procedure $Peterson(n, b)$.

$flag_n[b] \leftarrow true; \quad wait_n \leftarrow b;$
while $flag_n[1 - b] = true$ **and** $wait_n = b$ **do**
    $\{\};$
end while
if $n = 0$ **then**
    enter critical section;
    exit critical section;
else
    perform procedure $Peterson(\lceil n/2 \rceil - 1, (n + 1) \bmod 2);$
end if
$flag_n[b] \leftarrow false;$

The first four lines are simply Peterson's algorithm at node n. The next six lines express that at the root becoming privileged means entering the critical section, while at a nonroot it means moving to the parent node, where Peterson's algorithm is run once again. The last line makes sure that when a process exits its critical section, its flags at all the nodes it visited are set back to *false*, thus releasing processes that may be waiting at these nodes.

Example 16.2 We consider one possible execution of Peterson's algorithm in a tournament tree. Let $N = 8$, so $k = 2$. Suppose that p_1 and p_6 both want to enter their critical section; p_1 starts at node 3, side 1, and p_6 at node 6, side 0.

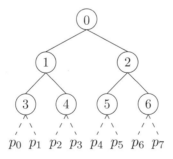

Initially, $flag_n[b] = false$ for all n and b.

- p_6 executes $Peterson(6, 0)$. It sets $flag_6[0]$ to *true* and $wait_6$ to 0, and (since $flag_6[1] = false$) continues with executing $Peterson(2, 1)$. It sets $flag_2[1]$ to *true* and $wait_2$ to 1, and (since $flag_2[0] = false$) continues with executing $Peterson(0, 1)$. It sets $flag_0[1]$ to *true*.
- p_1 executes $Peterson(3, 1)$. It sets $flag_3[1]$ to *true* and $wait_3$ to 1, and (since $flag_3[0] = false$) continues with executing $Peterson(1, 0)$. It sets $flag_1[0]$ to *true* and $wait_1$ to 0, and (since $flag_1[1] = false$) continues with executing

$Peterson(0, 0)$. It sets $flag_0[0]$ to $true$ and $wait_0$ to 0. Since $flag_0[1] = true$ and $wait_0 = 0$, p_1 must wait.
- p_6 finally sets $wait_0$ to 1. Since $flag_0[0] = true$ and $wait_0 = 1$, p_6 must wait.
- Since $wait_0 = 1$, p_1 can enter its critical section.
- When p_1 exits its critical section, it sets $flag_0[0]$, $flag_1[0]$, and $flag_3[1]$ to $false$.
- Since $flag_0[0] = false$, p_6 can enter its critical section.

We argue that the tournament tree provides mutual exclusion. Suppose that a process p has moved from a node n, at a side b, to its critical section (if $n = 0$) or to the parent of n (if $n > 0$). We show by induction on $k - \ell$, where ℓ is the depth of n in the tournament tree, that no other process can move away from n until p has left its critical section. For the process at side $1 - b$ of n this follows from the mutual exclusion property of Peterson's algorithm for two processes. Furthermore, if n is not a leaf, by induction, no process can move from the child of n at side b to n until p has left its critical section. Hence, at any time, and for any $\ell = -1, 0, \ldots, k$, at most $2^{\ell+1}$ processes can be at a node at a depth $\leq \ell$ in the tournament tree, where a critical section counts as depth -1. In particular, at any time, at most one process can be in its critical section.

The tournament tree moreover is starvation-free. Suppose that a process p has arrived at a node n in the tournament tree. We argue by induction on the depth of n in the tournament tree that p will eventually enter its critical section. Suppose that p is at the moment stuck at n. Then some other process q entered its critical section (in the base case $n = 0$) or moved to the parent of n (in the inductive case $n > 0$), thereby blocking p; in the case $n > 0$, by induction, q will eventually enter its critical section. When q exits its critical section, it will set the flag at its side of n to $false$, after which p can enter its critical section (if $n = 0$), or move to the parent of n (if $n > 0$); in the latter case, by induction, p will eventually enter its critical section.

The tournament tree does not let processes enter their critical section in a first-come, first-served manner. That is, if a process p completes Peterson's algorithm at its leaf before another process q starts running Peterson's algorithm at its leaf, in general this does not guarantee that p will enter its critical section before q.

16.2 Bakery algorithm

The bakery algorithm enforces mutual exclusion similar to the way customers in a shop are served in a first-come, first-served fashion. When entering say a bakery, each customer gets a ticket with a number, which is increased by one with each next ticket. The waiting customer with the smallest number is the next to be served.

Tickets could in principle be modeled by means of a multi-writer register of type integer. However, avoiding that multiple processes concurrently read the value of this register and increase it by one, would require the use of a read-modify-write operation. In the bakery algorithm, a process instead reads the numbers of all other processes, and selects as number the maximum of all those numbers plus one. To break ties between different processes that concurrently select the same number, the ticket of a process p_i that selects a number k consists of the pair (k, i), and tickets are ordered lexicographically: $(k, i) < (\ell, j)$ if either $k < \ell$, or $k = \ell$ and $i < j$. A process can enter its critical section if its ticket is the smallest among all processes that have a number greater than zero. When a process exits its critical section, it sets its number back to zero.

To be more precise, the bakery algorithm uses single-writer registers $choosing_i$ of type Boolean and $number_i$ of type integer, for $i = 0, \ldots, N-1$; only p_i can write to $choosing_i$ and $number_i$. Initially, $choosing_i = false$ and $number_i = 0$. A process p_i that wants to enter its critical section sets $choosing_i$ to $true$, reads the values of the registers $number_j$ for all $j \neq i$, writes $\max\{number_j \mid 0 \leq j < N\} + 1$ into $number_i$, and sets $choosing_i$ back to $false$. Next, for each $j \neq i$, p_i first spins on $choosing_j$ until it is $false$, and then on $number_j$ until either $number_j = 0$ or $(number_i, i) < (number_j, j)$. After that p_i can enter its critical section. When p_i exits its critical section, it sets $number_i$ to 0.

Example 16.3 We consider one possible execution of the bakery algorithm. Consider three processes p_0, p_1, p_2; initially $choosing_i = false$ and $number_i = 0$ for $i = 0, 1, 2$.

- p_1 wants to enter its critical section, sets $choosing_1$ to $true$, and reads $number_0$ and $number_2$.
- p_0 wants to enter its critical section, sets $choosing_0$ to $true$, and reads $number_1$ and $number_2$.
- p_0 sets $number_0$ to 1 and $choosing_0$ to $false$. p_0 does not yet enter its critical section, because $choosing_1 = true$.
- p_1 sets $number_1$ to 1 and $choosing_1$ to $false$. p_1 does not yet enter its critical section, because $(number_0, 0) < (number_1, 1)$ and $number_0 > 0$.
- Since $choosing_1 = choosing_2 = false$, $(number_0, 0) < (number_1, 1)$, and $number_2 = 0$, p_0 enters its critical section.
- p_0 exits its critical section and sets $number_0$ to 0.
- p_0 wants to enter its critical section, sets $choosing_0$ to $true$, and reads $number_1$ and $number_2$.
- p_0 sets $number_0$ to 2 and $choosing_0$ to $false$. p_0 does not yet enter its critical section, because $(number_1, 1) < (number_0, 0)$ and $number_1 > 0$.
- Since $choosing_0 = choosing_2 = false$, $number_1 < number_0$, and $number_2 = 0$, p_1 enters its critical section.

The bakery algorithm provides mutual exclusion. Suppose that p_i is in its critical section; then clearly $number_i > 0$. Moreover, let $number_j > 0$ for some $j \neq i$. We argue that then $(number_i, i) < (number_j, j)$. Before p_i entered its critical section, it must have read $choosing_j = false$, and either $number_j = 0$ or $(number_i, i) < (number_j, j)$. If p_j chooses a new ticket while p_i is in its critical section, then p_j is guaranteed to take $number_i$ into account, and so will choose a larger number. To conclude, since a privileged process always carries a positive number, and must have the smallest ticket among all processes with a positive number, only one process can be in its critical section at any time.

The bakery algorithm is starvation-free. If a process p_i wants to enter its critical section, and other processes keep on entering and exiting their critical section, then eventually p_i will have the smallest ticket. Namely, eventually all processes that want to enter their critical section will take the current value of $number_i$ into account, and will choose a number larger than $number_i$ for their own ticket.

Let us say that a process p_i enters its doorway when it sets $choosing_i$ to $true$, and exits its doorway when it sets $choosing_i$ back to $false$. The bakery algorithm treats processes in a first-come, first-served fashion, in the sense that if a process p_i exits its doorway before another process p_j enters its doorway, then p_i is guaranteed to enter its critical section before p_j.

The values of the $number$ fields grow without bound. The bakery algorithm can be adapted such that these values are limited to a finite range; see exercise 16.6.

16.3 N registers are required

In the bakery algorithm, a process that wants to enter its critical section reads the values of two registers at every other process. This renders the algorithm impractical in case of a large number of processes. The following theorem states that in principle it is impossible to solve mutual exclusion for N processes with fewer than N registers, with only read and write operations.

Theorem 16.1 *At least N registers are needed to solve livelock-free mutual exclusion for N processes, if only read and write operations are employed.*

Proof. We sketch a proof for the case $N = 2$; the general case is similar. Suppose, toward a contradiction, that a livelock-free mutual exclusion algorithm for two processes p and q uses only one multi-writer register R.

Before p can enter its critical section, it must write to R; for else q would not be able to recognize whether p is in its critical section. Likewise, before q can enter its critical section, it must write to R. Due to livelock-freeness, we can bring p and q in a position where they are both about to write to R, after which they will enter their critical section.

Suppose without loss of generality that p writes to R first and enters its critical section. The subsequent write by q obliterates the value p wrote to R, so that q cannot tell that p is in its critical section. Consequently q will also enter its critical section. This contradicts the mutual exclusion property. □

16.4 Fischer's algorithm

Fischer's algorithm circumvents the impossibility result from the previous section by means of time delays.

$turn$ is a multi-writer register, with range $\{-1, 0, \ldots, N-1\}$. Initially, it has the value -1. A process p_i that wants to enter its critical section, spins on $turn$ until its value is -1. Within one time unit of this read, p_i sets the value of *turn* to i. Next, p_i waits for more than one time unit, and then reads *turn*. If it still has the value i, then p_i enters its critical section. Otherwise, p_i returns to spinning on *turn* until its value is -1. When a process exits its critical section, it sets the value of *turn* to -1.

Example 16.4 We consider one possible execution of Fischer's algorithm. Consider three processes p_0, p_1, p_2, with p_0 in its critical section; so *turn* $= 0$. Processes p_1 and p_2 both want to enter their critical section and are spinning on *turn*.

When p_0 exits its critical section, it sets *turn* to -1. Now p_1 and p_2 concurrently read that *turn* $= -1$. First, p_1 sets the value of *turn* to 1, and less than one time unit later p_2 sets its value to 2. More than one time unit after it performed its write, p_1 reads *turn*, finds that its value was changed to 2, and returns to spinning on *turn*. On the other hand, more than one time unit after it performed its write, p_2 reads *turn*, finds that its value is still 2, and enters its critical section.

We argue that Fischer's algorithm guarantees mutual exclusion. When *turn* $= -1$, clearly no process is in its critical section. And when a process p_i sets the value of *turn* to i, other processes p_j can only set the value of *turn* to $j \neq i$ within one time unit. So if the value of *turn* remains i for more than one time unit, p_i can be certain that no other process can become privileged.

Fischer's algorithm is livelock-free: when the value of *turn* becomes -1, processes p_i that want to enter their critical section can freely write the value i in *turn*. The last process to set the value of *turn* within one time unit of the first write, will enter its critical section. However, there can be starvation, in case a process p_i wants to enter its critical section, infinitely often *turn* is set to -1 and p_i writes i in *turn*, but every time this value is overwritten by a $j \neq i$ within one time unit.

A strong requirement of this algorithm is the presence of a global clock. Another drawback is that processes all spin on the same register *turn*; why this can be problematic will be explained in the next section.

16.5 Test-and-test-and-set lock

Test-and-set lock

The test-and-set lock circumvents the impossibility result from section 16.3 by using a read-modify-write operation: *test-and-set*. This lock uses one Boolean multi-writer register *locked*, which initially holds the value *false*. A process that wants to acquire the lock, repeatedly applies *test-and-set* to *locked*: this operation sets the value of *locked* to *true* and returns the previous value of *locked*. The process obtains the lock (in other words, becomes privileged) as soon as *false* is returned by a *test-and-set* operation. To unlock, the process sets *locked* to *false*.

The test-and-set lock provides mutual exclusion. When *locked* contains *false*, clearly no process holds the lock. And when a process p acquires the lock, meaning that it applies a *test-and-set* that turns the value of *locked* from *false* to *true*, then no other process can acquire the lock until p unlocks by setting *locked* to *false*. The test-and-set lock moreover is livelock-free, but not starvation-free.

The test-and-set lock, although conceptually simple, tends to have a poor performance. The reason is that each *test-and-set* on *locked* comes with a memory barrier: at all processors it invalidates the cached value of *locked*. As a result, all processes that want to acquire the lock, and so are spinning on *locked*, take a cache miss and fetch the (mostly unchanged) value from main memory. This produces a continuous storm of unnecessary messages over the bus.

Test-and-test-and-set lock

The test-and-test-and-set lock improves upon the test-and-set lock by letting processes that want to acquire the lock spin on a cached copy of the Boolean register *locked*. When *false* is returned, the process applies *test-and-set* to *locked* itself. The process obtains the lock if *false* is returned; otherwise, it goes back to spinning on its cached copy of *locked*. To unlock, the process sets *locked* to *false*.

The test-and-test-and-set lock provides mutual exclusion and livelock-freeness. It avoids a considerable part of the bus traffic of the test-and-set lock, and therefore tends to have a much better performance. Still, the test-and-test-and-set lock generates unnecessary bus traffic when the lock is released. Then *false* is written in *locked*, invalidating all cached copies. As a result, all spinners take a cache miss and go to the bus to fetch the value of *locked*. Then they concurrently perform *test-and-set* to try to acquire the lock, invalidating the cached copies at other processes, and thus leading to another round of cache misses. Finally, the storm subsides and processes return to local spinning on their cached copy of *locked*.

The performance of the test-and-test-and-set lock can be improved by applying *exponential back-off* to reduce contention. The idea is that when a process applies *test-and-set* to *locked* but fails to get the lock, it backs off for a certain amount of time to avoid collisions. Each subsequent failure to get the lock by means of a *test-and-set* is interpreted as a sign that there is a high contention for the lock. Therefore, the waiting time is doubled at each failed attempt, up to some maximum. Two important parameters, for the performance of the lock, are the initial minimum delay and the maximum delay; optimal values for these parameters are platform-dependent. Waiting durations are randomized, to avoid that competing processes fall into lock-step.

Example 16.5 Consider three processes p_0, p_1, p_2 that all want to acquire the test-and-test-and-set lock. Initially, the Boolean register *locked* is *false*.

p_0, p_1, p_2 concurrently read that (their cached copy of) *locked* is *false*. Let p_1 apply *test-and-set* to *locked* first, setting it to *true*. Since this operation returns *false*, p_1 takes the lock. Next, p_0 and p_2 apply *test-and-set* to *locked*. In both cases this operation returns *true*, so p_0 and p_1 back off for (a randomization of) the minimum delay. After this delay, p_0 and p_1 start spinning on their cached copy of *locked*.

When p_1 releases the lock, it sets *locked* to *false*. Now p_0 and p_2 concurrently read that the value has changed, and apply *test-and-set* to *locked*. Let p_2 be the first to do so, setting its value to *true*. Since this operation returns *false*, p_2 takes the lock. The *test-and-set* by p_0 returns *true*, after which p_0 backs off for twice the minimum delay. After this delay, p_0 returns to spinning on its cached copy of *locked*.

The test-and-test-and-set lock with exponential back-off is easy to implement, and can give excellent performance in case of low contention. However, it may suffer from starvation, processes may be delayed longer than necessary due to back-off, and last but not least, all processes still spin on the same register *locked*, which creates a bottleneck and generates bus traffic, especially in case of high contention.

16.6 Queue locks

Queue locks overcome the drawbacks of the test-and-test-and-set lock by placing processes that want to acquire the lock in a queue. A process p in the queue spins on a register to check whether its predecessor in the queue has released the lock. When this is the case, p takes the lock. Key to the success of queue locks is that all processes in the queue spin on a different register. Queue locks provide mutual exclusion because only the head of the queue holds the lock. Moreover, processes are treated in a first-come, first-served manner: the sooner a process is added to the queue, the earlier it is served.

Anderson's lock

Anderson's lock places processes that want to acquire the lock in a queue by means of a Boolean array of size n. Here n is the maximal number of processes that can concurrently compete for the lock (so $n \leq N$). A counter is used to assign a slot in the array to every process that wants to acquire the lock; this counter is interpreted modulo n. Always at most one process is assigned to each slot in the array, and at most one slot in the array holds *true*; the process that is assigned to this slot holds the lock. The slots in the array and the counter are multi-writer registers. Initially, slot 0 of the array holds *true*, slots $1, \ldots, n-1$ hold *false*, and the counter is zero.

A process p that wants to acquire the lock applies the read-modify-write operation *get-and-increment* to the counter, which increases the counter by one and returns the previous value of the counter. The returned value modulo n is the slot of the process in the array. Now p spins on (a cached copy of) its slot in the array, until it holds *true*, at which moment p acquires the lock. To unlock, p first sets its slot in the array to *false*, and then the next slot modulo n to *true*, signaling to its successor (if any) that it can take the lock.

Example 16.6 Let $N = n = 3$, and suppose processes p, q, r all want to acquire Anderson's lock. Initially, only slot 0 in the array holds *true*, and the counter is 0.

- q applies *get-and-increment* to the counter, increasing it to 1. Since this operation returns 0, and slot 0 holds *true*, q takes the lock.

- p applies *get-and-increment* to the counter, increasing it to 2. Since this operation returns 1, and slot 1 holds *false*, p starts spinning on this slot.
- r applies *get-and-increment* to the counter, increasing it to 3. Since this operation returns 2, and slot 2 holds *false*, r starts spinning on this slot.
- When q releases the lock, it sets slot 0 to *false*, and slot 1 to *true*.
- p reads that the value of slot 1 has changed to *true* and takes the lock.
- q wants to acquire the lock again. It applies *get-and-increment* to the counter, increasing it to 4. Since this operation returns 3, and slot $3 \bmod 3 = 0$ holds *false*, q starts spinning on slot 0.

Anderson's lock resolves the weaknesses of the test-and-test-and-set lock. In particular, different processes spin on different registers. However, a risk is that different slots in the array may be kept on a single cache line, being the smallest unit of memory to be transferred between main memory and a cache. When a data item in the cache becomes invalid, the entire cache line where the data item is kept is invalidated. So if different slots of the array are kept on the same cache line, releasing the lock still gives rise to unnecessary bus traffic. This may be avoided by padding: the array size is, say, quadrupled, and slots are separated by three unused places in the array.

A drawback of Anderson's lock is that it requires an array of size n (or more, in case of padding), even when no process wants the lock. Especially in case of a large number of processes and multiple locks, this memory overhead can be costly.

CLH lock

The CLH lock does not use a fixed array. Instead, the queue of processes that are waiting for the lock is maintained by means of a dynamic list structure; each process that wants to acquire the lock places a node in the list. Each node ν contains a Boolean single-writer register $active_\nu$, which becomes *false* after the corresponding process has released the lock. Moreover, a multi-writer register *last* points to the most recently added node in the queue. Initially, *last* points to a dummy node, in which the *active* field is *false*.

A process p that wants to acquire the lock creates a node ν, with $active_\nu = true$. It applies *get-and-set*(ν) to *last*, to make ν the last node in the queue and get a pointer to the node of its predecessor. Next, p spins on (a cached copy of) the *active* field in its predecessor's node, until it becomes *false*. When this is the case, p can take the lock. To unlock, p sets $active_\nu$ to *false*, signaling to its successor (if any) that it can take the lock. After releasing the lock, p can reuse the node of its predecessor for a future lock access (but not its own node ν; see exercise 16.12).

Example 16.7 Processes p_0 and p_1 want to acquire the CLH lock; they create nodes ν_0 and ν_1, respectively, with $active_{\nu_0} = active_{\nu_1} = true$. Initially, *last* points to a dummy node, in which the *active* field is *false*.

- p_1 applies *get-and-set*(ν_1) to *last*, to let it point to ν_1. Since this operation returns the dummy node which contains *false*, p_1 takes the lock.

- p_0 applies $get\text{-}and\text{-}set(\nu_0)$ to $last$, to let it point to ν_0. Since this operation returns ν_1 which contains $true$, p_0 starts spinning on $active_{\nu_1}$.
- When p_1 releases the lock, it sets $active_{\nu_1}$ to $false$.
- p_0 reads that the value of $active_{\nu_1}$ has changed to $false$ and takes the lock.

The CLH lock exhibits the same good performance as Anderson's lock, and uses space more sparingly. The Achilles heel of the CLH lock is that due to remote spinning, on the $active$ field in the predecessor's node, its performance is heavily dependent on the presence of caches.

MCS lock

The MCS lock avoids remote spinning; instead, a process q waiting in the queue spins on a Boolean $wait$ field in its own node. To achieve this, q must inform its predecessor p in the queue that q is its successor, so that after p releases the lock, it will invert the $wait$ field in q's node. The price to pay is a more involved and expensive unlock procedure, to deal with the case where q joins the queue before p releases the lock, but informs p that q is its successor while p is releasing the lock.

Again, each process that wants to acquire the lock places a node ν in the list, containing two multi-writer registers: a Boolean $wait_\nu$, which is $true$ as long as the process must wait in the queue, and a pointer $succ_\nu$ to the successor node in the queue, or a null pointer in case ν is the last node in the queue. Moreover, the multi-writer register $last$ points to the last node in the queue. Initially, $last = $ null.

A process p that wants to acquire the lock creates a node ν, with $wait_\nu = false$ and $succ_\nu = $ null. It applies $get\text{-}and\text{-}set(\nu)$ to $last$, to make ν the last node in the queue and get a pointer to the node of its predecessor in the queue. If $last$ contained null, then p takes the lock immediately. Otherwise, p first sets $wait_\nu$ to $true$, and then lets the $succ$ field in the node of its predecessor point to ν. Next, p spins on $wait_\nu$ until it becomes $false$. When this is the case, p can take the lock.

When process p releases the lock, it checks whether $succ_\nu$ points to another node. If so, p sets the $wait$ field in the latter node to $false$, signaling to its successor that it can take the lock. If on the other hand $succ_\nu = $ null, then p applies $compare\text{-}and\text{-}set(\nu, \text{null})$ to $last$, signaling that the queue has become empty. If this operation fails, meaning that it returns $false$, then another process q which joined the queue in the meantime has written to $last$. In that case, p starts spinning on $succ_\nu$ until a node is returned, which is the node of q. Finally, p sets the $wait$ field in q's node to $false$. After releasing the lock, p can reuse ν for a future lock access

Example 16.8 Processes p_0 and p_1 want to acquire the MCS lock; they create nodes ν_0 and ν_1, respectively, containing $false$ and null. Initially, $last = $ null.

- p_1 applies $get\text{-}and\text{-}set(\nu_1)$ to $last$, to let it point to ν_1. Since this operation returns null, p_1 takes the lock.
- p_0 applies $get\text{-}and\text{-}set(\nu_0)$ to $last$, to let it point to ν_0. Since this operation returns ν_1, p_0 sets $wait_{\nu_0}$ to $true$, lets $succ_{\nu_1}$ point to ν_0, and starts spinning on $wait_{\nu_0}$.

- When p_1 releases the lock, it finds that $succ_{\nu_1}$ points to ν_0. Therefore, p_1 sets $wait_{\nu_0}$ to *false*.
- p_0 reads that the value of $wait_{\nu_0}$ has changed to *false* and takes the lock.

Example 16.9 Processes p_0 and p_1 want to acquire the MCS lock; they create nodes ν_0 and ν_1, respectively, containing *false* and null. Initially, $last = $ null.

- p_1 applies $get\text{-}and\text{-}set(\nu_1)$ to $last$, to let it point to ν_1. Since this operation returns null, p_1 takes the lock.
- p_0 applies $get\text{-}and\text{-}set(\nu_0)$ to $last$, to let it point to ν_0. This operation returns ν_1.
- When p_1 releases the lock, it finds that $succ_{\nu_1} = $ null. Therefore, it applies $compare\text{-}and\text{-}set(\nu_1, \text{null})$ to $last$. Since $last$ points to ν_0, this operation returns *false*. Therefore, p_1 starts spinning on $succ_{\nu_1}$.
- p_0 sets $wait_{\nu_0}$ to *true*, lets $succ_{\nu_1}$ point to ν_0, and starts spinning on $wait_{\nu_0}$.
- p_1 finds that $succ_{\nu_1}$ points to ν_0 and sets $wait_{\nu_0}$ to *false*.
- p_0 reads that the value of $wait_{\nu_0}$ has changed to *false* and takes the lock.

The MCS lock tends to outperform the CLH lock on so-called cacheless NUMA (Non-Uniform Memory Access) architectures, where each processor is provided with its own memory unit, instead of one shared-memory unit.

Timeouts

With queue locks, a process p in the queue cannot easily give up its attempt to acquire the lock, because its successor in the queue depends on p. We now explain how the CLH lock can be adapted to include such timeouts. The key is that p needs to tell its successor to start spinning on the node of p's predecessor in the queue.

Again, a process p that wants to acquire the lock places a node ν in the list, with a single-writer register $pred_\nu$ that contains either:

- null, in case p is waiting in the queue or is in its critical section; or
- a pointer to the node of p's predecessor in the queue, in case p has given up waiting for the lock; or
- a pointer to a special node called released, in case p has left its critical section.

The multi-writer register $last$ points to the last node in the queue. Initially, $last = $ null.

When p wants to acquire the lock, it creates a node ν with $pred_\nu = $ null. It applies $get\text{-}and\text{-}set(\nu)$ to $last$, to make ν the last node in the queue and get a pointer to the node of its predecessor. If $last$ contained null, then p takes the lock immediately. Otherwise, it spins on (a cached copy of) the $pred$ field in its predecessor's node until it is not null. If it points to the node released, then p takes the lock. Otherwise, it points to the node ν' of the new predecessor of p (meaning that p's original predecessor has timed out). In that case, p continues to spin on $pred_{\nu'}$ until it is not null.

If p quits its attempt to acquire the lock, it applies $compare\text{-}and\text{-}set(\nu, pred_p)$ to $last$. If this operation fails, then p has a successor in the queue; in that case, p sets

$pred_\nu$ to the node of its predecessor, signaling to the successor of p that it has a new predecessor.

When p releases the lock, it applies $compare\text{-}and\text{-}set(\nu, \texttt{null})$ to $last$. If this operation succeeds, then the queue has become empty. If it fails, then p has a successor in the queue. In the latter case p sets $pred_\nu$ to the node $\texttt{released}$, signaling to its successor that it can take the lock.

Example 16.10 Processes p_0, p_1, and p_2 want to acquire the CLH lock with timeouts; they create nodes ν_0, ν_1, and ν_2, respectively, containing $\texttt{null}$. Initially, $last = \texttt{null}$.

- p_1 applies $get\text{-}and\text{-}set(\nu_1)$ to $last$, to let it point to ν_1. Since this operation returns $\texttt{null}$, p_1 takes the lock.
- p_0 applies $get\text{-}and\text{-}set(\nu_0)$ to $last$, to let it point to ν_0. Since this operation returns ν_1, p_0 starts spinning on $pred_{\nu_1}$.
- p_2 applies $get\text{-}and\text{-}set(\nu_2)$ to $last$, to let it point to ν_2. Since this operation returns ν_0, p_2 starts spinning on $pred_{\nu_0}$.
- p_0 decides to abort its attempt to acquire the lock. It lets $pred_{\nu_0}$ point to ν_1.
- p_2 finds that $pred_{\nu_0}$ has changed from $\texttt{null}$ to ν_1 and starts spinning on $pred_{\nu_1}$.
- When p_1 releases the lock, it applies $compare\text{-}and\text{-}set(\nu_1, \texttt{null})$ to $last$. This operation fails, because $last$ points to ν_2 instead of ν_1. Therefore, p_1 lets $pred_{\nu_1}$ point to $\texttt{released}$.
- p_2 finds that $pred_{\nu_1}$ has changed from $\texttt{null}$ to $\texttt{released}$ and takes the lock.

Bibliographical notes

Peterson's mutual exclusion algorithm for two processes originates from [62], and the bakery algorithm from [44]. The fact that mutual exclusion for N processes requires N registers was proved in [13]. Fischer's algorithm was proposed in an email by Michael J. Fischer in 1985, and put forward in [46]. The test-and-test-and-set lock is due to [42]. Anderson's lock stems from [3], the CLH lock from [23, 51], the MCS lock from [58], and the CLH lock with timeouts from [69].

Exercises

Exercise 16.1 Explain why the following mutual exclusion algorithm is flawed. Let $flag$ be a multi-writer Boolean register. A process p wanting to enter its critical section waits until $flag = false$. Then p performs $flag \leftarrow true$ and becomes privileged. When p exits its critical section, it performs $flag \leftarrow false$.

Exercise 16.2 *2-mutual exclusion* is satisfied if at any time at most two processes are in their critical section. Modify the tournament tree (in which the nodes run Peterson's algorithm) to yield a solution for the 2-mutual exclusion problem.

Exercise 16.3 Present a starvation-free 2-mutual exclusion algorithm, using one register and a read-modify-write operation.

Exercise 16.4 Suppose that in the bakery algorithm a process could enter its critical section without waiting for all *choosing* registers to become *false*. Give an example to show that then mutual exclusion is no longer guaranteed.

Exercise 16.5 Describe an execution of the bakery algorithm in which the values of *number* registers grow without bound.

Exercise 16.6 Adapt the bakery algorithm such that the range of the *number* registers becomes finite.

Exercise 16.7 Argue the correctness of theorem 16.1 for the case $N = 3$.

Exercise 16.8 Explain why the proof of theorem 16.1 does not apply to Fischer's algorithm.

Exercise 16.9 Give an example of starvation with Fischer's algorithm.

Exercise 16.10 Argue in detail that Anderson's lock provides mutual exclusion and first-come, first-served fairness.

Exercise 16.11 Give an example (with $n = 3$) to show what could go wrong if in Anderson's lock a process that releases the lock would first set the next slot modulo n in the array to *true*, and only then its own slot to *false*.

Exercise 16.12 [37] Suppose that in the CLH lock, a process would reuse its own node (instead of the node of its predecessor). Give an execution to show that then the algorithm would be flawed.

Exercise 16.13 For each of the two read-modify-write operations in the MCS lock, replace this operation by read and write operations, and give an execution to show that the resulting lock is flawed. In both cases explain which property is violated.

Exercise 16.14 Argue in detail that (the unlock procedure of) the MCS lock does not suffer from deadlock.

Exercise 16.15 Consider for the MCS lock the situation where a process p wants to acquire the lock and finds that *last* points to a node. Suppose that p would first set the *succ* field of that node to its own node, and only then set the *wait* field in its own node to *true*. What could go wrong?

Exercise 16.16 Develop a variant of the MCS lock that includes timeouts, allowing a process to abandon its attempt to obtain the lock.

17
Barriers

Suppose processes must collectively wait at some point until all processes have arrived there, after which they can leave the barrier and resume execution. For example, this can be necessary for a soft real-time application, where a number of subtasks may have to be completed by the different processes before the overall application can proceed. This can be achieved by means of a barrier, which keeps track whether all processes have reached it. When the last process has reached the barrier, all processes can leave the barrier and resume execution.

Waiting at a barrier resembles waiting to enter a critical section. It can be based on spinning on local or (locally cached copies of) remote variables, or on falling asleep when the barrier is reached and being woken up when all processes have reached the barrier.

17.1 Sense-reversing barrier

A straightforward way to implement a barrier is to maintain a counter, being a multi-writer register, with initial value 0. Each process that reaches the barrier performs *get-and-increment* on the counter; a read-modify-write operation is needed, because otherwise multiple processes could concurrently increase the counter to the same value. When the counter equals the number N of processes that must reach the barrier, all processes can leave the barrier.

If a process reaches the barrier and applies a *get-and-increment* that returns a value smaller than $N - 1$, then it can fall asleep. The last process to reach the barrier, for which *get-and-increment* returns $N - 1$, first resets the value of the counter to 0, so that it can be reused, and then wakes up all other processes. A drawback of this approach is that the waking-up phase can be time-consuming.

A better idea may be to use a global Boolean sense field, a multi-writer register, which initially is *false*. Moreover, each process carries a local Boolean sense field, a single-reader/single-writer register, which initially is *true*. A process p that reaches the barrier applies *get-and-increment* to the counter. In case p is not the last to reach the barrier, meaning that *get-and-increment* returns a value smaller than $N - 1$, it starts spinning on the barrier's global sense field until it equals p's local sense, after which p can leave the barrier. On the other hand, in case p is the last to reach the barrier, it first resets the counter to 0, so that it can be reused, and then reverses the value of the global sense field, signaling to the other processes that they can leave the barrier. Processes resume execution with reversed local sense, so that not only the counter but also the (global and local) sense fields can be reused for a next barrier.

Example 17.1 We consider one possible execution of the sense-reversing barrier. Given three processes p, q, r, initially with local sense $true$. The barrier's counter initially has the value 0, and its global sense is $false$.

- Process q reaches the barrier and applies $get\text{-}and\text{-}increment$ to the counter, which returns 0. Therefore, q starts spinning on the global sense field until it is $true$.
- Process p reaches the barrier and applies $get\text{-}and\text{-}increment$ to the counter, which returns 1. Therefore, p starts spinning on the global sense field until it is $true$.
- Process r reaches the barrier and applies $get\text{-}and\text{-}increment$ to the counter, which returns 2. Therefore, r resets the value of the counter to 0, reverses the global sense field to $true$, and leaves the barrier with reversed local sense $false$.
- Processes p and q notice that the global sense of the barrier has become $true$, and also leave the barrier with reversed local sense $false$.

The main drawback of the sense-reversing barrier is, similar to the test-and-test-and-set lock, that processes that have arrived at the barrier are all spinning on (a cached copy of) the same global sense field.

17.2 Combining tree barrier

The combining tree barrier uses a tree structure to reduce contention on the global sense field. Each node represents a sense-reversing barrier; processes that are waiting at the barrier, are spinning on the global sense field of a node.

Let the tree have depth k, and let each node at a depth smaller than k have r children. The corresponding combining tree barrier can cope with r^{k+1} processes: to each leaf we assign at most r processes. For simplicity, we assume that $N = r^{k+1}$. Each node maintains a counter and a global sense field. At a leaf, the counter keeps track how many of its processes have reached the barrier, while at a nonleaf it keeps track at how many of the children of the node the counter has become r. As soon as the counter of a nonroot becomes r, the counter of the parent of this node is increased by one. When finally the counter at the root of the tree becomes r, we can be certain that all processes have reached the barrier. Then the counters are reset, and the global sense fields are reversed at all the nodes, from top (the root) to bottom (the leaves), after which all processes resume execution.

To be more precise, nodes in the tree are numbered as follows: the root carries number 0, and given a node with the number n, its children carry the numbers $rn +$

1 up to $rn + r$. To each node n we associate two multi-writer registers: $count_n$ of type integer and $gsense_n$ of type Boolean. We assume that there are processes $p_0, \ldots, p_{N-1}$. Each process p_i maintains a single-reader/single-writer local sense field $lsense_i$. Initially, $count_n = 0$, $gsense_n = false$, and $lsense_i = true$. Process p_i is assigned to leaf $r^{k-1} + r^{k-2} + \cdots + 1 + \lfloor i/r \rfloor$ in the tree. That is, when p_i reaches the barrier, it performs the following procedure $CombiningTree(n)$ with $n = r^{k-1} + r^{k-2} + \cdots + 1 + \lfloor i/r \rfloor$.

if $counter_n.\textit{get-and-increment} < r - 1$ **then**
    while $gsense_n \neq lsense_i$ **do**
        $\{\}$;
    end while
else
    if $n > 0$ **then**
        perform procedure $CombiningTree(\lceil \frac{n}{r} \rceil - 1)$;
    end if
    $count_n \leftarrow 0$; $gsense_n \leftarrow lsense_i$;
end if

A process p_i performing $CombiningTree(n)$ first applies $get\text{-}and\text{-}increment$ to the counter at node n. If the counter is increased to a value smaller than r, then p_i starts spinning on the global sense field of n until it equals p_i's local sense. On the other hand, if p_i increases the counter at n to r, then we distinguish the case where n is a nonroot from the case where n is the root of the tree. If n is a nonroot, then p_i moves to the parent of n in the tree, where it performs $CombiningTree$ again. If n is the root of the tree, then all processes have reached the barrier. In this case p_i resets the counter at the root to 0, so that it can be reused, and next reverses the value of the global sense field at the root, signaling to the $r - 1$ processes spinning on this field that they can leave the barrier.

Processes that find the global sense field they are spinning on reversed, and the process that reverses the global sense at the root, reset the counter and reverse the global sense field at all the nodes they visited before, signaling to the $r - 1$ processes spinning on such a field that they can leave the barrier. Processes resume execution with reversed local sense, so that the counters and sense fields can be reused for a next barrier.

Example 17.2 We consider one possible execution of the combining tree barrier. Let $k = 2$, $r = 2$, and $N = 8$. The processes p_0 up to p_7 are assigned to the leaves of the tree as depicted below. Initially, the counters at the nodes are 0, the global sense fields at the nodes are $false$, and all processes have local sense $true$.

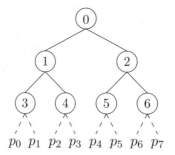

- Let p_0, p_2, p_4, and p_7 arrive at the barrier. They apply *get-and-increment* to the counter of their leaf, increasing it to 1. Next, they start spinning on the global sense field of their leaf, until it becomes *true*.
- Let p_1 and p_6 arrive at the barrier. They apply *get-and-increment* to the counter of leaf 3 and 6, respectively, increasing it to 2. Next, they move to node 1 and 2 respectively, where they apply *get-and-increment* to the counter, increasing it to 1. They start spinning on the global sense field of node 1 and 2 respectively, until it becomes *true*.
- Let p_3 arrive at the barrier. It applies *get-and-increment* to the counter of leaf 4, increasing it to 2. Next, it moves to node 1, where it applies *get-and-increment* to the counter, increasing it to 2. Next, it moves to the root, where it applies *get-and-increment* to the counter, increasing it to 1. It starts spinning on the global sense field of the root, until it becomes *true*.

The resulting situation is as follows.

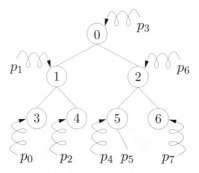

- Finally, p_5 arrives at the barrier. It applies *get-and-increment* to the counter of leaf 5, increasing it to 2. Next, it proceeds to node 2, where it applies *get-and-increment* to the counter, increasing it to 2. Next, it moves to the root, where it applies *get-and-increment* to the counter, increasing it to 2. It reverses the global sense field of the root to *true*.
- p_5 moves to node 2, where it reverses the global sense field to *true*. And p_3, which finds that the global sense field of the root has become *true*, moves to node 1, where it reverses the global sense field to *true*.
- p_5 and p_3 move to leaf 5 and 4, respectively, where they reverse the global sense field to *true*. And p_1 and p_6, which find that the global sense field of node 1 and

2, respectively, has become *true*, move to leaf 3 and 6, respectively, where they reverse the global sense field to *true*.
- p_0, p_2, p_4, and p_7 find that the global sense field they are spinning on has become *true*. All eight processes leave the barrier and continue their execution with reversed local sense *false*.

We argue that the combining tree barrier is correct. It is easy to see, by induction on depth, that the counter at a node n becomes r if and only if the processes assigned to the leaves below n have all reached the barrier: in the base case of the induction, n is a leaf, and in the inductive case, the claim has already been proved for the children of n. So in particular, the counter at the root becomes r if and only if all processes have reached the barrier. Furthermore, when this happens, it is guaranteed that the global sense fields at all nodes are reversed, so that all processes leave the barrier.

17.3 Tournament barrier

The tournament barrier is an improvement over the combining tree barrier in the sense that it allows processes to spin on local variables, and does not use any read-modify-write operations.

Consider a tournament tree of a depth $k > 0$, being a binary tree in which each node represents a barrier of size two. The corresponding tournament barrier can cope with 2^{k+1} processes: to each leaf we assign at most two processes. For simplicity, we assume that $N = 2^{k+1}$. Each node is divided into an active and a passive side; both sides of the node carry a global sense field. The active and passive side of every nonleaf in the tree have one child each, and to both the active and the passive side of every leaf in the tree one process is assigned.

The idea behind the tournament barrier is that a process p at the passive side of a node signals to (the global sense field of) its active partner at this node that p has arrived at the barrier. Next, p starts spinning on the global sense field of its passive side until it has been reversed, after which p can leave the barrier. Conversely, a process at the active side of a node waits until it receives a signal that its passive partner at this node has arrived at the barrier, and then either moves on to the parent of this node, at a nonroot, or concludes that the barrier has been completed, at the root. In the latter case the passive global sense fields are reversed at all the nodes, from top (the root) to bottom (the leaves), after which all processes resume execution, with reversed local sense.

To be more precise, nodes in the tree are numbered similar to the combining tree barrier with $r = 2$ (and the binary tree in Peterson's algorithm). To each node n we associate two Boolean multi-writer registers: $asense_n$ and $psense_n$. We assume that there are processes $p_0, \ldots, p_{N-1}$. Each process p_i maintains a single-reader/single-writer local sense field $lsense_i$. Initially, $asense_n = psense_n = false$ and $lsense_i = true$. Process p_i is assigned to leaf $(2^k - 1) + \lfloor i/2 \rfloor$ in the tree, at the active side if i is even and at the passive side if i is odd. That is, when p_i reaches the barrier, it performs the following procedure $Tournament(n, b)$ with $n = (2^k - 1) + \lfloor i/2 \rfloor$ and $b = i \bmod 2$; here, $b = 0$ represents the active and $b = 1$ the passive side of node n.

```
if b = 1 then
    asense_n ← lsense_i;
    while psense_n ≠ lsense_i do
        {};
    end while
else
    while asense_n ≠ lsense_i do
        {};
    end while
    if n > 0 then
        perform procedure Tournament(⌈n/2⌉ − 1, (n + 1) mod 2);
    end if
    psense_n ← lsense_i;
end if
```

A process p_i that performs $Tournament(n, b)$ acts as follows.

- If $b = 1$, then p_i sets the active sense field of n to p_i's local sense, and starts spinning on the passive sense field of n until it equals p_i's local sense. When this is the case, p_i reverses the passive sense fields of nodes it visited before and leaves the barrier.
- If $b = 0$, then p_i starts spinning on the active sense field of n until it equals p_i's local sense. In case n is not the root of the tree, p_i moves to the parent of n, where it performs $Tournament$ again. On the other hand, in case n is the root of the tree, p_i reverses the passive sense fields of nodes it has visited and leaves the barrier.

As we said before, processes resume execution with reversed local sense.

It is determined beforehand on which global sense fields a process will spin while waiting for the barrier to complete. And for each global sense field of each active or passive part of a node there is exactly one process that will spin on this field. Therefore, each of these fields can be kept in the local memory of the process that spins on it.

Example 17.3 We consider one possible execution of the tournament barrier. Let $k = 2$ and $N = 8$. The processes p_0 up to p_7 are assigned to the leaves of the tree as depicted below, whereby p_0, p_2, p_4, p_6 are assigned to the active and p_1, p_3, p_5, p_7 to the passive side of their leaf. For each nonleaf, its even and odd child are assigned to its active and passive side, respectively. Initially, the sense fields at both sides of the nodes are *false*, and all processes have local sense *true*.

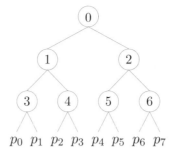

- Let p_0, p_2, p_4, and p_7 arrive at the barrier. Then p_0, p_2, and p_4 move to their leaf, and start spinning on the active sense field, until it equals *true*. And p_7 moves to its leaf 6, sets the active sense field to *true*, and starts spinning on the passive sense field, until it equals *true*.
- Let p_1 arrive at the barrier. It moves to its leaf 3, sets the active sense field to *true*, and starts spinning on the passive sense field.
- When p_0 finds that the active sense field of leaf 3 has become *true*, it moves to node 1, where it starts spinning on the active sense field.
- Let p_6 arrive at the barrier. It moves to its leaf 6, where it finds that the active sense field is *true*. Therefore, it moves to node 2, sets the active sense field to *true*, and starts spinning on the passive sense field.
- Let p_3 arrive at the barrier. It moves to its leaf 4, sets the active sense field to *true*, and starts spinning on the passive sense field.
- When p_2 finds that the active sense field of leaf 4 has become *true*, it moves to node 1, where it sets the active sense field to *true*, and starts spinning on the passive sense field.
- When p_0 finds that the active sense field of node 1 has become *true*, it moves to the root, and starts spinning on the active sense field.

  The resulting situation is depicted in the following diagram; p_0 is spinning on the active sense field of the root, while six other processes are spinning on a passive sense field.

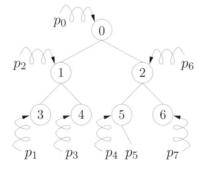

- Finally, p_5 arrives at the barrier. It moves to its leaf 5, sets the active sense field to *true*, and starts spinning on the passive sense field.

- When p_4 finds that the active sense field of leaf 5 has become *true*, it moves to node 2. Since the active sense field of node 2 is *true*, p_4 moves on to the root, where it sets the active sense field to *true*, and starts spinning on the passive sense field.
- When p_0 finds that the active sense field of the root has become *true*, it sets the passive sense fields at nodes 0, 1, and 3 to *true*.
- When p_4 finds that the passive sense field of the root has become *true*, it sets the passive sense fields at nodes 2 and 5 to *true*.
- When p_2 and p_6 find that the passive sense field of node 1 and 2, respectively, has become *true*, they set the passive sense field at leaf 4 and 6, respectively, to *true*.
- p_1, p_3, p_5, and p_7 find that the passive sense field they are spinning on has become *true*. All eight processes leave the barrier and continue their execution with reversed local sense *false*.

Correctness of the tournament tree can be argued in a similar fashion as for the combining tree barrier.

17.4 Dissemination barrier

The dissemination barrier progresses in rounds; in each round, every process that has reached the barrier notifies some other process, and waits for notification by some other process. Just as in the tournament barrier, no read-modify-write operations are used.

Suppose that N processes $p_0, \ldots, p_{N-1}$ are to reach the barrier. A process that reaches the barrier starts with executing round 0. In a round $n \geq 0$, each process p_i that has reached the barrier:

- notifies process $p_{(i+2^n) \bmod N}$,
- waits for notification by process $p_{(i-2^n) \bmod N}$, and
- progresses to round $n + 1$.

When a process completes round $\lceil \log_2 N \rceil - 1$, all N processes have reached the barrier. So then the process can leave the barrier.

Example 17.4 We consider one execution of the dissemination barrier, with $N = 5$. Since $\lceil \log_2 5 \rceil = 3$, the barrier is completed after round 2.

- In round 0, each process p_i notifies process $p_{(i+1) \bmod 5}$, and waits for notification by process $p_{(i-1) \bmod 5}$.
- In round 1, each process p_i notifies process $p_{(i+2) \bmod 5}$, and waits for notification by process $p_{(i-2) \bmod 5}$.
- In round 2, each process p_i notifies process $p_{(i+4) \bmod 5}$, and waits for notification by process $p_{(i-4) \bmod 5}$.

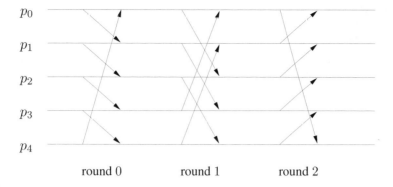

When a process has completed round 2, it can leave the barrier.

Note that if, for instance, p_0 has not yet reached the barrier, then p_1 cannot complete round 0, p_2 and p_3 cannot complete round 1, and p_4 cannot complete round 2. So no process can leave the barrier.

We argue the correctness of the dissemination barrier. When all N processes have reached the barrier, clearly all $\lceil \log_2 N \rceil$ rounds can be completed by all processes. Now suppose that some process p_i has not yet reached the barrier; we argue that then no process can have completed round $\lceil \log_2 N \rceil - 1$. For simplicity, we take $N = 2^k$ for some $k > 0$, so that $\lceil \log_2 N \rceil = k$. In the following explanation, subscripts of processes are to be interpreted modulo 2^k.

- Since p_i has not reached the barrier, p_{i+1} has not completed round 0.
- Since p_i, p_{i+1} have not completed round 0, p_{i+2}, p_{i+3} have not completed round 1.
- Since $p_i, p_{i+1}, p_{i+2}, p_{i+3}$ have not completed round 1, $p_{i+4}, p_{i+5}, p_{i+6}, p_{i+7}$ have not completed round 2.
- ...
- Since $p_i, \ldots, p_{i+2^{k-1}-1}$ have not completed round $k-2$, $p_{i+2^{k-1}}, \ldots, p_{i+2^k-1}$ have not completed round $k-1$.

Since subscripts are interpreted modulo 2^k, p_{i+2^k-1} is p_{i-1}. So no process has left the barrier.

Bibliographical notes

The combining tree barrier originates from [81]. The tournament barrier and the dissemination barrier stem from [36].

Exercises

Exercise 17.1 Explain under which circumstances it is more favorable to let processes that have arrived at the barrier fall asleep, and under which circumstances it is better to use spinning.

Exercise 17.2 Consider the sense-reversing barrier. Suppose that the last process to reach the barrier would first reverse the value of the global sense field, and only then reset the counter to 0. What could go wrong?

Exercise 17.3 Continue the application of the sense-reversing barrier in example 17.1, by reusing the counter and the sense fields (with their reversed values) for a next barrier. Give one possible execution.

Exercise 17.4 Argue that the sense-reversing barrier is a correct barrier. Take into account that the counter and sense fields are reused for multiple subsequent barriers.

Exercise 17.5 [37] Argue that the combining tree barrier can employ any barrier algorithm in its nodes (so not just the sense-reversing barrier).

Exercise 17.6 Consider the tournament barrier, with $k = 2$ and $N = 8$. Give an execution in which at some point only one process has not yet reached the barrier, and all other processes are spinning on a passive sense field.

Exercise 17.7 Argue the correctness of the dissemination barrier for any N.

18
Self-Stabilization

A distributed algorithm is *self-stabilizing* if it will always end up in a correct configuration, even if it is initialized in an incorrect (possibly unreachable) configuration. A strong advantage of self-stabilization is that it provides fault-tolerance in circumstances where the system moves to an incorrect configuration, for example, due to a hardware error or a malicious intruder. Self-stabilization can offer an attractive solution in case failures are infrequent and temporary malfunction is acceptable, as is often the case in operating systems and database systems. An important requirement is that failures are resolved within a relatively short period of time.

The self-stabilizing algorithms that are discussed in this chapter target a network of N processes. Self-stabilizing algorithms are generally presented in a shared-memory framework. The reason is that in a message-passing framework, all processes might be initialized in a state in which they are waiting for a message to arrive, in which case the network would exhibit no behavior at all. In shared memory, processes take into account the values of variables at their neighbors, so that such deadlocks can be avoided. We assume that the local variables at the processes are single-writer registers and that processes can read values of variables at their neighbors.

We will discuss self-stabilizing algorithms for mutual exclusion, where initially multiple processes may be privileged, and for computing a spanning tree, where initially there may, for instance, be a cycle in the spanning tree.

18.1 Dijkstra's token ring for mutual exclusion

Dijkstra's self-stabilizing token ring for mutual exclusion assumes a directed ring of processes $p_0, \ldots, p_{N-1}$. Each process p_i holds a single-writer register x_i with values in $\{0, \ldots, K-1\}$, where $K \geq N$; process p_i can read the value of the register at its predecessor $p_{(i-1) \bmod N}$ in the ring. The privileged processes are defined as follows:

- p_i for $i = 1, \ldots, N-1$ is privileged if $x_i \neq x_{i-1}$.
- p_0 is privileged if $x_0 = x_{N-1}$.

Since Dijkstra's token ring can be initialized in any configuration, clearly there can be multiple privileged processes at the start (if $N \geq 3$).

Each privileged process is allowed to change its value, causing the loss of its privilege:

- p_i can perform $x_i \leftarrow x_{i-1}$ if $x_i \neq x_{i-1}$, for any $i = 1, \ldots, N-1$.
- p_0 can perform $x_0 \leftarrow (x_0 + 1) \bmod K$ if $x_0 = x_{N-1}$.

Example 18.1 Consider a ring of size three, with $K = 3$. Initially, each process has the value 0, so that only process p_0 is privileged. Then p_0 can pass on the privilege to p_1, by setting x_0 to 1. Next, p_1 can pass on the privilege to p_2, by setting x_1 to 1. Now p_2 can pass on the privilege to p_0, by setting x_2 to 1, and so on.

In Dijkstra's token ring, always at least one process is privileged. Namely, if $p_1, \ldots, p_{N-1}$ are not privileged, then it must be the case that the registers $x_0, \ldots, x_{N-1}$ all contain the same value. But then p_0 is privileged, because $x_0 = x_{N-1}$. Furthermore, an event at a process p_i never increases the number of privileged processes, because p_i loses its privilege, and the event can at most cause p_i's successor $p_{(i+1) \bmod N}$ in the ring to become privileged. So if the initial configuration is correct, in the sense that only one process is privileged, then mutual exclusion is guaranteed.

Example 18.2 Let $N = K = 4$, and consider the following initial configuration.

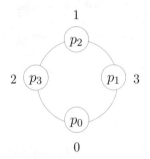

Initially, p_1, p_2, and p_3 are privileged. Each computation will eventually lead to a configuration in which only one process is privileged. The value at p_0 is different from the values at p_1, p_2, and p_3. In the proof of theorem 18.1 it will be argued that in each infinite computation, p_0 must eventually perform an event. The only way p_0 can perform an event is if the register at p_3 attains the value 0. This can happen only if first the register at p_2 attains this value. And in turn this can happen only if first the register at p_1 attains the value 0. Then the registers at p_1, p_2, and p_3 have attained the value 0, so only p_0 is privileged.

For instance, first $x_3 \leftarrow 1$. Next, $x_2 \leftarrow 3$ and $x_3 \leftarrow 3$. And finally, $x_1 \leftarrow 0$, $x_2 \leftarrow 0$, and $x_3 \leftarrow 0$. Now only p_0 is privileged.

Theorem 18.1 *If $K \geq N$, then Dijkstra's token ring for mutual exclusion always eventually reaches a correct configuration, in which starvation-free mutual exclusion is guaranteed.*

Proof. Consider an infinite computation; we need to argue that eventually a configuration is reached in which only one process is privileged. The longest possible sequence of transitions without an event at p_0 consists of $\frac{1}{2}(N-1)N$ events at $p_1, \ldots, p_{N-1}$: one event at p_1 (copying p_0's value), two events at p_2 (copying p_1's first and second value), and so on, up to $N-1$ events at p_{N-1}. So the infinite computation involves infinitely many events at p_0. Since at each such event p_0 increases its value by one modulo K, this implies that during the execution, x_0 ranges over all values in $\{0, \ldots, K-1\}$. Since $p_1, \ldots, p_{N-1}$ only copy values from their predecessors, and $K \geq N$, it follows that in some configuration of the computation, $x_0 \neq x_i$ for all $i = 1, \ldots, N-1$. The next time p_0 becomes privileged, that is, when $x_{N-1} = x_0$, clearly $x_i = x_0$ for all $i = 1, \ldots, N-1$. Then only p_0 is privileged, so mutual exclusion has been achieved.

Starvation-freeness follows from the fact if $N \geq 2$, then in a correct configuration the privileged process always passes on the privilege to its successor. □

For $N \geq 3$, theorem 18.1 also holds if $K = N - 1$. (In case $N = 2$ and $K = 1$, starvation-freeness is violated.) Let us revisit the argumentation in the proof of theorem 18.1. When p_{N-1} copies the value from p_{N-2}, the processes $p_1, \ldots, p_{N-1}$ hold at most $N - 2$ different values (because $N \geq 3$). Since $p_1, \ldots, p_{N-1}$ only copy values, they are then restricted to these $N - 2$ values, as long as the value of x_0 is also among these $N - 2$ values. Since $K \geq N - 1$, and in each infinite computation p_0 performs infinitely many events, it follows that in some configuration of the computation, $x_0 \neq x_i$ for all $i = 1, \ldots, N-1$. The next time p_0 becomes privileged, $x_i = x_0$ for all $i = 1, \ldots, N-1$. Then only p_0 is privileged.

The value $K = N - 1$ is sharp; the next example shows that if $K = N - 2$, then there are infinite computations in which mutual exclusion is never achieved.

Example 18.3 Let $N \geq 4$ and $K = N - 2$, and consider the following initial configuration.

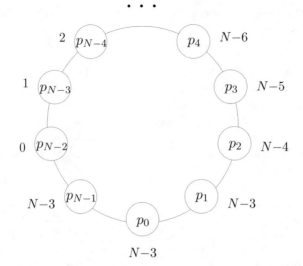

In this configuration only p_1 is not privileged. We consider one possible computation of Dijkstra's token ring. First, p_0 sets x_0 to $((N-3)+1) \bmod (N-2) = 0$. Next, p_{N-1} sets x_{N-1} to 0, then p_{N-2} sets x_{N-2} to 1, and so on. This sequence of events proceeds in a clockwise fashion, until finally p_1 sets x_1 to 0. Then we have reached the following configuration.

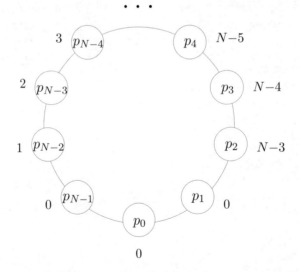

The only difference with the initial configuration is that the values of the registers have increased by one, modulo $N-2$. In particular, in the configuration above again only p_1 is not privileged. This execution pattern can be repeated over and over again, leading to an infinite computation in which always $N-1$ processes are privileged at the same time.

18.2 Arora-Gouda spanning tree algorithm

In the Arora-Gouda self-stabilizing spanning tree algorithm for undirected networks, the process with the largest ID eventually becomes the root of a spanning tree of the network. The algorithm requires that all processes know an upper bound K on the network size.

Each process keeps track of its parent in the spanning tree, which process is the root, and its distance to the root via the spanning tree. Due to arbitrary initialization, there are three complications: first, multiple processes may consider themselves the root; second, there may be a cycle in the spanning tree; and third, there may be a "false" root, meaning that processes may consider a process q the root while q is not in the network at all. The idea behind the Arora-Gouda algorithm is that these inconsistencies can be resolved if a process declares itself the root of the spanning tree, and adapts its local variables accordingly, every time it detects an inconsistency in the values of its local variables. Moreover, a process may resolve inconsistencies between the values of its own local variables and those of its neighbors.

Each process p maintains the following variables.

$parent_p$: p's parent in the spanning tree.
$root_p$: the root of the spanning tree.
$dist_p$: p's distance from the root, via the spanning tree.

The value $\perp$ for $parent_p$ means that p's parent is undefined (in particular when p considers itself the root). A process p declares itself root, that is,

$$parent_p \leftarrow \perp \qquad root_p \leftarrow p \qquad dist_p \leftarrow 0,$$

when it detects an inconsistency in the values of its local variables:

- $root_p < p$; or
- $parent_p = \perp$, and $root_p \neq p$ or $dist_p \neq 0$; or
- $parent_p \neq \perp$ and $parent_p$ is not a neighbor of p; or
- $dist_p \geq K$.

In the first case, $root_p$ is not the largest ID in the network. In the second case, $parent_p$ says p is the root, while $root_p$ or $dist_p$ says not. In the third case, $parent_p$ has an improper value. And the fourth case is in contradiction with the fact that K is an upper bound on the network size.

Suppose there is no such inconsistency in the local variables of p. Let q be a neighbor of p with $dist_q < K$. If $q = parent_p$ and p detects an inconsistency between its own and q's variables, then p can bring its root and distance value in line with those of q:

$$root_p \leftarrow root_q \qquad dist_p \leftarrow dist_q + 1.$$

Furthermore, if $q \neq parent_p$ and $root_p < root_q$, then p can make q its parent:

$$parent_p \leftarrow q \qquad root_p \leftarrow root_q \qquad dist_p \leftarrow dist_q + 1.$$

18 Self-Stabilization

Example 18.4 We consider one possible computation of the Arora-Gouda algorithm on the following undirected network, with $K = 5$. Arrows point from a child to its parent. Note that all processes consider process 8 the root, but that this is a false root.

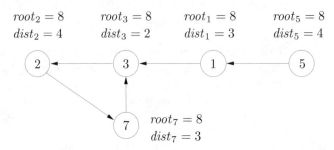

First, process 3 notes that it has distance 2 to the root, while its parent 2 has distance 4. Therefore, process 3 sets its distance to 5. Then it has a distance equal to $K = 5$, so it declares itself root: $parent_3 \leftarrow \bot$, $root_3 \leftarrow 3$, and $dist_3 \leftarrow 0$. As a result, processes 7 and 1 set their root to 3 and their distance to 1, and next processes 2 and 5 set their root to 3 and their distance to 2.

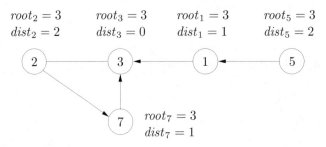

Now process 5 finds an inconsistency in its local variables: its root value is smaller than its own ID. Therefore, it declares itself root: $parent_5 \leftarrow \bot$, $root_5 \leftarrow 5$, and $dist_5 \leftarrow 0$. As a result, first process 1 makes process 5 its parent: $parent_1 \leftarrow 5$, $root_1 \leftarrow 5$, and $dist_1 \leftarrow 1$; next process 3 makes process 1 its parent: $parent_3 \leftarrow 1$, $root_3 \leftarrow 5$, and $dist_3 \leftarrow 2$; and next process 2 makes process 3 its parent: $parent_2 \leftarrow 3$, $root_2 \leftarrow 5$, and $dist_2 \leftarrow 3$.

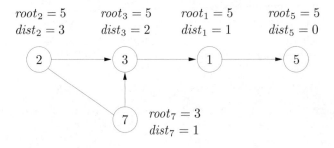

Now process 7 finds an inconsistency in its local variables: its root value is smaller than its own ID. Therefore, it declares itself root: $parent_7 \leftarrow \perp$, $root_7 \leftarrow 7$, and $dist_7 \leftarrow 0$. As a result, processes 2 and 3 make process 7 their parent; next, process 1 makes process 3 its parent; and finally, process 5 makes process 1 its parent.

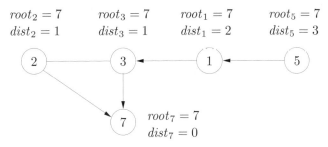

The resulting configuration, depicted above, is stable.

We argue that the Arora-Gouda spanning tree algorithm is self-stabilizing, if only fair computations are considered (see exercise 18.5). The key is that false root values, which are not an ID of any process in the network, will eventually disappear. Namely, such false roots can survive only if there is a cycle of processes that all have this root value. Distance values of processes on such a cycle will keep on increasing, until one of them gets distance K and declares itself root. Then the cycle is broken, and by fairness the cycle can be reestablished only a finite number of times. Hence, the false root of the (former) cycle will eventually be eradicated. Since false roots are guaranteed to disappear, the process with the largest ID in the network will eventually declare itself root. Then the network will converge to a spanning tree with this process as the root.

To obtain a breadth-first search tree, in the Arora-Gouda algorithm, the case where $q \neq parent_p$ is a neighbor of p with $dist_q < K$ has one extra subcase: if $root_p = root_q$ and $dist_p > dist_q + 1$, then $parent_p \leftarrow q$ and $dist_p \leftarrow dist_q + 1$. That is, a process can select a new parent if it offers a shorter path to the root.

18.3 Afek-Kutten-Yung spanning tree algorithm

The Afek-Kutten-Yung self-stabilizing spanning tree algorithm for undirected networks does not require a known upper bound on the network size. Moreover, it does not exhibit (unfair) infinite computations. Again, the process with the largest ID eventually becomes the root of a spanning tree of the network.

Each process p again maintains the variables $parent_p$, $root_p$, and $dist_p$. A process p declares itself root, that is,

$$parent_p \leftarrow \perp \qquad root_p \leftarrow p \qquad dist_p \leftarrow 0,$$

if it does not yet consider itself root, and detects an inconsistency in the values of its local variables, or between these values and those of its parent:

- $root_p \leq p$; or
- $parent_p = \bot$; or
- $parent_p \neq \bot$, and $parent_p$ is not a neighbor of p or $root_p \neq root_{parent_p}$ or $dist_p \neq dist_{parent_p} + 1$.

Note that if there is a cycle in the spanning tree, then always a process on this cycle will declare itself root. Namely, there is always some process p on this cycle with $dist_p \neq dist_{parent_p} + 1$.

A process p that considers itself root can make a neighbor q its parent, if $root_q$ is larger than p. In case several neighbors of p have a root value greater than $root_p$, p selects a neighbor q with the largest root value among all p's neighbors. Before p can make q its parent, p must wait until q's component of the spanning tree has a proper root. For otherwise processes could infinitely often join a component of the spanning tree with a false root, as shown in the next example.

Example 18.5 Consider the initial following configuration.

$$root_0 = 2 \quad \boxed{0} \longleftrightarrow \boxed{1} \quad root_1 = 2$$
$$dist_0 = 0 \qquad\qquad\qquad\qquad dist_1 = 1$$

Since $dist_0 \neq dist_1 + 1$, process 0 declares itself root: $parent_0 \leftarrow \bot$, $root_0 \leftarrow 0$, and $dist_0 \leftarrow 0$. Next, since $root_0 < root_1$, process 0 makes process 1 its parent: $parent_0 \leftarrow 1$, $root_0 \leftarrow 2$, and $dist_0 \leftarrow 2$. Next, since $dist_1 \neq dist_0 + 1$, process 1 declares itself root: $parent_1 \leftarrow \bot$, $root_1 \leftarrow 1$, and $dist_1 \leftarrow 0$. Next, since $root_1 < root_0$, process 1 makes process 0 its parent: $parent_1 \leftarrow 0$, $root_1 \leftarrow 2$, and $dist_1 \leftarrow 3$. And so on.

Therefore, before p makes q its parent, if first sends a join request to q, which is forwarded through the spanning tree to the root, which sends back an acknowledgment to p via the spanning tree. When p receives this acknowledgment, p makes q its parent, that is,

$$parent_p \leftarrow q \qquad root_p \leftarrow root_q \qquad dist_p \leftarrow dist_q + 1.$$

Since we are in a shared-memory framework, join requests and acknowledgments need to be encoded in shared variables; see the pseudocode in the appendix. The path of a join request is remembered in local variables, so that the resulting acknowledgment can follow this path in the reverse order. A process can be forwarding and awaiting an acknowledgment for at most one join request at a time. As the encoding of join requests in shared variables is rather involved, they are presented in the examples in a message-passing style.

Example 18.6 We revisit the initial configuration from example 18.5, but now with join requests and acknowledgments. We consider one possible computation of the Afek-Kutten-Yung algorithm.

Since $dist_0 \neq dist_1 + 1$, process 0 declares itself root: $parent_0 \leftarrow \bot$, $root_0 \leftarrow 0$, and $dist_0 \leftarrow 0$. Next, since $root_0 < root_1$, process 0 sends a join request to process

1. Note that process 1 cannot forward this join request to its parent 0, because 0 is awaiting an acknowledgment. Next, since $dist_1 \neq dist_0 + 1$, process 1 declares itself root: $parent_1 \leftarrow \bot$, $root_1 \leftarrow 1$, and $dist_1 \leftarrow 0$. Since process 1 is now a proper root, it replies to the join request of process 0 with an acknowledgment. As a result, process 0 makes process 1 its parent: $parent_0 \leftarrow 1$, $root_0 \leftarrow 1$, and $dist_0 \leftarrow 1$. The resulting spanning tree, with process 1 as root, is stable.

Join requests are forwarded only between processes of which the local variables have consistent values; else there could be infinite computations, as shown in example 18.7. And processes forward an acknowledgment only if they sent a corresponding join request previously. This check avoids spurious acknowledgments due to improper initial values of local variables.

Example 18.7 Given an undirected ring with three processes $0, 1, 2$. Initially, processes 0 and 1 consider themselves root, while process 2 has process 0 as parent, considers the (nonexistent) process 3 the root, and has some distance value k.

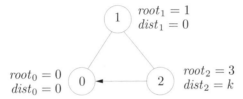

Since $root_2 > root_1$ (and $root_2 > root_0$), process 1 sends a join request to process 2. Without the consistency check, process 2 would forward this join request to process 0. Since process 0 considers itself root, it would send back an acknowledgment to process 1 (via process 2), and process 1 would make process 2 its parent and consider process 3 the root. Next, since $root_2 \neq root_0$, process 2 could make itself root.

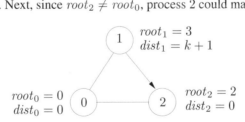

Now we would have a (nearly) symmetrical configuration to the initial one. This scenario could be repeated to obtain an infinite computation that never reaches a stable configuration.

We argue that the Afek-Kutten-Yung spanning tree algorithm is self-stabilizing. Each component in the network with a false root contains an inconsistency, so a process in this component will declare itself root. Since join requests are forwarded only between consistent processes, and processes can be involved in only one join request at a time, each join request is eventually acknowledged. Join requests guarantee that processes only finitely often join a component with a false root, each time due to improper initial values of local variables. These observations together imply that eventually false roots will disappear. Therefore, the process with the largest ID in the network will declare itself root, and the network will converge to a spanning tree with this process as the root.

Bibliographical notes

Dijkstra's token ring originates from [24]; a proof that the ring is self-stabilizing for $K = N - 1$ is presented in [31]. The Arora-Gouda algorithm stems from [5], and the Afek-Kutten-Yung algorithm from [1].

Exercises

Exercise 18.1 Give a computation of Dijkstra's token ring with $N = K = 4$ that takes as long as possible before it reaches a correct configuration.

Exercise 18.2 Argue that from any configuration of Dijkstra's token ring (with $K \geq N$) it takes at most $O(N^2)$ transitions to reach a correct configuration.

Exercise 18.3 Given an undirected ring of three processes with IDs 0, 1, and 2. In the initial configuration, $parent_0 = 1$, $parent_1 = 2$, and $parent_2 = 0$; $root_0 = root_1 = root_2 = 3$; $dist_0 = 1$, $dist_1 = 0$, and $dist_2 = 2$. Describe one possible computation of the Arora-Gouda algorithm on this network, with $K = 4$.

Exercise 18.4 One part of the Arora-Gouda algorithm considers a neighbor q of process p with $dist_q < K$. Show that if the side condition "with $dist_q < K$" were omitted, then the algorithm might not stabilize.

Exercise 18.5 Give an unfair infinite computation of the Arora-Gouda algorithm that never stabilizes. Let only one process perform events.

Exercise 18.6 Adapt the Arora-Gouda algorithm so that it no longer exhibits (unfair) infinite computations.

Exercise 18.7 Describe one possible computation of the Afek-Kutten-Yung algorithm on the network from exercise 18.3.

Exercise 18.8 Argue that in the Afek-Kutten-Yung algorithm, each join request eventually results in an acknowledgment.

Exercise 18.9 Argue that the Afek-Kutten-Yung algorithm takes at most $O(N^2)$ transitions to stabilize.

19
Online Scheduling

So far we have mostly ignored timing aspects. Logical clocks were used for termination detection and mutual exclusion, and local clocks with bounded drift were employed to build a synchronous system in the presence of Byzantine processes. But these were abstract representations of time. In this chapter we will consider jobs, meaning units of work, that need to be scheduled and executed and are for this purpose divided over the processors. These jobs have time constraints and resource requirements.

One important application of real-time computing is computer graphics in video games, where it is vital to produce and analyze images in real time, and where there is very little time available per image. Typically, every image is then decomposed into triangles, and special hardware is employed to generate the pixels inside each of the triangles separately. Another important application is air traffic control to direct planes on the ground and through the air, based on information from different sources such as radars, weather stations, and pilots.

19.1 Jobs

The *arrival time* of a job is the moment in time it arrives at a processor, while the *release time* of a job is the moment in time it becomes available for execution. In many cases these two times will coincide, but sometimes it can be useful to postpone the release time of a job, notably for avoiding resource competition (see section 19.3). The *execution time* of a job at a processor is the amount of time needed to perform the job (assuming it executes alone and all resources are available).

We disregard the functional behavior of jobs, and focus on their deadlines, meaning the time by which they must have been completed. This can be expressed as an *absolute deadline*, that is, as a fixed moment in real time, or as a *relative deadline*, that is, the maximum allowed time between arrival and completion of a job. A deadline can be *hard*, meaning that late completion is not allowed, or *soft*, meaning that late completion is allowed but comes at some penalty.

A scheduler at a processor decides in which order jobs are performed at this processor, and which resources they can claim. A scheduler aims to meet all hard deadlines, meet soft deadlines as much as possible, and avoid deadlocks. Of course, a job cannot be scheduled before its release time, and the total amount of time assigned to a job should equal its (maximum) execution time.

In this chapter, the communication paradigm, message passing versus shared memory, is not of the essence. In view of the fact that real-time scheduling plays an important role in operating systems, it is placed in the shared-memory part.

A task is a set of related jobs. Three types of tasks can be distinguished:

- *Periodic*: such a task is known at the start of the system; the jobs have hard deadlines.
- *Aperiodic*: such a task is executed in response to some external event; the jobs have soft deadlines.
- *Sporadic*: such a task is executed in response to some external event; the jobs have hard deadlines.

A periodic task is defined by three parameters:

- The *release time* r of the first periodic job.
- The *period* p, which is a periodic time interval, at the start of which a periodic job is released.
- The *execution time* e of each periodic job.

For simplicity, we assume that the relative deadline of each periodic job equals its period. The *utilization* of a periodic task (r, p, e) is $\frac{e}{p}$, representing the relative amount of execution time on a processor that will be consumed by this periodic task. The utilization at a processor is the sum of utilizations of its periodic tasks. Clearly, scheduling of the periodic tasks at a processor is possible only if its utilization does not exceed one.

Example 19.1 Consider the periodic tasks $T_1 = (1, 2, 1)$ and $T_2 = (0, 3, 1)$ at a processor. The utilization at the processor is $\frac{1}{2} + \frac{1}{3} = \frac{5}{6}$. The periodic jobs can be executed as follows.

```
| J_2 | J_1 |   | J_1 | J_2 | J_1 | • • •
 0     1     2   3     4     5     6      time axis
```

The conflict at time 3, when periodic jobs of both T_1 and T_2 are released, must be resolved by some scheduler. In this example, T_1 is given priority over T_2. Different schedulers will be discussed in section 19.2.

19.2 Schedulers

An offline scheduler determines the order in which jobs will be executed beforehand, typically with an algorithm for an NP-complete graph problem. In such schedulers, time is usually divided into regular time intervals called frames, and in each frame, a predetermined set of periodic tasks is executed. Jobs may be sliced into subjobs to accommodate frame length. Offline scheduling is conceptually relatively simple, but cannot cope so well with jitter (that is, imprecise release and execution times), extra workload, nondeterminism, and system modifications.

Here we focus on online schedulers, where the schedule is computed at run-time. Scheduling decisions are taken when jobs are released, when aperiodic/sporadic tasks arrive, when jobs are completed, or when resources are required or released. Released jobs are placed in priority queues, ordered by for instance release time, execution time, period of the task, deadline, or slack. The latter means the available idle time of a job until the next deadline. For example, if at time 2 a job with a deadline at time 6 still needs three time units to complete, then its slack at time 2 is $(6-2) - 3 = 1$.

For simplicity, we consider aperiodic and sporadic jobs instead of tasks. Such jobs are offered to processors at run-time. Sporadic jobs are only accepted at a processor if they can be completed in time, without causing the processor to miss hard deadlines of other jobs. We assume that aperiodic jobs are always accepted and are performed such that periodic and accepted sporadic jobs do not miss their deadlines. Sporadic and aperiodic jobs that need to be executed at a processor are placed in job queues. The queueing discipline of aperiodic jobs tries to minimize the penalty associated to missed soft deadlines (for example, minimize the number of missed soft deadlines, or the average tardiness, being the amount of time by which an aperiodic job misses its deadline).

Unless stated otherwise, we assume that there is no resource competition and that jobs are preemptive, meaning that they can be suspended at any time in their execution.

Scheduling periodic jobs

A popular scheduler for periodic tasks is the *rate-monotonic* scheduler, which gives periodic jobs with a shorter period a higher priority. A strong point of this scheduler is that the static priority at the level of tasks makes its schedules relatively easy to compute and predict. The idea behind the rate-monotonic scheduler is that if a periodic job J_1 has a shorter period than a periodic job J_2, then the relative deadline of J_1 is shorter than the relative deadline of J_2. However, it may be the case that J_2 has been released before J_1, in which case J_s has an earlier deadline than J_1. As a result, the rate-monotonic scheduler is not optimal, in the sense that it may cause periodic jobs to miss their deadline, even in cases where the utilization of the periodic tasks at a processor is less than one.

Example 19.2 Consider a single processor, with periodic tasks $T_1 = (0, 4, 2)$ and $T_2 = (0, 6, 3)$. Note that utilization is $\frac{2}{4} + \frac{3}{6} = 1$. The rate-monotonic scheduler, which gives jobs from T_1 a higher priority than jobs from T_2, schedules the periodic jobs as follows.

| J_1 | J_2 | J_1 | J_2 | J_2 | J_1 | J_2 | ... |

0   1   2   3   4   5   6   7   8   9   10   11   12

Note that T_2 is preempted by T_1 at times 4 and 8. The first periodic job of T_2 misses its deadline at time 6.

The *earliest deadline first* scheduler gives a job a higher priority if its deadline is earlier. In case of preemptive jobs and no competition for resources, this scheduler is optimal, in the sense that if utilization at a processor does not exceed one, then periodic jobs will be scheduled in such a way that no deadlines are missed.

Example 19.3 Consider the setting of example 19.2: a single processor, with periodic tasks $T_1 = (0, 4, 2)$ and $T_2 = (0, 6, 3)$. The earliest deadline first scheduler may schedule the periodic jobs as follows.

| J_1 | J_2 | J_1 | J_2 | J_1 | ... |

0   1   2   3   4   5   6   7   8   9   10   11   12

No deadlines are missed. Note that at time 8 it would also be possible to let J_1 preempt J_2, because both jobs have their deadline at time 12.

The *least slack-time first* scheduler gives a job a higher priority if it has less slack. This scheduler is also optimal: if utilization at a processor does not exceed one, then periodic jobs will be scheduled in such a way that no deadlines are missed.

Slack of a job gives precise information how much time can be spent on other jobs without this job missing its deadline. However, it is computationally expensive. Another drawback of the least slack-time first scheduler is that priority between jobs is dynamic, in the sense that it may change over time. Continuous scheduling decisions would lead to so-called context switch overhead in case of two jobs with the same amount of slack, because they would interrupt each other repeatedly.

In case of nonpreemptive jobs, or resource competition, it may be impossible to schedule periodic jobs in such a way that no deadlines are missed, even in cases where utilization at a processor is (much smaller than) one. For instance, suppose there are two nonpreemptive periodic tasks $(0, 1, e)$ and $(0, p, 2)$. No matter how small $e > 0$ and how large p are chosen, as soon as a job of the second periodic task is executed, a job of the first periodic task will miss its deadline. The same holds if these periodic tasks are preemptive, but they both require the same resource from start to finish. Moreover, nonpreemptive jobs or resource competition can give rise to so-called scheduling anomalies: shorter execution times may lead to violation of deadlines. This is shown in the next example.

Example 19.4 Let three nonpreemptive jobs be executed at the same processor: job J_1 is released at time 0 with a deadline at time 2 and execution time 1; job J_2 is released at time 1 with a deadline at time 5 and execution time 2; and job J_3 is released at time 2 with a deadline at time 3 and execution time 1. The earliest deadline first and least slack-time first schedulers both schedule these three jobs as follows.

$$
\begin{array}{|c|c|c|}
\hline
J_1 & J_2 & J_3 \\
\hline
\end{array}
$$
0 1 2 3 4

Job J_3 misses its deadline at time 3.

If the execution time of J_1 is increased from 1 to 2, then the earliest deadline first and least slack-time first schedulers both schedule these three jobs as follows.

$$
\begin{array}{|c|c|c|}
\hline
J_1 & J_3 & J_2 \\
\hline
\end{array}
$$
0 1 2 3 4 5

In this case no deadlines are missed.

Scheduling aperiodic jobs

We assume that aperiodic jobs are always accepted for execution at a processor and that they are executed in such a way that periodic and accepted sporadic jobs do not miss their hard deadlines. The challenge is to execute aperiodic jobs in such a way that they adhere to their soft deadlines as much as possible.

A straightforward solution is the *background* server, which schedules aperiodic jobs only in idle time, when no periodic and sporadic jobs are available for execution. The drawback is that this server may needlessly let an aperiodic job miss its deadline.

Example 19.5 Let aperiodic job A have execution time 1 and a deadline one time unit away, while sporadic job S has execution time 1 and a deadline ten time units away. Although A could easily be scheduled before S, the background server would schedule S first, causing A to miss its deadline.

In the *slack stealing* server, an aperiodic job may be executed as long as the processor has slack, meaning that it could idle without causing periodic or sporadic jobs to miss their deadline. The drawback of this server is that the amount of slack of a processor is difficult to compute, because it changes over time, and in practice one would have to take jitter into account.

Example 19.6 Suppose that a processor is executing periodic tasks $T_1 = (0, 2, \frac{1}{2})$ and $T_2 = (0, 3, \frac{1}{2})$, and that aperiodic jobs are available for execution at this processor in the time interval $[0, 6]$. The following graph depicts how, with the slack stealing server, the amount of slack of the processor changes over time.

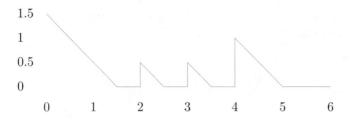

In the time intervals $\langle 0, 1\frac{1}{2}\rangle$, $\langle 2, 2\frac{1}{2}\rangle$, $\langle 3, 3\frac{1}{2}\rangle$, and $\langle 4, 5\rangle$, aperiodic jobs are executed. A periodic job from T_1 is executed in $\langle 1\frac{1}{2}, 2\rangle$, $\langle 3\frac{1}{2}, 4\rangle$, and $\langle 5, 5\frac{1}{2}\rangle$ and a periodic job from T_2 in $\langle 2\frac{1}{2}, 3\rangle$ and $\langle 5\frac{1}{2}, 6\rangle$.

We discuss three more servers, which are based on utilization. Suppose that periodic tasks $T_k = (r_k, p_k, e_k)$ for $k = 1, \ldots, n$ are being executed at the processor under consideration. For simplicity, we ignore sporadic jobs.

The *polling* server carries two parameters p_s and e_s: in each period of length p_s, *the first e_s time units* can be used to execute aperiodic jobs. The polling server works correctly if

$$\sum_{k=1}^{n} \frac{e_k}{p_k} + \frac{e_s}{p_s} \leq 1. \tag{19.1}$$

For the correctness of the polling server it is essential that in a period p_s, aperiodic jobs are executed only in the first e_s time units; see example 19.7. A drawback of the polling server is that aperiodic jobs released just after the first e_s time units of a period p_s may be delayed needlessly.

The *deferrable* server is similar to the polling server, but allows aperiodic jobs to be executed for e_s time units in the entire period p_s, so not only at the start. The following example shows that for the deferrable server, criterion (19.1) for the values p_s and e_s would be incorrect.

Example 19.7 Consider a processor with one periodic task $T = (2, 5, 3\frac{1}{3})$, and let $p_s = 3$ and $e_s = 1$. Note that criterion (19.1) is satisfied.

Let an aperiodic job A with execution time 2 arrive at time 2. The deferrable server would allow A to execute at the end of the first period p_s, from time 2 until time 3, and at the start of the second period p_s from time 3 until time 4. As a result, the first periodic job, which is released at time 2, can start execution only at time 4, until time $7\frac{1}{3}$. So it misses its deadline at time 7.

A drawback of the deferrable server is that it is not easy to determine optimal values for p_s and e_s.

The *total bandwidth* server fixes a utilization rate $\tilde{u}_s$ for aperiodic jobs, such that

$$\sum_{k=1}^{n} \frac{e_k}{p_k} + \tilde{u}_s \leq 1.$$

When the queue of aperiodic jobs gets a new head, a deadline d is determined for this head as follows. If, at a time t, either a job arrives at the empty aperiodic queue, or an aperiodic job completes and the tail of the aperiodic queue is nonempty, then

$$d \leftarrow \max\{d, t\} + \frac{e}{\tilde{u}_s}$$

where e denotes the execution time of the new head of the aperiodic queue. Initially, $d = 0$.

Aperiodic jobs can now be treated in the same way as periodic jobs, by the earliest deadline first scheduler. Periodic jobs are guaranteed to meet their deadlines (in the absence of sporadic jobs), and aperiodic jobs meet the deadlines assigned to them (which may differ from their actual soft deadlines).

Example 19.8 Consider a processor with two periodic tasks $T_1 = (0, 2, 1)$ and $T_2 = (0, 3, 1)$. We fix $\tilde{u}_s = \frac{1}{6}$.

J_1	J_2	A_1	J_1	J_2	J_1	A_2	J_1	J_2	J_1	A_3	J_1	J_2
0	1	2	3	4	5	6	7	8	9	10	11	12

- Aperiodic job A_1, released at time 1 with execution time $\frac{1}{2}$, gets (at 1) deadline $1 + 3 = 4$.
- Aperiodic job A_2, released at time 2 with execution time $\frac{2}{3}$, gets (at $2\frac{1}{2}$) deadline $4 + 4 = 8$.
- Aperiodic job A_3, released at time 3 with execution time $\frac{2}{3}$, gets (at $6\frac{1}{6}$) deadline $8 + 4 = 12$.

Scheduling sporadic jobs

We now present an acceptance test for sporadic jobs. A sporadic job can be accepted at a processor only if it can be executed before its (hard) deadline, without causing the violation of deadlines of periodic and accepted sporadic jobs at this processor.

A sporadic job with deadline d and execution time e that is offered to a processor at time t, is accepted if utilization of the periodic and accepted sporadic jobs in the time interval $[t, d]$ is never more than $1 - \frac{e}{d-t}$. If accepted, utilization in $[t, d]$ is increased with $\frac{e}{d-t}$. Periodic and accepted sporadic jobs can be scheduled according to the earliest deadline first scheduler.

Example 19.9 Consider a processor with one periodic task $T = (0, 2, 1)$. Utilization of this periodic task over the entire time domain is $\frac{1}{2}$.

- Sporadic job S_1 with execution time 2 and a deadline 6 is offered to the processor at time 1. S_1 is accepted, and utilization in $[1, 6]$ is increased to $\frac{1}{2} + \frac{2}{5} = \frac{9}{10}$.
- Sporadic job S_2 with execution time 2 and a deadline 20 is offered to the processor at time 2. S_2 is rejected, because utilization in the time interval $[2, 6]$ would increase beyond 1.

188   19 Online Scheduling

- Sporadic job S_3 with execution time 1 and a deadline 13 is offered to the processor at time 3. S_3 is accepted, and utilization in $[3, 6]$ is increased to $\frac{9}{10} + \frac{1}{10} = 1$, and utilization in $[6, 13]$ is increased to $\frac{1}{2} + \frac{1}{10} = \frac{3}{5}$.

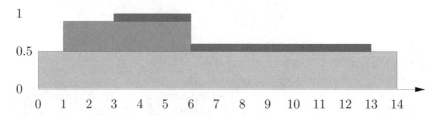

The acceptance test may reject schedulable sporadic jobs. In particular, sporadic job S_2 in the previous example is schedulable, but it is nevertheless rejected.

The total bandwidth server can be integrated with the acceptance test for sporadic jobs, for example, by making the allowed utilization rate $\tilde{u}_s$ for the total bandwidth server dynamic.

19.3 Resource access control

So far we have ignored competition for resources, such as a block of memory. In this section we consider resource units that can be requested by jobs during their execution, and are allocated to jobs in a mutually exclusive fashion. When a requested resource is refused, the job is preempted.

One danger of resource sharing is that it may give rise to deadlock, when two jobs block each other because they hold a different resource, and these jobs require both resources. A second danger is that a high-priority job J may be blocked by a sequence of low-priority jobs, when J requires a resource that is being held by a job with a very low priority. We give examples of these two situations.

Example 19.10 Consider two jobs J_1 and J_2, where J_1 has a higher priority than J_2, and two resources R and R'.

First, J_2 is executing, and claims R. Then J_1 arrives at the same processor, preempts J_2, starts executing, and claims R'. Next, J_1 requires R; since this resource is held by J_2, J_1 is preempted and J_2 continues its execution. Next, J_2 requires R'; since this resource is held by J_1, J_2 is preempted. Now J_1 is blocked because J_2 holds R, while J_2 is blocked because J_1 holds R'. So J_1 and J_2 are deadlocked.

Example 19.11 Consider jobs $J_0, J_1, \ldots, J_k$, with as priorities $J_0 > J_1 > \cdots > J_k$. There is a resource R, which will be required by both J_0 and J_k.

First, J_k is executing, and claims R. Then J_{k-1} arrives at the same processor, preempts J_k, and starts executing. Next, J_{k-2} arrives at the same processor, preempts J_{k-1}, and starts executing. This pattern is repeated, until finally J_0 arrives at the same processor, preempts J_1, and starts executing. Next, J_0 requires R; since this resource is held by J_k, J_0 is preempted, and J_1 (which has the highest priority of the available jobs) continues its execution. When J_1 is completed, J_2 continues its execution; upon completion of J_2, J_3 continues its execution, and so on, until finally J_k continues its execution, completes, and releases R. Only then J_0 can claim R and continue its execution.

| J_k | J_{k-1} | $\bullet\bullet\bullet$ | J_1 | J_0 | J_1 | $\bullet\bullet\bullet$ | J_{k-1} | J_k | J_0 |

Priority inheritance makes blocking of a high-priority job J by a sequence of low-priority jobs less likely. The idea is that when a job J_1 is blocked because it requires a resource that is held by a job J_2, and J_1 has a higher priority than J_2, then J_2 inherits the priority of J_1 as long as it is blocking the execution of J_1.

Example 19.12 We revisit example 19.11, with priority inheritance. When J_0 requires R, J_k inherits the priority of J_k. So instead of J_1, now J_k continues its execution. When J_k completes and releases R, J_0 can claim R and continue its execution.

| J_k | J_{k-1} | $\bullet\bullet\bullet$ | J_1 | J_0 | J_k | J_0 | J_1 | $\bullet\bullet\bullet$ | J_{k-1} |

However, with priority inheritance a deadlock can still occur. For instance, priority inheritance has no effect on the execution discussed in example 19.10. Such deadlocks can be avoided by *priority ceiling*. The priority ceiling of a resource R at a time t is the highest priority of (known) jobs that will require R at some time $\geq t$. The priority ceiling of a processor at a time t is the highest priority ceiling of resources that are in use at time t. The priority ceiling of a processor has a special bottom value Ω when no resources are in use. In case of priority ceiling, from the arrival of a job at a processor, this job is not released until its priority is higher than the priority ceiling of the processor.

The idea behind priority ceiling is that a job J is released only if all the resources it will require during its execution are not in use. Because otherwise at the arrival of J the priority ceiling of the processor increases to the priority of J, if this priority ceiling is not at or beyond this level already. Of course, this approach works properly only if all the resources a job will require during its execution are always known beforehand. If priorities of jobs do not change over time (as is the case for the earliest deadline first scheduler, but not for the least slack-time first scheduler), then deadlocks like the one in example 19.10 cannot occur.

Example 19.13 We revisit example 19.10, with priority ceiling. When J_1 arrives at the processor, the priority ceiling is increased to the priority of J_1, because J_1 will require R, and this resource is in use by J_2. So J_1 is not yet released. When J_2 completes and releases R, the priority ceiling goes down to Ω, so that J_1 is released and starts executing.

With priority ceiling, blocking of a high-priority job by a sequence of lower-priority jobs becomes less likely.

Example 19.14 We revisit example 19.11, with priority ceiling, under the assumption that the future arrival of J_0 is known from the start. Since J_0 will require R, and J_k holds R, the priority ceiling becomes the priority of J_0. Therefore, J_{k-1} is not released at its arrival, and J_k continues its execution. When J_k completes and releases R, the priority ceiling drops to Ω, so that jobs are released. When J_0 arrives, it can claim R, and start executing straightaway.

| J_k | J_{k-2} | $\cdots$ | J_1 | J_0 | J_1 | $\cdots$ | J_{k-2} | J_{k-1} |

Priority ceiling has no effect on jobs that have been released. For instance, if in example 19.11 the arrival of J_0 is known only at its arrival, priority ceiling does not help. Therefore, priority inheritance tends to be imposed on top of priority ceiling.

Priority ceiling can be extended to a setting with multiple units of the same resource type. Then the definition of priority ceiling needs to be adapted as follows. The priority ceiling of a resource R with k free units at a time t is the highest priority level of known jobs that require more than k units of R at some time $\geq t$.

Bibliographical notes

The slack stealing server originates from [48], the deferrable server from [74], and the total bandwidth server in [73]. Priority inheritance was introduced in [71], and priority ceiling in [65].

Exercises

In these exercises, all jobs are assumed to be preemptive.

Exercise 19.1 [50] Consider a system with two processors. Suppose jobs J_1, J_2, and J_3 are released at time 0, with execution times 1, 1, and 2, and deadlines at times 1, 2, and 3, respectively.

(a) Let jobs J_4 and J_5 be released at time 2, both with execution time 1 and a deadline at time 3.
(b) Let job J_4 be released at time 1, with execution time 2 and a deadline at time 3. (In this case there is no J_5.)

In both cases, give a schedule such that all deadlines are met.

Exercise 19.2 [50] Which of the following collections of periodic tasks are schedulable on one processor by the earliest deadline first scheduler? And which ones by the rate-monotonic scheduler?

(a) $(0, 8, 4)$, $(0, 10, 2)$, $(0, 12, 3)$.
(b) $(0, 8, 4)$, $(0, 12, 4)$, $(0, 20, 4)$.

(c) $(0, 8, 3)$, $(0, 9, 3)$, $(0, 15, 3)$.

Exercise 19.3 Consider a processor with one periodic task $(0, 5, 3\frac{1}{3})$, and with the earliest deadline first scheduler.

(a) Given a polling server with $p_s = 3$, what is the maximum value for e_s?
(b) Given a deferrable server with $p_s = 3$, what is the maximum value for e_s?
(c) Given a total bandwidth server, what is the maximum utilization rate $\tilde{u}_s$?
(d) Suppose aperiodic jobs A_1, A_2, and A_3 arrive at times 3, 5, and 13, with execution times 1, 2, and 1, respectively. Explain how these aperiodic jobs are executed in case of the deferrable server (with e_s maximal) and the total bandwidth server (with $\tilde{u}_s$ maximal).

Exercise 19.4 Suppose that the total bandwidth server is adapted as follows. When at time t an aperiodic job (with execution time e) arrives at the aperiodic queue while it is empty, $d \leftarrow t + \frac{e}{\tilde{u}_s}$. Give an example to show that then, with the earliest deadline first scheduler, periodic jobs may miss their deadlines.

Exercise 19.5 Consider a processor with one periodic task $(0, 3, 1)$. Suppose sporadic jobs S_1, S_2, S_3, and S_4 arrive at times 0, 1, 3, and 6, with execution times 1, 3, 1, and 2, and with deadlines at times 1, 12, 7, and 14, respectively. Explain which of these jobs pass the acceptance test.

Exercise 19.6 Give an example where the acceptance test for sporadic jobs rejects a sporadic job at a time t, while it accepts this same job at a time $t' > t$.

Exercise 19.7 Suggest an adaptation of the acceptance test for sporadic jobs that accepts more sporadic jobs (without computing slack). Give an example of a sporadic job that is accepted by your test, but not by the original test. Does your test accept all schedulable sporadic jobs?

Exercise 19.8 Jobs J_1 and J_2 arrive at times 1 and 0, with execution times 1 and 2, respectively. Let J_1 and J_2 use resource R for their entire execution, and J_2 resource R' for the last time unit of its execution.

(a) Job J_3 arrives at time 1, with execution time 100. Let $J_1 > J_3 > J_2$. Explain how J_1, J_2, J_3 are executed with and without priority inheritance.
(b) Job J_4 arrives at time 1, with execution time 2. Let J_4 use resource R' for its entire execution and resource R for the last time unit of its execution. Let $J_1 > J_4 > J_2$. Explain how J_1, J_2, J_4 are executed with and without priority inheritance.

Exercise 19.9 Let preemptive jobs J_1, J_2, and J_3 arrive at times 2, 1, and 0, respectively, with execution time 2. Let the priorities be $J_1 > J_2 > J_3$. Let J_1 and J_3 use resource R for their entire execution. The jobs are executed using priority ceiling.

(a) Explain how the three jobs are executed if the arrival of J_1 is known from the start.
(b) Explain how the three jobs are executed if the arrival of J_1 is not known before time 2. Consider the cases with and without priority inheritance.

Exercise 19.10 Give an example to show that with priority ceiling, a job can still be blocked by a sequence of lower-priority jobs, even if there is priority inheritance and the arrival of all jobs is known from the start.

Exercise 19.11 Give an example to show that a deadlock can occur if priority ceiling is applied in combination with the least slack-time first scheduler. (The resources a job requires during its execution are assumed to be known beforehand.)

Pseudocode Descriptions

Pseudocode descriptions are presented for a considerable number of distributed algorithms discussed in the main body of this book. Several algorithms are excluded here, either because their pseudocode description is trivial or very similar to another algorithm that is included, or because the main body contains a description that resembles the pseudocode.

Each piece of pseudocode is presented for a process p or p_i; its local variables are subscripted with p or i, respectively. We use $Neighbors_p$ to denote the set of neighbors of process p in the network, and $Processes$ for the set of processes in the network.

Each pseudocode description starts with a variable declaration section. Let **bool**, **nat**, **int**, and **real** denote the data type of Booleans, natural numbers, integers, and reals, with as default initial value *false* and 0 (for the latter three). The operations $\wedge$, $\vee$, and $\neg$ on Booleans denote conjunction, disjunction, and negation, respectively. The data type **dist**, representing distance, consists of the natural numbers extended with infinity ∞, where $\infty + d = d + \infty = \infty$ for all distance values d, and $d < \infty$ for all $d \neq \infty$; its default initial value is ∞.

The data type of processes in the network, **proc**, has as default initial value $\perp$ (i.e., undefined). The data types **mess-queue** and **proc-queue** represent FIFO queues of basic messages and processes, respectively. Likewise, **mess-set**, **proc-set**, **proc-nat-set**, **proc-real-nat-set**, and **proc-dist-set** represent sets of basic messages, processes, pairs of a process and a natural number, triples of a process, a natural number, and a real value, and pairs of a process and a distance value, respectively. Variables containing queues or sets have as default initial value $\emptyset$, that is, empty. There are three operations on queues: $head$ produces the head and $tail$ the tail of the queue (on the empty queue these operations are undefined), while $append(Q, e)$ appends element e at the end of queue Q.

We recall that assignment of a new value to a variable is written as $\leftarrow$. Equality between two data elements, $d_1 = d_2$ (or between two sets, $S_1 = S_2$), represents a Boolean value, which is *true* if and only if the two elements (or sets) are equal. We also recall that the network topology is supposed to be strongly connected. In the pseudocode it is assumed that the network size N is greater than one.

A process is supposed to interrupt the execution of a procedure call (under a boxed text, such as "If p receives [...]") only if it has to wait for an incoming message, or in case of a **while** b **do** *statement* **end while** construct after performing *statement* if the Boolean b is $true$, or when it enters its critical section.

In general, pseudocode tends to be error-prone, because on one hand it is condensed and intricate, while on the other hand it has never been executed. I welcome any comments on the pseudocode descriptions, as well as on the main body of the book.

Chandy-Lamport snapshot algorithm

The Boolean variable $recorded_p$ in the following pseudocode is set (to $true$) when p takes a local snapshot of its state. For each incoming channel c of p, the Boolean variable $marker_p[c]$ is set when a **marker** message arrives at p through c, and the queue $state_p[c]$ keeps track of the basic messages that arrive through channel c after p has taken its local snapshot and before a **marker** message arrives through c.

bool $recorded_p$, $marker_p[c]$ for all incoming channels c of p;
mess-queue $state_p[c]$ for all incoming channels c of p;

If p wants to initiate a snapshot

perform procedure $TakeSnapshot_p$;

If p receives a basic message m through an incoming channel c_0

if $recorded_p = true$ and $marker_p[c_0] = false$ **then**
    $state_p[c_0] \leftarrow append(state_p[c_0], m)$;
end if

If p receives $\langle$**marker**$\rangle$ through an incoming channel c_0

perform procedure $TakeSnapshot_p$;
$marker_p[c_0] \leftarrow true$;
if $marker_p[c] = true$ for all incoming channels c of p **then**
    $terminate$;
end if

Procedure $TakeSnapshot_p$

if $recorded_p = false$ **then**
    $recorded_p \leftarrow true$;
    send $\langle$**marker**$\rangle$ into each outgoing channel of p;
    take a local snapshot of the state of p;
end if

Lai-Yang snapshot algorithm

$recorded_p$ is set when p takes a local snapshot of its state. The set $State_p[qp]$ keeps track of the basic messages that arrive at p through its incoming channel qp after p

has taken its local snapshot and that were sent by q before it took its local snapshot. The variable $counter_q[qp]$ counts how many basic messages process q has sent into its outgoing channel qp before taking its local snapshot. Right before taking its local snapshot, q sends the control message $\langle \textbf{presnap}, counter_q[qp] + 1 \rangle$ to p (the $+1$ is present because the control message itself is also counted), and p stores the value within this message in the variable $counter_p[qp]$. Finally, p terminates when it has received a control message $\langle \textbf{presnap}, k \rangle$ and $k - 1$ basic messages with the tag *false* through each incoming channel qp.

bool $recorded_p$;
nat $counter_p[c]$ for all channels c of p;
mess-set $State_p[c]$ for all incoming channels c of p;

If p wants to initiate a snapshot

perform procedure $TakeSnapshot_p$;

If p sends a basic message m into an outgoing channel c_0

send $\langle m, recorded_p \rangle$ into c_0;
if $recorded_p = false$ **then**
    $counter_p[c_0] \leftarrow counter_p[c_0] + 1$;
end if

If p receives $\langle m, b \rangle$ through an incoming channel c_0

if $b = true$ **then**
    perform procedure $TakeSnapshot_p$;
else if $recorded_p = true$ **then**
    $State_p[c_0] \leftarrow State_p[c_0] \cup \{m\}$;
    if $|State_p[c]| + 1 = counter_p[c]$ for all incoming channels c of p **then**
        terminate;
    end if
end if

If p receives $\langle \textbf{presnap}, \ell \rangle$ through an incoming channel c_0

$counter_p[c_0] \leftarrow \ell$;
perform procedure $TakeSnapshot_p$;
if $|State_p[c]| + 1 = counter_p[c]$ for all incoming channels c of p **then**
    terminate;
end if

Procedure $TakeSnapshot_p$

if $recorded_p = false$ **then**
    $recorded_p \leftarrow true$;
    send $\langle \textbf{presnap}, counter_p[c] + 1 \rangle$ into each outgoing channel c;
    take a local snapshot of the state of p;
end if

Cidon's depth-first search algorithm

$parent_p$ is the parent of p in the spanning tree rooted at the initiator (or $\perp$ if p has no parent). $info_p$ is set when p sends the token for the first time, and $token_p[q]$ is set when p is certain that neighbor q will receive or has received the token. In $forward_p$ the neighbor is stored to which p forwarded the token last.

bool $info_p$, $token_p[r]$ for all $r \in Neighbors_p$;
proc $parent_p$, $forward_p$;

$\boxed{\text{If } p \text{ is the initiator}}$
perform procedure $ForwardToken_p$;

$\boxed{\text{If } p \text{ receives } \langle \mathbf{info} \rangle \text{ from a neighbor } q}$
if $forward_p \neq q$ **then**
$\quad token_p[q] \leftarrow true$;
else
$\quad$ perform procedure $ForwardToken_p$;
end if

$\boxed{\text{If } p \text{ receives } \langle \mathbf{token} \rangle \text{ from a neighbor } q}$
if $forward_p = \perp$ **then**
$\quad parent_p \leftarrow q; \quad token_p[q] \leftarrow true$;
$\quad$ perform procedure $ForwardToken_p$;
else if $forward_p = q$ **then**
$\quad$ perform procedure $ForwardToken_p$;
else
$\quad token_p[q] \leftarrow true$;
end if

$\boxed{\text{Procedure } ForwardToken_p}$
if $\{r \in Neighbors_p \mid token_p[r] = false\} \neq \emptyset$ **then**
$\quad$ choose a q from this set, and send $\langle \mathbf{token} \rangle$ to q;
$\quad forward_p \leftarrow q; \quad token_p[q] \leftarrow true$;
$\quad$ **if** $info_p = false$ **then**
$\quad\quad$ send $\langle \mathbf{info} \rangle$ to each $r \in Neighbors_p \setminus \{q, parent_p\}$;
$\quad\quad info_p \leftarrow true$;
$\quad$ **end if**
else if $parent_p \neq \perp$ **then**
$\quad$ send $\langle \mathbf{token} \rangle$ to $parent_p$;
else
$\quad decide$;
end if

Tree algorithm

$parent_p$ is the parent of p in the spanning tree. $received_p[q]$ is set when p receives a wave message from neighbor q. Messages are included to inform all processes of the decision.

bool $received_p[r]$ for all $r \in Neighbors_p$;
proc $parent_p$;

$\boxed{\text{Initialization of } p}$

perform procedure $SendWave_p$;

$\boxed{\text{If } p \text{ receives } \langle \text{wave} \rangle \text{ from a neighbor } q}$

$received_p[q] \leftarrow true$;
perform procedure $SendWave_p$;

$\boxed{\text{Procedure } SendWave_p}$

if $|\{r \in Neighbors_p \mid received_p[r] = false\}| = 1$ **then**
    send $\langle \text{wave} \rangle$ to the only $q \in Neighbors_p$ with $received_p[q] = false$;
    $parent_p \leftarrow q$;
else if $|\{r \in Neighbors_p \mid received_p[r] = false\}| = 0$ **then**
    decide;
    send $\langle \text{info} \rangle$ to each $r \in Neighbors_p \setminus \{parent_p\}$;
end if

$\boxed{\text{If } p \text{ receives } \langle \text{info} \rangle \text{ from } parent_p}$

send $\langle \text{info} \rangle$ to each $r \in Neighbors_p \setminus \{parent_p\}$;

Echo algorithm

$parent_p$ is the parent of p in the spanning tree rooted at the initiator. The variable $received_p$ counts how many wave messages have arrived at p.

nat $received_p$;
proc $parent_p$;

$\boxed{\text{If } p \text{ is the initiator}}$

send $\langle \text{wave} \rangle$ to each $r \in Neighbors_p$;

$\boxed{\text{If } p \text{ receives } \langle \text{wave} \rangle \text{ from a neighbor } q}$

$received_p \leftarrow received_p + 1$;
if $parent_p = \bot$ and p is a noninitiator **then**
    $parent_p \leftarrow q$;
    if $|Neighbors_p| > 1$ **then**
        send $\langle \text{wave} \rangle$ to each $r \in Neighbors_p \setminus \{q\}$;
    else

```
            send ⟨wave⟩ to q;
        end if
    else if received_p = |Neighbors_p| then
        if parent_p ≠ ⊥ then
            send ⟨wave⟩ to parent_p;
        else
            decide;
        end if
    end if
end if
```

Shavit-Francez termination detection algorithm

$parent_p$ is the parent of p in a tree in the forest, and cc_p keeps track of (or better, estimates from above) the number of children of p in its tree. $active_p$ is set when p becomes active, and reset when p becomes passive.

bool $active_p$;
nat cc_p;
proc $parent_p$;

<u>If p is an initiator</u>

$active_p \leftarrow true$;

<u>If p sends a basic message</u>

$cc_p \leftarrow cc_p + 1$;

<u>If p receives a basic message from a neighbor q</u>

```
if active_p = false then
    active_p ← true;   parent_p ← q;
else
    send ⟨ack⟩ to q;
end if
```

<u>If p receives ⟨ack⟩</u>

$cc_p \leftarrow cc_p - 1$;
perform procedure $LeaveTree_p$;

<u>If p becomes passive</u>

$active_p \leftarrow false$;
perform procedure $LeaveTree_p$;

<u>Procedure $LeaveTree_p$</u>

```
if active_p = false and cc_p = 0 then
    if parent_p ≠ ⊥ then
        send ⟨ack⟩ to parent_p;
        parent_p ← ⊥;
    else
```

start a wave, tagged with p;
   end if
end if

If p receives a wave message

---
if $active_p = false$ **and** $cc_p = 0$ **then**
   act according to the wave algorithm;
   in case of a *decide* event, call *Announce*;
end if

Weight-throwing termination detection algorithm

$active_p$ is set when p becomes active, and reset when p becomes passive. $weight_p$ contains the weight at p, and $total$ the total amount of weight in the network. The constant $minimum$, a real value between 0 and $\frac{1}{2}$, represents the minimum allowed weight at a process. In case of underflow, a noninitiator informs the initiator that it has added one extra unit of weight to the system, and waits for an acknowledgment from the initiator. For simplicity, we assume that there is an undirected channel between the initiator and every other process in the network.

bool $active_p$;
real $weight_p$, $total$ only at the initiator;

If p is the initiator

$active_p \leftarrow true$; $weight_p \leftarrow 1$; $total \leftarrow 1$;

If p sends a basic message m to a neighbor q

---
if $\frac{1}{2} \cdot weight_p < minimum$ **then**
   if p is a noninitiator **then**
      send $\langle \textbf{more-weight} \rangle$ to the initiator, to ask for extra weight;
      wait for an acknowledgment from the initiator to arrive;
   else
      $total \leftarrow total + 1$;
   end if
   $weight_p \leftarrow weight_p + 1$;
end if
send $\langle m, \frac{1}{2} \cdot weight_p \rangle$ to q;
$weight_p \leftarrow \frac{1}{2} \cdot weight_p$;

If p receives a basic message $\langle m, w \rangle$

$active_p \leftarrow true$; $weight_p \leftarrow weight_p + w$;

If p becomes passive

$active_p \leftarrow false$;
if p is a noninitiator **then**
   send $\langle \textbf{return-weight}, weight_p \rangle$ to the initiator;

$weight_p \leftarrow 0;$
else if $total = weight_p$ **then**
    call *Announce*;
end if

If initiator p receives $\langle \textbf{more-weight} \rangle$ from a process q

---
$total \leftarrow total + 1;$
send an acknowledgment to q;

If initiator p receives $\langle \textbf{return-weight}, w \rangle$

$weight_p \leftarrow weight_p + w;$
if $active_p = false$ **and** $total = weight_p$ **then**
    call *Announce*;
end if

Rana's termination detection algorithm

$active_p$ is set when p becomes active, and reset when p becomes passive. $clock_p$ represents the clock value at p, and $unack_p$ the number of unacknowledged basic messages that were sent by p.

bool $active_p$;
nat $clock_p, unack_p$;

If p is an initiator

$active_p \leftarrow true;$

If p sends a basic message

$unack_p \leftarrow unack_p + 1;$

If p receives a basic message from a neighbor q

$active_p \leftarrow true;$
send $\langle \textbf{ack}, clock_p \rangle$ to q;

If p receives $\langle \textbf{ack}, t \rangle$

$clock_p \leftarrow \max\{clock_p, t+1\}; \quad unack_p \leftarrow unack_p - 1;$
if $active_p = false$ **and** $unack_p = 0$ **then**
    start a wave, tagged with p and $clock_p$;
end if

If p becomes passive

$active_p \leftarrow false;$
if $unack_p = 0$ **then**
    start a wave, tagged with p and $clock_p$;
end if

If p receives a wave message tagged with q and t

if $active_p = false$ **and** $unack_p = 0$ **and** $clock_p \leq t$ **then**
    act according to the wave algorithm, for the wave tagged with q and t;
    in case of a *decide* event, call *Announce*;
end if
$clock_p \leftarrow \max\{clock_p, t\}$;

Safra's termination detection algorithm

$active_p$ is set when p becomes active, and reset when p becomes passive. $black_p$ is set when p receives a basic message, and reset when p forwards the token. Moreover, the initiator of the control algorithm at the start sets this variable, to make sure it sends out the token when it becomes passive for the first time. As long as p is holding the token, $token_p$ is set. When p sends/receives a basic message, $mess\text{-}counter_p$ is increased/decreased by one. The variable $token\text{-}counter_p$ is used to store the counter value of the token. For simplicity, we assume that the initiator of the control algorithm is also an initiator of the basic algorithm.

bool $active_p$, $token_p$, $black_p$;
int $mess\text{-}counter_p$, $token\text{-}counter_p$;

If p is the initiator of the control algorithm
$token_p \leftarrow true$; $black_p \leftarrow true$;

If p is an initiator of the basic algorithm
$active_p \leftarrow true$;

If p sends a basic message
$mess\text{-}counter_p \leftarrow mess\text{-}counter_p + 1$;

If p receives a basic message
$active_p \leftarrow true$; $black_p \leftarrow true$; $mess\text{-}counter_p \leftarrow mess\text{-}counter_p - 1$;

If p becomes passive
$active_p \leftarrow false$;
perform procedure $TreatToken_p$;

If p receives $\langle \text{token}, b, k \rangle$
$token_p \leftarrow true$; $black_p \leftarrow black_p \vee b$; $token\text{-}counter_p \leftarrow k$;
perform procedure $TreatToken_p$;

Procedure $TreatToken_p$
if $active_p = false$ **and** $token_p = true$ **then**
    if p is a noninitiator **then**
        forward $\langle \text{token}, black_p, mess\text{-}counter_p + token\text{-}counter_p \rangle$;
        $token_p \leftarrow false$; $black_p \leftarrow false$;
    else if $black_p = true$ **or** $mess\text{-}counter_p + token\text{-}counter_p \neq 0$ **then**

send ⟨**token**, $false, 0$⟩ on a round trip through the network;
$token_p \leftarrow false$; $black_p \leftarrow false$;
else
   call *Announce*;
end if
end if

Chandy-Misra routing algorithm

$parent_p$ is the parent of p in the spanning tree rooted at the initiator, and $dist_p$ the distance value of p toward the initiator.

dist $dist_p$;
proc $parent_p$;

$\boxed{\text{If } p \text{ is the initiator}}$
$dist_p \leftarrow 0$;
send ⟨**dist**, 0⟩ to each $r \in Neighbors_p$;

$\boxed{\text{If } p \text{ receives } \langle \mathbf{dist}, d \rangle \text{ from a neighbor } q}$
if $d + weight(pq) < dist_p$ **then**
   $dist_p \leftarrow d + weight(pq)$; $parent_p \leftarrow q$;
   send ⟨**dist**, $dist_p$⟩ to each $r \in Neighbors_p \setminus \{q\}$;
end if

Merlin-Segall routing algorithm

$parent_p$ is the parent of p in the spanning tree rooted at the initiator, and $dist_p$ the distance value of p toward the initiator. In $new\text{-}parent_p$ the process is stored that sent the message to p on which the current value of $dist_p$ is based; at the end of a round, the value of $new\text{-}parent_p$ is passed on to $parent_p$. In $counter_p$, p keeps track of how many messages it has received in the current round.

nat $counter_p$;
dist $dist_p$;
proc $parent_p, new\text{-}parent_p$;

$\boxed{\text{If } p \text{ is the initiator}}$
$dist_p \leftarrow 0$;
initiate a wave that determines a spanning tree of the network,
captured by values of $parent_r$ for all $r \in Processes$, with p as root;
wait until this wave has terminated;
for $k = 1$ **to** $N - 1$ **do**
   send ⟨**dist**, 0⟩ to each $r \in Neighbors_p$;
   while $counter_p < |Neighbors_p|$ **do**

wait for a message $\langle \mathbf{dist}, d \rangle$ to arrive;
        $counter_p \leftarrow counter_p + 1$;
    end while
    $counter_p \leftarrow 0$;
end for

$\boxed{\text{If } p \text{ is a noninitiator}}$

take part in the wave, and provide $parent_p$ with the resulting parent value;
for $k = 1$ **to** $N - 1$ **do**
    while $counter_p < |Neighbors_p|$ **do**
        wait for a message $\langle \mathbf{dist}, d \rangle$ from a $q \in Neighbors_p$;
        $counter_p \leftarrow counter_p + 1$;
        if $d + weight(pq) < dist_p$ **then**
            $dist_p \leftarrow d + weight(pq)$; $new\text{-}parent_p \leftarrow q$;
        end if
        if $q = parent_p$ **then**
            send $\langle \mathbf{dist}, dist_p \rangle$ to each $r \in Neighbors_p \setminus \{parent_p\}$;
        end if
    end while
    send $\langle \mathbf{dist}, dist_p \rangle$ to $parent_p$;
    $parent_p \leftarrow new\text{-}parent_p$; $counter_p \leftarrow 0$;
end for

Toueg's routing algorithm

$parent_p[q]$ is the parent of p in the spanning tree rooted at process q, and $dist_p[q]$ the distance value of p toward destination q. In $round_p$, p keeps track of its round number. The distance values of the pivot in round k are stored in $Distances_p[k]$. Each process that sends a request to p for the distance values of the pivot in the current or a future round k is stored in $Forward_p[k]$. We assume that p only treats incoming requests when it is idle, to avoid that a request could be stored in $Forward_p[k]$ after p forwarded the distance values of the pivot in round k. The pivot in round k is denoted by $pivot(k)$. We include the optimization that a process, at the reception of distance values from the pivot, first checks which of its distance values are improved, and then forwards only those elements of the set that gave rise to an improved distance value.

nat $round_p$;
dist $dist_p[r]$ for all $r \in Processes$;
proc $parent_p[r]$ for all $r \in Processes$;
proc-set $Forward_p[k]$ for all $k \in \{0, \ldots, N-1\}$;
proc-dist-set $Distances_p[k]$ for all $k \in \{0, \ldots, N-1\}$;

$\boxed{\text{Initialization of } p}$

$dist_p[p] \leftarrow 0$; $parent_p[r] \leftarrow r$ and $dist_p[r] \leftarrow weight(pr)$ for all $r \in Neighbors_p$;
perform procedure $Request_p$;

> **Procedure $Request_p$**

if $p = pivot(round_p)$ **then**
    send $\langle \textbf{dist-set}, \{(r, dist_p[r]) \mid r \in Processes \text{ and } dist_p[r] < \infty\}\rangle$
    to each $q \in Forward_p[round_p]$;
    perform procedure $NextRound_p$;
else if $parent_p[pivot(round_p)] \neq \bot$ **then**
    send $\langle \textbf{request}, round_p\rangle$ to $parent_p[pivot(round_p)]$;
else
    perform procedure $NextRound_p$;
end if

> **If p receives $\langle \textbf{request}, k\rangle$ from a neighbor q**

if $k < round_p$ **then**
    send $\langle \textbf{dist-set}, Distances_p[k]\rangle$ to q;
else
    $Forward_p[k] \leftarrow Forward_p[k] \cup \{q\}$;
end if

> **If p receives $\langle \textbf{dist-set}, Distances\rangle$ from $parent_p[pivot(round_p)]$**

for each $s \in Processes$ **do**
    if there is a pair (s, d) in $Distances$ **then**
        if $d + dist_p[pivot(round_p)] < dist_p[s]$ **then**
            $parent_p[s] \leftarrow parent_p[pivot(round_p)]$;
            $dist_p[s] \leftarrow d + dist_p[pivot(round_p)]$;
        else
            remove entry (s, d) from $Distances$;
        end if
    end if
end for
send $\langle \textbf{dist-set}, Distances\rangle$ to each $r \in Forward_p[round_p]$;
$Distances_p[round_p] \leftarrow Distances$;
perform procedure $NextRound_p$;

> **Procedure $NextRound_p$**

if $round_p < N - 1$ **then**
    $round_p \leftarrow round_p + 1$;
    perform procedure $Request_p$;
else
    terminate;
end if

Frederickson's breadth-first search algorithm

$parent_p$ is the parent of p in the spanning tree rooted at the initiator, and $dist_p$ the distance value of p toward the initiator. In $dist_p[r]$, p stores the best-known distance value of neighbor r. After p has sent **forward** or **explore** messages, it keeps track in Ack_p of the neighbors that should still send a (positive or negative) reply. In

$Reported_p$, p remembers to which neighbors it should send a **forward** message in the next round. The initiator maintains the round number in *counter*. Each round, ℓ levels are explored. For uniformity, messages $\langle \textbf{reverse}, b \rangle$ are always supplied with the distance value of the sender.

nat $counter$ only at the initiator;
dist $dist_p$, $dist_p[r]$ for all $r \in Neighbors_p$;
proc $parent_p$;
proc-set Ack_p, $Reported_p$;

If p is the initiator

send $\langle \textbf{explore}, 1 \rangle$ to each $r \in Neighbors_p$;
$dist_p \leftarrow 0$; $\quad Ack_p \leftarrow Neighbors_p$; $\quad counter \leftarrow 1$;

If p receives $\langle \textbf{explore}, k \rangle$ from a neighbor q

$dist_p[q] \leftarrow \min\{dist_p[q], k-1\}$;
if $k < dist_p$ **then**
$\quad parent_p \leftarrow q$; $\quad dist_p \leftarrow k$; $\quad Reported_p \leftarrow \emptyset$;
$\quad$ **if** $k \bmod \ell \neq 0$ **then**
$\quad\quad$ send $\langle \textbf{explore}, k+1 \rangle$ to each $r \in Neighbors_p \setminus \{q\}$;
$\quad\quad Ack_p \leftarrow \{r \in Neighbors_p \mid dist_p[r] > k+1\}$;
$\quad\quad$ **if** $Ack_p = \emptyset$ **then**
$\quad\quad\quad$ send $\langle \textbf{reverse}, k, true \rangle$ to q;
$\quad\quad$ **end if**
$\quad$ **else**
$\quad\quad$ send $\langle \textbf{reverse}, k, true \rangle$ to q;
$\quad$ **end if**
else if $k \bmod \ell \neq 0$ **then**
$\quad$ **if** $k \leq dist_p + 2$ and $q \in Ack_p$ **then**
$\quad\quad Ack_p \leftarrow Ack_p \setminus \{q\}$;
$\quad\quad$ perform procedure $ReceivedAck_p$;
$\quad$ **else if** $k = dist_p$ **then**
$\quad\quad Reported_p \leftarrow Reported_p \setminus \{q\}$;
$\quad$ **end if**
else
$\quad$ send $\langle \textbf{reverse}, k, false \rangle$ to q;
end if

If p receives $\langle \textbf{reverse}, k, b \rangle$ from a neighbor q

$dist_p[q] \leftarrow \min\{dist_p[q], k\}$;
if $k = dist_p + 1$ **then**
$\quad$ **if** $b = true$ and $dist_p[q] = k$ **then**
$\quad\quad Reported_p \leftarrow Reported_p \cup \{q\}$;
$\quad$ **end if**
$\quad$ **if** $q \in Ack_p$ **then**
$\quad\quad Ack_p \leftarrow Ack_p \setminus \{q\}$;
$\quad\quad$ perform procedure $ReceivedAck_p$;
$\quad$ **end if**

end if

> Procedure $ReceivedAck_p$

if $Ack_p = \emptyset$ **then**
    if $parent_p \neq \bot$ **then**
        send $\langle \mathbf{reverse}, dist_p, Reported_p \neq \emptyset \rangle$ to $parent_p$;
    else if $Reported_p \neq \emptyset$ **then**
        send $\langle \mathbf{forward}, \ell \cdot counter \rangle$ to each $r \in Reported_p$;
        $Ack_p \leftarrow Reported_p$; $Reported_p \leftarrow \emptyset$; $counter \leftarrow counter + 1$
    else
        terminate;
    end if
end if

> If p receives $\langle \mathbf{forward}, k \rangle$ from a neighbor q

if $q = parent_p$ **then**
    if $k < depth_p$ **then**
        send $\langle \mathbf{forward}, k \rangle$ to each $r \in Reported_p$;
        $Ack_p \leftarrow Reported_p$; $Reported_p \leftarrow \emptyset$;
    else
        $Ack_p \leftarrow \{r \in Neighbors_p \mid dist_p[r] = \infty\}$;
        if $Ack_p \neq \emptyset$ **then**
            send $\langle \mathbf{explore}, k+1 \rangle$ to each $r \in Ack_p$;
        else
            send $\langle \mathbf{reverse}, k, \mathit{false} \rangle$ to q;
        end if
    end if
end if

Dolev-Klawe-Rodeh election algorithm

$active_p$ is set when p is an initiator, and reset when p becomes passive. If p terminates as the leader, it sets $leader_p$. Since messages of two consecutive rounds can overtake each other, p keeps track of the parity of its round number in $parity_p$, and attaches this Boolean value to its message. In $election\text{-}id_p$, p stores the ID it assumes for the current election round. In $neighb\text{-}id_p[0,b]$ and $neighb\text{-}id_p[1,b]$, p stores the process IDs of its two nearest active predecessors in the directed ring, with b the parity of the corresponding election round. We assume a total order $<$ on process IDs.

bool $active_p, leader_p, parity_p$;
proc $election\text{-}id_p, neighb\text{-}id_p[n,b]$ for $n = 0, 1$ and Booleans b;

> If p is an initiator

$active_p \leftarrow \mathit{true}$; $election\text{-}id_p \leftarrow p$;
send $\langle \mathbf{id}, p, 0, b \rangle$;

> If p receives $\langle \mathbf{id}, q, n, b \rangle$

if $active_p = true$ **then**
    if $n = 0$ **then**
        send $\langle \mathbf{id}, q, 1, b \rangle$;
    end if
    $neighb\text{-}id_p[n, b] \leftarrow q$;
    if $neighb\text{-}id_p[n, parity_p] \neq \bot$ for $n = 0$ and $n = 1$ **then**
        perform procedure $CompareIds_p$;
    end if
else
    send $\langle \mathbf{id}, q, n, b \rangle$;
end if

Procedure $CompareIds_p$

if $\max\{election\text{-}id_p, neighb\text{-}id_p[1, parity_p]\} < neighb\text{-}id_p[0, parity_p]$ **then**
    $election\text{-}id_p \leftarrow neighb\text{-}id_p[0, parity_p]$;
    $neighb\text{-}id_p[n, parity_p] \leftarrow \bot$ for $n = 0$ and $n = 1$; $parity_p \leftarrow \neg parity_p$;
    send $\langle \mathbf{id}, election\text{-}id_p, 0, parity_p \rangle$;
    if $neighb\text{-}id_p[n, parity_p] \neq \bot$ for $n = 0$ and $n = 1$ **then**
        perform procedure $CompareIds_p$;
    end if
else if $neighb\text{-}id_p[0, parity_p] < election\text{-}id_p$ **then**
    $active_p \leftarrow false$;
else
    $leader_p \leftarrow true$;
end if

Gallager-Humblet-Spira minimum spanning tree algorithm

$parent_p$ is p's parent toward the core edge of p's fragment. The name and level of p's fragment are stored in $name_p$ and $level_p$. Initially, $state_p$ has the value *find*; for simplicity, the state *sleep* and the corresponding wake-up phase are omitted. The channel states, $state_p[q]$ for each $q \in Neighbors_p$, initially are *basic*. While looking for a least-weight outgoing edge, p stores the optimal intermediate result in $best\text{-}weight_p$. If the optimal result was reported through the basic or branch edge pq, then $best\text{-}edge_p$ has the value q. While p is testing whether basic edge pq is outgoing, $test\text{-}edge_p$ has the value q. In $counter_p$, p keeps track of how many branch edges have reported their minimal value; it starts at 1 to account for the fact that p's parent in general does not report a value (except for the core nodes). In $parent\text{-}report_p$, a core node p can keep the value reported by its parent; if there is no report yet its value is 0, while the value ∞ means that p's parent has reported there are no outgoing edges at its side. In $Connects_p$ and $Tests_p$, p stores incoming **connect** and **test** messages to which a reply is delayed until the level of p's fragment is high enough.

    $\{find, found\}\ state_p$;
    $\{basic, branch, rejected\}\ state_p[r]$ for all $r \in Neighbors_p$;
    real $name_p$;

nat $level_p$, $counter_p$;
dist $best\text{-}weight_p$, $parent\text{-}report_p$;
proc $parent_p$, $test\text{-}edge_p$, $best\text{-}edge_p$;
proc-nat-set $Connects_p$;
proc-real-nat-set $Tests_p$;

Initialization of p
---

determine the lowest-weight channel pq;
$state_p \leftarrow found$; $state_p[q] \leftarrow branch$; $counter_p \leftarrow 1$; $parent\text{-}report_p \leftarrow 0$;
send $\langle \mathbf{connect}, 0 \rangle$ to q;

If p receives $\langle \mathbf{connect}, \ell \rangle$ from a neighbor q
---

if $\ell < level_p$ **then**
    send $\langle \mathbf{initiate}, name_p, level_p, state_p \rangle$ to q;
    $state_p[q] \leftarrow branch$;
else if $state_p[q] = branch$ **then**
    send $\langle \mathbf{initiate}, weight(pq), level_p + 1, find \rangle$ to q;
else
    $Connects_p = Connects_p \cup \{(q, \ell)\}$;
end if

If p receives $\langle \mathbf{initiate}, fn, \ell, st \rangle$ from a neighbor q
---

$name_p \leftarrow fn$; $level_p \leftarrow \ell$; $state_p \leftarrow st$; $parent_p \leftarrow q$;
$best\text{-}edge_p \leftarrow \bot$; $best\text{-}weight_p \leftarrow \infty$; $counter_p \leftarrow 1$; $parent\text{-}report_p \leftarrow 0$;
for each $(q_0, \ell_0) \in Connects_p$ **do**
    if $\ell_0 < level_p$ **then**
        $state_p[q_0] \leftarrow branch$; $Connects_p \leftarrow Connects_p \setminus \{(q_0, \ell_0)\}$;
    end if
end for
send $\langle \mathbf{initiate}, fn, \ell, st \rangle$ to each $r \in Neighbors_p \setminus \{q\}$ with $state_p[r] = branch$;
for each $(q_1, fn_1, \ell_1) \in Tests_p$ **do**
    if $\ell_1 \leq level_p$ **then**
        perform procedure $ReplyTest_p(q_1)$;
        $Tests_p \leftarrow Tests_p \setminus \{(q_1, fn_1, \ell_1)\}$;
    end if
end for
if $st = find$ **then**
    perform procedure $FindMinimalOutgoing_p$;
end if

Procedure $FindMinimalOutgoing_p$
---

if $\{pr \mid r \in Neighbors_p$ and $state_p(pr) = basic\} \neq \emptyset$ **then**
    send $\langle \mathbf{test}, name_p, level_p \rangle$ into the lowest-weight channel pq in this collection;
    $test\text{-}edge_p \leftarrow q$;
else
    $test\text{-}edge_p \leftarrow \bot$;
end if

If p receives $\langle \mathbf{test}, fn, \ell \rangle$ from a neighbor q
---

if $\ell \leq level_p$ **then**
    perform procedure $ReplyTest_p(q)$;
else
    $Tests_p = Tests_p \cup \{(q, fn, \ell)\}$;
end if

Procedure $ReplyTest_p(q)$

---

if $name_p \neq fn$ **then**
    send $\langle \textbf{accept} \rangle$ to q;
else
    $state_p[pq] \leftarrow rejected$;
    if $test\text{-}edge_p \neq q$ **then**
        send $\langle \textbf{reject} \rangle$ to q;
    else
        perform procedure $FindMinimalOutgoing_p$;
    end if
end if

If p receives $\langle \textbf{reject} \rangle$ from a neighbor q

---

$state_p[q] \leftarrow rejected$;
perform procedure $FindMinimalOutgoing_p$;

If p receives $\langle \textbf{accept} \rangle$ from a neighbor q

---

$test\text{-}edge_p \leftarrow \bot$;
if $weight(pq) < best\text{-}weight_p$ **then**
    $best\text{-}edge_p \leftarrow q$; $best\text{-}weight_p \leftarrow weight(pq)$;
end if
if $counter_p = |\{r \in Neighbors_p \mid state_p[r] = branch\}|$ **then**
    perform procedure $SendReport_p$
end if

Procedure $SendReport_p$

$state_p \leftarrow found$;
send $\langle \textbf{report}, best\text{-}weight_p \rangle$ to $parent_p$;
if $parent\text{-}report_p > 0$ and $best\text{-}weight_p < parent\text{-}report_p$ **then**
    perform procedure $ChangeRoot_p$;
end if

If p receives $\langle \textbf{report}, \lambda \rangle$ from a neighbor q

---

if $q \neq parent_p$ **then**
    $counter_p \leftarrow counter_p + 1$;
    if $\lambda < best\text{-}weight_p$ **then**
        $best\text{-}edge_p \leftarrow q$; $best\text{-}weight_p \leftarrow \lambda$;
    end if
    if $counter_p = |\{r \in Neighbors_p \mid state_p[r] = branch\}|$ and $test\text{-}edge_p = \bot$ **then**
        perform procedure $SendReport_p$
    end if
else if $state_p = find$ **then**

$parent\text{-}report_p \leftarrow \lambda$;
else
    if $best\text{-}weight_p < \lambda$ **then**
        perform procedure $ChangeRoot_p$;
    else if $\lambda = \infty$ **then**
        terminate;
    end if
end if

Procedure $ChangeRoot_p$

---

if $state_p[best\text{-}edge_p] = branch$ **then**
    send $\langle \textbf{changeroot} \rangle$ to $best\text{-}edge_p$;
else
    $state_p[best\text{-}edge_p] \leftarrow branch$;
    send $\langle \textbf{connect}, level_p \rangle$ to $best\text{-}edge_p$;
    if $(best\text{-}edge_p, level_p) \in Connects_p$ **then**
        send $\langle \textbf{initiate}, best\text{-}weight_p, level_p + 1, find \rangle$ to $best\text{-}edge_p$;
        $Connects_p \leftarrow Connects_p \setminus \{(best\text{-}edge_p, level_p)\}$;
    end if
end if

If p receives $\langle \textbf{changeroot} \rangle$

---

perform procedure $ChangeRoot_p$;

IEEE 1394 election algorithm

$parent_p$ is the parent of p in the spanning tree. $received_p[q]$ is set when p receives a parent request from a neighbor q to which p has not sent a parent request. If p gets into root contention and chooses to start a timer, it sets $waiting_p$. If p terminates as the leader, it sets $leader_p$.

bool $leader_p$, $waiting_p$, $received_p[r]$ for all $r \in Neighbors_p$;
proc $parent_p$;

Initialization of p

---

perform procedure $SendRequest_p$;

Procedure $SendRequest_p$

---

if $|\{r \in Neighbors_p \mid received_p[r] = false\}| = 1$ **then**
    send $\langle \textbf{parent-req} \rangle$ to the only $q \in Neighbors_p$ with $received_p[q] = false$;
    $parent_p \leftarrow q$;
end if

If p receives $\langle \textbf{parent-req} \rangle$ from a neighbor q

---

if $q \neq parent_p$ **then**
    $received_p[q] \leftarrow true$;
    send $\langle \textbf{ack} \rangle$ to q;

perform procedure $SendRequest_p$;
else if $waiting_p = false$ **then**
    perform procedure $RootContention_p$;
else
    $leader_p \leftarrow true$;
end if

| If p receives $\langle \mathbf{ack} \rangle$ from $parent_p$ |

terminate;

| Procedure $RootContention_p$ |

either send $\langle \mathbf{parent\text{-}req} \rangle$ to q and $waiting_p \leftarrow false$,
or start a timer and $waiting_p \leftarrow true$;

| If a *timeout* occurs at p |

perform procedure $RootContention_p$;

Awerbuch's synchronizer

$parent_p$ is the parent of p in the spanning tree within its cluster, $Children_p$ contains the children of p in this spanning tree, and $Designated_p$ the processes q for which there is a designated channel pq. Note that these three values are fixed after the initialization phase. In $1st\text{-}counter_p$ and $2nd\text{-}counter_p$, p keeps track of how many messages still need to be received in the first and second phase of this synchronizer, respectively.

nat $1st\text{-}counter_p$, $2nd\text{-}counter_p$;
proc $parent_p$;
proc-set $Children_p$, $Designated_p$;

| Initialization |

The network is divided into clusters, and within each cluster a spanning tree is built. Between each pair of distinct clusters that are connected by a channel, one of these connecting channels is labeled as *designated*. Furthermore, a wake-up phase makes sure that all processes start their first pulse, meaning that they perform the procedure $NewPulse$.

| Procedure $NewPulse_p$ |

send $k \geq 0$ basic messages;
$1st\text{-}counter_p \leftarrow k + |Children_p|$; $2nd\text{-}counter_p \leftarrow |Children_p| + |Designated_p|$;
perform procedure $FirstReport_p$;

| If p receives a basic message from a neighbor q |

send $\langle \mathbf{ack} \rangle$ to q;

| If p receives $\langle \mathbf{ack} \rangle$ or $\langle \mathbf{safe} \rangle$ |

$1st\text{-}counter_p \leftarrow 1st\text{-}counter_p - 1$;

perform procedure $FirstReport_p$;

Procedure $FirstReport_p$

if $1st\text{-}counter_p = 0$ then
    if $parent_p \neq \perp$ then
        send $\langle\mathbf{safe}\rangle$ to $parent_p$;
    else
        perform procedure $SendNext_p$;
    end if
end if

Procedure $SendNext_p$

send $\langle\mathbf{next}\rangle$ to each $q \in Children_p$;
send $\langle\mathbf{cluster\text{-}safe}\rangle$ to each $r \in Designated_p$;
perform procedure $SecondReport_p$;

If p receives $\langle\mathbf{next}\rangle$

perform procedure $SendNext_p$;

If p receives $\langle\mathbf{cluster\text{-}safe}\rangle$

$2nd\text{-}counter_p \leftarrow 2nd\text{-}counter_p - 1$;
perform procedure $SecondReport_p$;

Procedure $SecondReport_p$

if $2nd\text{-}counter_p = 0$ then
    if $parent_p \neq \perp$ then
        send $\langle\mathbf{cluster\text{-}safe}\rangle$ to $parent_p$;
    else
        perform procedure $SendClusterNext_p$;
    end if
end if

Procedure $SendClusterNext_p$

send $\langle\mathbf{cluster\text{-}next}\rangle$ to each $q \in Children_p$;
perform procedure $NewPulse_p$;

If p receives $\langle\mathbf{cluster\text{-}next}\rangle$

perform procedure $SendClusterNext_p$;

Ricart-Agrawala mutual exclusion algorithm

We use the lexicographical order on pairs (t, i) with t a time stamp and i a process index. $clock_i$ represents the clock value at p_i; it starts at 1. In $req\text{-}stamp_i$, p_i stores the time stamp of its current request; if there is none, $req\text{-}stamp_i = 0$. The number of permissions that p_i has received for its current request is maintained in $counter_i$. In $Pending_i$, p_i remembers from which processes it has received a request but to which it has not yet sent permission. The Carvalho-Roucairol optimization is taken into account. In $Requests_i$, p_i stores to which processes it must send (or has sent) its next (or current) request.

nat $clock_i$, $req\text{-}stamp_i$, $counter_i$;
proc-set $Pending_i$, $Requests_i$;

---Initialization of p_i---

$Requests_i \leftarrow Neighbors_i$; $clock_i \leftarrow 1$;

---If p_i wants to enter its critical section---

if $Requests_i \neq \emptyset$ **then**
    send $\langle \textbf{request}, clock_i, i \rangle$ to each $q \in Requests_i$;
    $req\text{-}stamp_i \leftarrow clock_i$; $counter_i \leftarrow 0$;
else
    perform procedure $CriticalSection_p$;
end if

---If p_i receives $\langle \textbf{permission} \rangle$---

$counter_i \leftarrow counter_i + 1$;
if $counter_i = |Requests_i|$ **then**
    perform procedure $CriticalSection_p$;
end if

---Procedure $CriticalSection_p$---

enter critical section;
exit critical section;
send $\langle \textbf{permission} \rangle$ to each $q \in Pending_i$;
$req\text{-}stamp_i \leftarrow 0$; $Requests_i \leftarrow Pending_i$; $Pending_i \leftarrow \emptyset$;

---If p_i receives $\langle \textbf{request}, t, j \rangle$ from a p_j---

$clock_i \leftarrow \max\{clock_i, t+1\}$;
if $req\text{-}stamp_i = 0$ or $(t, j) < (req\text{-}stamp_i, i)$ **then**
    send $\langle \textbf{permission} \rangle$ to p_j;
    $Requests_i \leftarrow Requests_i \cup \{p_j\}$;
    if $req\text{-}stamp_i > 0$ **then**
        send $\langle \textbf{request}, req\text{-}stamp_i, i \rangle$ to p_j;
    end if
else
    $Pending_i \leftarrow Pending_i \cup \{p_j\}$;
end if

Raymond's mutual exclusion algorithm

$parent_p$ is the parent of p in the spanning tree. The queue $pending_p$ contains the children of p in the tree that have asked for the token, and possibly p itself.

proc $parent_p$;
proc-queue $pending_p$;

If p is the initiator

Initiate a wave that determines a spanning tree of the network, captured by values of $parent_r$ for all $r \in Processes$, with p as root;

If p wants to enter its critical section

if $parent_p \neq \bot$ **then**
    $pending_p \leftarrow append(pending_p, p)$;
    if $head(pending_p) = p$ **then**
        send $\langle \textbf{request} \rangle$ to $parent_p$;
    end if
else
    perform procedure $CriticalSection_p$;
end if

If p receives $\langle \textbf{request} \rangle$ from a neighbor q

$pending_p \leftarrow append(pending_p, q)$;
if $head(pending_p) = q$ **then**
    if $parent_p \neq \bot$ **then**
        send $\langle \textbf{request} \rangle$ to $parent_p$;
    else if p is not in its critical section **then**
        perform procedure $SendToken_p$;
    end if
end if

If p receives $\langle \textbf{token} \rangle$

if $head(pending_p) \neq p$ **then**
    perform procedure $SendToken_p$;
else
    $parent_p \leftarrow \bot$; $pending_p \leftarrow tail(pending_p)$;
    perform procedure $CriticalSection_p$;
end if

Procedure $SendToken_p$

$parent_p \leftarrow head(pending_p)$; $pending_p \leftarrow tail(pending_p)$;
send $\langle \textbf{token} \rangle$ to $parent_p$;
if $pending_p \neq \emptyset$ **then**
    send $\langle \textbf{request} \rangle$ to $parent_p$;
end if

Procedure $CriticalSection_p$

enter critical section;
exit critical section;
if $pending_p \neq \emptyset$ **then**
    perform procedure $SendToken_p$;
end if

Agrawal-El Abbadi mutual exclusion algorithm

$requests_p$ is a queue of processes from which p must still obtain permission to enter its critical section. The set $Permissions_p$ contains the processes from which p has received permission during its current attempt to become privileged. The queue $pending_p$ contains the processes from which p has received a request; it has only sent permission to the head of this queue. (We recall that p may have to ask permission from itself.) We assume that $N = 2^k - 1$ for some $k > 1$, so that the binary tree has depth $k - 1$. $root$ denotes the root node of the binary tree, and for any nonleaf q in the tree, $left\text{-}child(q)$ and $right\text{-}child(q)$ denote its child at the left and right, respectively. Processes may crash, and are provided with a complete and strongly accurate failure detector. When p detects that another process has crashed, it puts the corresponding process ID in the set $Crashed_p$.

proc-queue $requests_p$, $pending_p$;
proc-set $Permissions_p$, $Crashed_p$;

If p wants to enter its critical section

$requests_p \leftarrow append(\emptyset, root)$;
perform procedure $SendRequest_p$;

Procedure $SendRequest_p$
---

if $head(requests_p) \notin Crashed_p$ **then**
    send $\langle\mathbf{request}\rangle$ to $head(requests_p)$;
else
    perform procedure $HeadRequestsCrashed_p$;
end if

Procedure $HeadRequestsCrashed_p$
---

if $head(requests_p)$ is not a leaf of the binary tree **then**
    $requests_p \leftarrow append(append(tail(requests_p), left\text{-}child(head(requests_p))),$
            $right\text{-}child(head(requests_p)))$;
    perform procedure $SendRequest_p$;
else
    $Permissions_p \leftarrow \emptyset$;
    start a new attempt to enter the critical section;
end if

If p receives $\langle\mathbf{request}\rangle$ from a process q
---

$pending_p \leftarrow append(pending_p, q)$;
if $head(pending_p) = q$ **then**
    perform procedure $SendPermission_p$;
end if

Procedure $SendPermission_p$
---

if $pending_p \neq \emptyset$ **then**
    if $head(pending_p) \notin Crashed_p$ **then**

            send $\langle$**permission**$\rangle$ to $head(pending_p)$;
        else
            $pending_p \leftarrow tail(pending_p)$;
            perform procedure $SendPermission_p$;
        end if
end if

If p receives $\langle$**permission**$\rangle$ from process q

$Permissions_p \leftarrow Permissions_p \cup \{q\}$; $requests_p \leftarrow tail(requests_p)$;
if q is not a leaf of the binary tree **then**
    either $requests_p \leftarrow append(requests_p, \textit{left-child}(q))$
    or $requests_p \leftarrow append(requests_p, \textit{right-child}(q))$;
end if
if $requests_p \neq \emptyset$ **then**
    perform procedure $SendRequest_p$;
else
    enter critical section;
    exit critical section;
    send $\langle$**released**$\rangle$ to each $r \in Permissions_p$;
    $Permissions_p \leftarrow \emptyset$;
end if

If p receives $\langle$**released**$\rangle$

$pending_p \leftarrow tail(pending_p)$;
perform procedure $SendPermission_p$;

If p detects that a process q has crashed

$Crashed_p \leftarrow Crashed_p \cup \{q\}$;
if $head(requests_p) = q$ **then**
    perform procedure $HeadRequestsCrashed_p$;
end if
if $head(pending_p) = q$ **then**
    $pending_p \leftarrow tail(pending_p)$;
    perform procedure $SendPermission_p$;
end if

MCS queue lock

Since processes can use the same node for each lock access, we take the liberty to represent the queue of waiting processes using process IDs instead of nodes. The multi-writer register $wait_p$ is $true$ as long as p must wait to get the lock. The multi-writer register $succ_p$ points to the successor of p in the queue of waiting processes. The single-writer register $pred_p$ points to the predecessor of p in the queue of waiting processes. When a process arrives at this queue, it assigns its process ID to the multi-writer register $last$. The operation $last.get\text{-}and\text{-}set(p)$ assigns the value p to $last$, and returns the previous value of $last$, all in one atomic step. And $last.compare\text{-}and\text{-}set(p, \bot)$ in one atomic operation reads the value of $last$, and either assigns the value $\perp$ to *last*, if its current value is p, or leaves the value of *last* unchanged otherwise. In the first case this operation returns *true*, while in the second case it returns *false*.

bool $wait_p$;
proc $last$, $succ_p$, $pred_p$;

If p wants to enter its critical section

$pred_p \leftarrow last.get\text{-}and\text{-}set(p)$;
if $pred_p \neq \perp$ **then**
    $wait_p \leftarrow true$; $succ_{pred_p} \leftarrow p$;
    while $wait_p = true$ **do**
        $\{\}$;
    end while
end if
enter critical section;
exit critical section;
if $succ_p \neq \perp$ **then**
    $wait_{succ_p} \leftarrow false$;
else if $last.compare\text{-}and\text{-}set(p, \perp)$ returns *false* **then**
    while $succ_p = \perp$ **do**
        $\{\}$;
    end while
    $wait_{succ_p} \leftarrow false$;
end if

CLH queue lock with timeouts

The data type **pointer** consists of pointers to a node, with as default initial value null. If p want to enter its critical section, it creates a node ν containing a pointer $pred_\nu$. Let node ν' denote the nearest nonabandoned predecessor of ν in the queue. $pred_p$ points to ν'. In $pred\text{-}pred_p$, p repeatedly stores the value of $pred_{\nu'}$. If p decides to abandon its attempt to get the lock, and it has a successor in the queue, then it lets $pred_\nu$ point to ν'. The multi-writer register *last* points to the last node in the queue.

pointer $last$, $pred_p$, $pred\text{-}pred_p$, $pred_\nu$ for all nodes ν;

If p wants to enter its critical section

---
create a node ν;
$pred_p \leftarrow last.get\text{-}and\text{-}set(\nu)$;
if $pred_p = $ null **then**
    perform procedure $CriticalSection_p(\nu)$;
else
    while no *timeout* occurs **do**
        $pred\text{-}pred_p \leftarrow pred_{pred_p}$;
        if $pred\text{-}pred_p = $ released **then**

                    perform procedure $CriticalSection_p(\nu)$;
            else if $pred\text{-}pred_p \neq$ `null` then
                $pred_p \leftarrow pred\text{-}pred_p$;
            end if
        end while
        if $last.compare\text{-}and\text{-}set(\nu, pred_p)$ returns *false* then
            $pred_\nu \leftarrow pred_p$;
        end if
        abandon the attempt to take the lock;
    end if

> Procedure $CriticalSection_p(\nu)$

enter critical section;
exit critical section;
if $last.compare\text{-}and\text{-}set(\nu, \texttt{null})$ returns *false* then
    $pred_\nu \leftarrow$ `released`;
end if
terminate;

Afek-Kutten-Yung spanning tree algorithm

Self-stabilizing algorithms are always defined in a shared-memory framework. Therefore, the message-passing description of the Afek-Kutten-Yung spanning tree algorithm in section 18.3 is here cast in shared variables. We recall that variables can be initialized with any value in their domain.

$root_p$ is the root of the spanning tree according to p, $parent_p$ represents the parent of p in the spanning tree, and $dist_p$ is the distance value of p toward the root. The variables req_p, $from_p$, to_p, and $direction_p$ deal with join requests and corresponding grant messages. In req_p the process ID of the process that originally issued the request is stored, in $from_p$ the neighbor from which p received the request, in to_p the neighbor to which p forwarded the request, and in $direction_p$ whether a request is being forwarded to the root of the fragment, or a grant message is being forwarded to the process that originally issued the request. $toggle_p$ makes sure that p performs an event only when all its neighbors have copied the current values of p's local variables; $toggle_q(p)$ represents the copy at neighbor q of the value of $toggle_p$. It is assumed that a process copies the values of all local variables of a neighbor in one atomic step.

We use the following abbreviations. $AmRoot_p$ states that p considers itself root:

$$parent_p = \bot \;\wedge\; root_p = p \;\wedge\; dist_p = 0.$$

$NotRoot_p$ states that p does not consider itself root, and that the values of p's local variables are in line with those of its parent:

$$parent_p \in Neighbors_p \;\wedge\; root_p > p$$
$$\wedge\; root_p = root_{parent_p} \;\wedge\; dist_p = dist_{parent_p} + 1.$$

$MaxRoot_p$ states that no neighbor of p has a root value greater than $root_p$:

$$root_p \geq root_r \text{ for all } r \in Neighbors_p.$$

The network is stable, with the process with the largest ID as root, if at each process p either $AmRoot_p$ or $NotRoot_p$ holds, as well as $MaxRoot_p$.

In the following pseudocode, p repeatedly copies the values of the local variables of its neighbors, checks whether all its neighbors have copied the current values of p's local variables, and if so, tries to perform one of several possible events. First of all, if $NotRoot_p \wedge MaxRoot_p$ does not hold and p does not yet consider itself root, then p makes itself root. The second kind of events arises if $MaxRoot_p$ does not hold (and so, since p skipped the first case, $AmRoot_p$ does hold). Then either p asks a neighbor with a maximal root value to become its parent, if p is not already making such a request to a neighbor q, expressed by (the negation of) the predicate $Asking_p(q)$:

$$root_q \geq root_r \text{ for all } r \in Neighbors_p$$
$$\wedge \; req_p = from_p = p \wedge to_p = q \wedge direction_p = \texttt{ask}.$$

Or such a request by p may be granted by a neighbor q, expressed by the predicate $Granted_p(q)$:

$$req_q = req_p \wedge from_q = from_p \wedge direction_q = \texttt{grant} \wedge direction_p = \texttt{ask},$$

where we take q to be to_p. It is moreover required that p issued a request to to_p, expressed by the predicate $Requestor_p$:

$$to_p \in Neighbors_p \wedge root_{to_p} > p \wedge req_p = from_p = p.$$

In this case to_p becomes p's parent. The third kind of events arises when p is not yet handling a request from a neighbor q, expressed by (the negation of) the predicate $Handling_p(q)$:

$$req_q = req_p \wedge from_p = q \wedge to_q = p \wedge to_p = parent_p \wedge direction_q = \texttt{ask}.$$

Here q should be either a root that issued a join request, or a child of p in the spanning tree, expressed by the predicate $Request_p(q)$:

$$(AmRoot_q \wedge req_q = from_q = q) \vee (parent_q = p \wedge req_q \notin \{q, \bot\}).$$

If the four variables that capture requests are not all undefined, expressed by (the negation of) the predicate $NotHandling_p$,

$$req_p = \bot \wedge from_p = \bot \wedge to_p = \bot \wedge direction_p = \bot,$$

then p sets the values of these four variables to $\bot$. Otherwise, p forwards a request, but only if $from_{parent_p} \neq p$ (allowing $parent_p$ to first reset its join request variables). The fourth kind of event is that a root p that is handling a request of a neighbor sets

$direction_p$ to grant. Finally, the fifth kind of event is that a nonroot p that finds that its request has been granted by its parent sets $direction_p$ to grant. Note that for the third, fourth, and fifth kinds of events, $AmRoot_p \vee NotRoot_p$ (because p skipped the first case) and $MaxRoot_p$ (because p skipped the second case). And for the fourth and fifth kinds of events, $Request_p(q) \wedge Handling_p(q)$ for some $q \in Neighbors_p$ (because p skipped the third case).

bool $toggle_p$, $toggle_p(r)$ for all $r \in Neighbors_p$;
dist $dist_p$;
proc $parent_p$, $root_p$, req_p, $from_p$, to_p;
$\{\text{ask}, \text{grant}, \bot\}$ $direction_p$;

while $true$ **do**
    copy the values of variables of all neighbors into a local copy;
    if $toggle_r(p) = toggle_p$ for all $r \in Neighbors_p$ **then**
        if $\neg(NotRoot_p \wedge MaxRoot_p) \wedge \neg AmRoot_p$ **then**
            $parent_p \leftarrow \bot$; $root_p \leftarrow p$; $dist_p \leftarrow 0$;
        else if $\neg MaxRoot_p$ **then**
            if $\neg Asking_p(r)$ for all $r \in Neighbors_p$ **then**
                $req_p \leftarrow p$; $from_p \leftarrow p$; $direction_p \leftarrow \text{ask}$;
                $to_p \leftarrow q$ for a $q \in Neighbors_p$ with $root_q$ as large as possible;
            else if $Requestor_p \wedge Granted_p(to_p)$ **then**
                $parent_p \leftarrow to_p$; $root_p \leftarrow root_{to_p}$; $dist_p \leftarrow dist_{to_p} + 1$;
                $req_p \leftarrow \bot$; $from_p \leftarrow \bot$; $to_p \leftarrow \bot$; $direction_p \leftarrow \bot$;
            end if
        else if $\neg(Request_p(r) \wedge Handling_p(r))$ for all $r \in Neighbors_p$ **then**
            if $\neg NotHandling_p$ **then**
                $req_p \leftarrow \bot$; $from_p \leftarrow \bot$; $to_p \leftarrow \bot$; $direction_p \leftarrow \bot$;
            else if $from_{parent_p} \neq p \wedge Request_p(q)$ for some $q \in Neighbors_p$ **then**
                $req_p \leftarrow req_q$; $from_p \leftarrow q$; $to_p \leftarrow parent_p$; $direction_p \leftarrow \text{ask}$;
            end if
        else if $AmRoot_p \wedge direction_p = \text{ask}$ **then**
            $direction_p \leftarrow \text{grant}$;
        else if $Granted_p(parent_p)$ **then**
            $direction_p \leftarrow \text{grant}$;
        end if
        $toggle_p \leftarrow \neg toggle_p$;
    end if
end while

References

1. Y. AFEK, S. KUTTEN, AND M. YUNG (1997), *The local detection paradigm and its applications to self-stabilization*, Theoretical Computer Science, 186, pp. 199–229.
2. D. AGRAWAL AND A. EL ABBADI (1991), *An efficient and fault-tolerant solution for distributed mutual exclusion*, ACM Transactions on Computer Systems, 9, pp. 1–20.
3. T.E. ANDERSON (1990), *The performance of spin lock alternatives for shared-memory multiprocessors*, IEEE Transactions on Parallel and Distributed Systems, 1, pp. 6–16.
4. D. ANGLUIN (1980), *Local and global properties in networks of processors*, in Proc. 12th Symposium on Theory of Computing, pp. 82–93, ACM.
5. A. ARORA AND M.G. GOUDA (1994), *Distributed reset*, IEEE Transactions on Computers, 43, pp. 1026–1038.
6. B. AWERBUCH (1985), *Complexity of network synchronization*, Journal of the ACM, 32, pp. 804–823.
7. B. AWERBUCH (1985), *A new distributed depth-first-search algorithm*, Information Processing Letters, 20, pp. 147–150.
8. R. BAKHSHI, J. ENDRULLIS, W. FOKKINK, AND J. PANG (2011) *Fast leader election in anonymous rings with bounded expected delay*, Information Processing Letters, 111, pp. 864–870.
9. R. BAKHSHI, W. FOKKINK, J. PANG, AND J. VAN DE POL (2008), *Leader election in anonymous rings: Franklin goes probabilistic*, in Proc. 5th IFIP Conference on Theoretical Computer Science, pp. 57–72, Springer.
10. D.I. BEVAN (1987), *Distributed garbage collection using reference counting*, in Proc. 1st Conference on Parallel Architectures and Languages Europe, vol. 259 of Lecture Notes in Computer Science, pp. 176–187, Springer.
11. G. BRACHA AND S. TOUEG (1985), *Asynchronous consensus and broadcast protocols*, Journal of the ACM, 32, pp. 824–840.
12. G. BRACHA AND S. TOUEG (1987), *Distributed deadlock detection*, Distributed Computing, 2, pp. 127–138.
13. J.E. BURNS AND N.A. LYNCH (1993), *Bounds on shared memory for mutual exclusion*, Information and Computation, 107, pp. 171–184.
14. O.S.F. CARVALHO AND G. ROUCAIROL (1983), *On mutual exclusion in computer networks*, Communications of the ACM, 26, pp. 146–147.
15. T.D. CHANDRA AND S. TOUEG (1996), *Unreliable failure detectors for reliable distributed systems*, Journal of the ACM, 43, pp. 225–267.

16. K.M. CHANDY AND L. LAMPORT (1985), *Distributed snapshots: Determining global states of distributed systems*, ACM Transactions on Computer Systems, 3, pp. 63–75.
17. K.M. CHANDY AND J. MISRA (1982), *Distributed computation on graphs: Shortest path algorithms*, Communications of the ACM, 25, pp. 833–837.
18. E.J.H. CHANG (1982), *Echo algorithms: Depth parallel operations on general graphs*, IEEE Transactions on Software Engineering, 8, pp. 391–401.
19. E.J.H. CHANG AND R. ROBERTS (1979), *An improved algorithm for decentralized extrema-finding in circular configurations of processes*, Communications of the ACM, 22, pp. 281–283.
20. T.-Y. CHEUNG (1983), *Graph traversal techniques and the maximum flow problem in distributed computation*, IEEE Transactions on Software Engineering, 9, pp. 504–512.
21. C.-T. CHOU, I. CIDON, I.S. GOPAL, AND S. ZAKS (1990), *Synchronizing asynchronous bounded delay networks*, IEEE Transactions on Communications, 38, pp. 144–147.
22. I. CIDON (1988), *Yet another distributed depth-first-search algorithm*, Information Processing Letters, 26, pp. 301–305.
23. T.S. CRAIG (1993), *Building FIFO and priority-queueing spin locks from atomic swap*, Tech. Rep. TR 93-02-02, University of Washington.
24. E.W. DIJKSTRA (1974), *Self-stabilizing systems in spite of distributed control*, Communications of the ACM, 17, pp. 643–644.
25. E.W. DIJKSTRA (1987), *Shmuel Safra's version of termination detection*, vol. 998 of EWD manuscripts, The University of Texas at Austin.
26. E.W. DIJKSTRA AND C.S. SCHOLTEN (1980), *Termination detection for diffusing computations*, Information Processing Letters, 11, pp. 1–4.
27. D. DOLEV, M.M. KLAWE, AND M. RODEH (1982), *An $O(n \log n)$ unidirectional distributed algorithm for extrema finding in a circle*, Journal of Algorithms, 3, pp. 245–260.
28. D. DOLEV AND H.R. STRONG (1983), *Authenticated algorithms for Byzantine agreement*, SIAM Journal on Computing, 12, pp. 656–666.
29. C.J. FIDGE (1988), *Timestamps in message-passing systems that preserve the partial ordering*, in Proc. 11th Australian Computer Science Conference, pp. 56–66.
30. M.J. FISCHER, N.A. LYNCH, AND M. PATERSON (1985), *Impossibility of distributed consensus with one faulty process*, Journal of the ACM, 32, pp. 374–382.
31. W. FOKKINK, J.-H. HOEPMAN, AND J. PANG (2005), *A note on K-state self-stabilization in a ring with $K = N$*, Nordic Journal of Computing, 12, pp. 18–26.
32. W. FOKKINK AND J. PANG (2006), *Variations on Itai-Rodeh leader election for anonymous rings and their analysis in PRISM*, Journal of Universal Computer Science, 12, pp. 981–1006.
33. W.R. FRANKLIN (1982), *On an improved algorithm for decentralized extrema-finding in circular configurations of processes*, Communications of the ACM, 25, pp. 336–337.
34. G.N. FREDERICKSON (1985), *A single source shortest path algorithm for a planar distributed network*, in Proc. 2nd Symposium of Theoretical Aspects of Computer Science, vol. 182 of Lecture Notes in Computer Science, pp. 143–150, Springer.
35. R.G. GALLAGER, P.A. HUMBLET, AND P.M. SPIRA (1983), *A distributed algorithm for minimum-weight spanning trees*, ACM Transactions on Programming Languages and Systems, 5, pp. 66–77.
36. D. HENSGEN, R.A. FINKEL, AND U. MANBER (1988), *Two algorithms for barrier synchronization*, International Journal of Parallel Programming, 17, pp. 1–17.
37. M. HERLIHY AND N. SHAVIT (2008), *The Art of Multiprocessor Programming*, Morgan Kaufmann.
38. IEEE COMPUTER SOCIETY (1996), *IEEE standard for a high performance serial bus*, Tech. Rep. Std. 1394-1995, IEEE.

39. A. ITAI AND M. RODEH (1990), *Symmetry breaking in distributed networks*, Information and Computation, 88, pp. 60–87.
40. V. JACOBSON (1988), *Congestion avoidance and control*, in Proc. 3rd Symposium on Communications Architectures and Protocols, pp. 314–329, ACM.
41. E. KREPSKA, T. KIELMANN, W. FOKKINK, AND H. BAL (2011), *HipG: Parallel processing of large-scale graphs*, ACM SIGOPS Operating Systems Review, 45, pp. 3–13.
42. C.P. KRUSKAL, L. RUDOLPH, AND M. SNIR (1988), *Efficient synchronization on multiprocessors with shared memory*, ACM Transactions on Programming Languages and Systems, 10, pp. 579–601.
43. T.H. LAI AND T.H. YANG (1987), *On distributed snapshots*, Information Processing Letters, 25, pp. 153–158.
44. L. LAMPORT (1974), *A new solution of Dijkstra's concurrent programming problem*, Communications of the ACM, 17, pp. 453–455.
45. L. LAMPORT (1978), *Time, clocks, and the ordering of events in a distributed system*, Communications of the ACM, 21, pp. 558–565.
46. L. LAMPORT (1987), *A fast mutual exclusion algorithm*, ACM Transactions on Computer Systems, 5, pp. 1–11.
47. L. LAMPORT, R.E. SHOSTAK, AND M.C. PEASE (1982), *The Byzantine generals problem*, ACM Transactions on Programming Languages and Systems, 4, pp. 382–401.
48. J.P. LEHOCZKY AND S. RAMOS-THUEL (1992), *An optimal algorithm for scheduling soft-aperiodic tasks in fixed-priority preemptive systems*, in Proc. 13th Real-Time Systems Symposium, pp. 110–123, IEEE.
49. H. LIEBERMAN AND C. HEWITT (1983), *A real-time garbage collector based on the lifetimes of objects*, Communications of the ACM, 26, pp. 419–429.
50. J.W. LIU (2000), *Real-Time Systems*, Prentice-Hall.
51. P.S. MAGNUSSON, A. LANDIN, AND E. HAGERSTEN (1994), *Queue locks on cache coherent multiprocessors*, in Proc. 8th Symposium on Parallel Processing, pp. 165–171, IEEE.
52. S.R. MAHANEY AND F.B. SCHNEIDER (1985), *Inexact agreement: Accuracy, precision, and graceful degradation*, in Proc. 4th Symposium on Principles of Distributed Computing, pp. 237–249, ACM.
53. G. MALEWICZ, M.H. AUSTERN, A.J.C. BIK, J.C. DEHNERT, I. HORN, N. LEISER, AND G. CZAJKOWSKI (2010), *Pregel: A system for large-scale graph processing*, in Proc. 10th Conference on Management of Data, pp. 135–146, ACM.
54. F. MATTERN (1989), *Global quiescence detection based on credit distribution and recovery*, Information Processing Letters, 30, pp. 195–200.
55. F. MATTERN (1989), *Virtual time and global states of distributed systems*, in Proc. Workshop on Parallel and Distributed Algorithms, pp. 215–226, North-Holland/Elsevier.
56. J.M. MCQUILLAN (1974), *Adaptive Routing for Distributed Computer Networks*, PhD thesis, Harvard University.
57. J.M. MCQUILLAN, I. RICHER, AND E.C. ROSEN (1980), *The new routing algorithm for ARPANET*, IEEE Transactions on Communications, 28, pp. 711–719.
58. J.M. MELLOR-CRUMMEY AND M.L. SCOTT (1991), *Algorithms for scalable synchronization on shared-memory multiprocessors*, ACM Transactions on Computer Systems, 9, pp. 21–65.
59. P.M. MERLIN AND P.J. SCHWEITZER (1980), *Deadlock avoidance in store-and-forward networks I: Store-and-forward deadlock*, IEEE Transactions on Communications, 28, pp. 345–354.
60. P.M. MERLIN AND A. SEGALL (1979), *A failsafe distributed routing protocol*, IEEE Transactions on Communications, 27, pp. 1280–1287.

61. J.K. PACHL, E. KORACH, AND D. ROTEM (1984), *Lower bounds for distributed maximum-finding algorithms*, Journal of the ACM, 31, pp. 905–918.
62. G.L. PETERSON (1981), *Myths about the mutual exclusion problem*, Information Processing Letters, 12, pp. 115–116.
63. G.L. PETERSON (1982), *An $O(n \log n)$ unidirectional algorithm for the circular extrema problem*, ACM Transactions on Programming Languages and Systems, 4, pp. 758–762.
64. J.M. PIQUER (1991), *Indirect reference counting: A distributed garbage collection algorithm*, in Proc. 3rd Conference on Parallel Architectures and Languages Europe, vol. 505 of Lecture Notes in Computer Science, pp. 150–165, Springer.
65. R. RAJKUMAR, L. SHA, AND J.P. LEHOCZKY (1988), *Real-time synchronization protocols for multiprocessors*, in Proc. 9th Real-Time Systems Symposium, pp. 259–269, IEEE.
66. S.P. RANA (1983), *A distributed solution of the distributed termination problem*, Information Processing Letters, 17, pp. 43–46.
67. K. RAYMOND (1989), *A tree-based algorithm for distributed mutual exclusion*, ACM Transactions on Computer Systems, 7, pp. 61–77.
68. G. RICART AND A.K. AGRAWALA (1981), *An optimal algorithm for mutual exclusion in computer networks*, Communications of the ACM, 24, pp. 9–17.
69. M.L. SCOTT AND W.N. SCHERER III (2001), *Scalable queue-based spin locks with timeout*, in Proc. 8th Symposium on Principles and Practice of Parallel Programming, pp. 44–52, ACM.
70. A. SEGALL (1983), *Distributed network protocols*, IEEE Transactions on Information Theory, 29, pp. 23–34.
71. L. SHA, R. RAJKUMAR, AND J.P. LEHOCZKY (1990), *Priority inheritance protocols: An approach to real-time synchronization*, IEEE Transactions on Computers, 39, pp. 1175–1185.
72. N. SHAVIT AND N. FRANCEZ (1986), *A new approach to detection of locally indicative stability*, in Proc. 13th Colloquium on Automata, Languages and Programming, vol. 226 of Lecture Notes in Computer Science, pp. 344–358, Springer.
73. M. SPURI AND G.C. BUTTAZZO (1996), *Scheduling aperiodic tasks in dynamic priority systems*, Real-Time Systems, 10, pp. 179–210.
74. J.K. STROSNIDER, J.P. LEHOCZKY, AND L. SHA (1995), *The deferrable server algorithm for enhanced aperiodic responsiveness in hard real-time environments*, IEEE Transactions on Computers, 44, pp. 73–91.
75. G. TARRY (1895), *Le problème des labyrinthes*, Nouvelles Annales de Mathématiques, 14, pp. 187–190.
76. G. TEL (2000), *Introduction to Distributed Algorithms*, Cambridge University Press, 2nd edition.
77. G. TEL AND F. MATTERN (1993), *The derivation of distributed termination detection algorithms from garbage collection schemes*, ACM Transactions on Programming Languages and Systems, 15, pp. 1–35.
78. S. TOUEG (1980), *An all-pairs shortest-path distributed algorithm*, Tech. Rep. RC-8397, IBM Thomas J. Watson Research Center.
79. S.C. VESTAL (1987), *Garbage Collection: An Exercise in Distributed, Fault-Tolerant Programming*, PhD thesis, University of Washington.
80. P. WATSON AND I. WATSON (1987), *An efficient garbage collection scheme for parallel computer architectures*, in Proc. 1st Conference on Parallel Architectures and Languages Europe, vol. 259 of Lecture Notes in Computer Science, pp. 432–443, Springer.
81. P.-C. YEW, N.-F. TZENG, AND D.H. LAWRIE (1987), *Distributing hot-spot addressing in large-scale multiprocessors*, IEEE Transactions on Computers, 36, pp. 388–395.

Index

0-potent, 112
1-potent, 112
N-out-of-M request, 27
α synchronizer, 102
β synchronizer, 102
γ synchronizer, 103
ρ-bounded drift, 105
k-Byzantine broadcast, 128
k-Byzantine clock synchronization, 126
k-Byzantine consensus, 121
k-crash consensus, 112

absolute deadline, 181
active process, 73
acyclic orientation, 66
acyclic orientation cover, 66
acyclic orientation cover controller, 66
Afek-Kutten-Yung spanning tree algorithm, 177, 218
Agrawal-El Abbadi mutual exclusion algorithm, 140, 215
agreement, 111
algorithm, 1
   basic, 11
   centralized, 8
   control, 11
   decentralized, 8
   distributed, 8
   Las Vegas, 88
   Monte Carlo, 88
   probabilistic, 88
   self-stabilizing, 171
Anderson's lock, 155
anonymous network, 87
   echo algorithm with extinction, 91
   Itai-Rodeh election algorithm, 89
   Itai-Rodeh ring size algorithm, 94
   resuscitation election algorithm, 107
aperiodic job, 182
aperiodic task, 182
Arora-Gouda spanning tree algorithm, 175
arrival time, 181
assertion, 9
asynchronous communication, 7
Awerbuch's depth-first search algorithm, 22
Awerbuch's synchronizer, 102, 211

background server, 185
bakery mutual exclusion algorithm, 150
barrier, 161
   combining tree, 162
   dissemination, 168
   sense-reversing, 161
   tournament, 165
basic algorithm, 11
basic message, 13
bivalent configuration, 111
blocked node, 27
Boolean, 2
bounded delay network, 105
bounded expected delay network, 106
Bracha-Toueg Byzantine consensus algorithm, 122
Bracha-Toueg crash consensus algorithm, 113
Bracha-Toueg deadlock detection algorithm, 30

breadth-first search, 55
  Frederickson's algorithm, 62, 204
breadth-first search tree, 55
bus, 145
busy-waiting, 147
Byzantine broadcast, 127
  Lamport-Shostak-Pease algorithm, 128
  Lamport-Shostak-Pease authentication algorithm, 131
    Dolev-Strong optimization, 132
Byzantine clock synchronization
  Lamport-Melliar-Smith synchronizer, 133
  Mahaney-Schneider synchronizer, 126
Byzantine consensus, 121
  Bracha-Toueg algorithm, 122
Byzantine failure, 121

cache, 146
cache line, 156
Carvalho-Roucairol optimization, 136
causal order, 9
centralized algorithm, 8
Chandra-Toueg crash consensus algorithm, 117
Chandy-Lamport snapshot algorithm, 14, 194
Chandy-Misra routing algorithm, 53, 202
Chang-Roberts election algorithm, 73
channel, 7
  directed, 7
  FIFO, 7
  undirected, 7
channel state, 13
child node, 7
Cidon's depth-first search algorithm, 22, 196
CLH lock, 156
CLH lock with timeouts, 158, 217
clock, 7, 105
  local, 105
  logical, 10
combining tree barrier, 162
communication, 7
  asynchronous, 7
  synchronous, 8
communication deadlock, 27
compare-and-set, 145
complete failure detector, 115
complete network, 7
computation, 10

concurrent event, 10
configuration, 8
  bivalent, 111
  initial, 8
  reachable, 8
  symmetric, 87
  terminal, 8
congestion window, 68
consensus, 111
  k-Byzantine, 121
  k-crash, 112
  Byzantine, 121
  crash, 111
consistent snapshot, 13
control algorithm, 11
control message, 13
controller, 65
  acyclic orientation cover, 66
  destination, 65
  hops-so-far, 66
core edge, 81
core node, 81
correct process, 111, 121
crash consensus, 111
  Bracha-Toueg algorithm, 113
  Chandra-Toueg algorithm, 117
  rotating coordinator algorithm, 116
crash failure, 111
crashed process, 111
critical section, 135
cyclic garbage, 47

deadline, 181
  absolute, 181
  hard, 181
  relative, 181
deadlock, 27
  communication, 27
  resource, 27
  store-and-forward, 65
deadlock detection
  Bracha-Toueg algorithm, 30
decentralized algorithm, 8
decide event, 19
deferrable server, 186
dependence, 128
depth-first search, 21
  Awerbuch's algorithm, 22
  Cidon's algorithm, 22, 196

depth-first search tree, 21
destination controller, 65
Dijkstra's token ring, 171
Dijkstra-Scholten termination detection algorithm, 38
directed channel, 7
directed network, 7
dissemination barrier, 168
distributed algorithm, 8
Dolev-Klawe-Rodeh election algorithm, 75, 206
Dolev-Strong optimization, 132

earliest deadline first scheduler, 184
echo algorithm, 24, 197
echo algorithm with extinction, 79, 91
edge, 7
    core, 81
    frond, 7
    outgoing, 80
    tree, 7
election, 73
    Chang-Roberts algorithm, 73
    Dolev-Klawe-Rodeh algorithm, 75, 206
    echo algorithm with extinction, 79, 91
    Franklin's algorithm, 74
    IEEE 1394 election algorithm, 96, 210
    Itai-Rodeh algorithm, 89
    resuscitation algorithm, 107
    tree algorithm, 77
event, 8
    concurrent, 10
    decide, 19
    postsnapshot, 13
    presnapshot, 13
    receive, 8
    send, 8
eventually strongly accurate failure detector, 116
eventually weakly accurate failure detector, 117
execution, 8
    fair, 9
execution time, 181
exponential back-off, 154

failure
    Byzantine, 121
    crash, 111

failure detector, 115
    complete, 115
    eventually strongly accurate, 116
    eventually weakly accurate, 117
    strongly accurate, 115
    weakly accurate, 116
failure detector history, 115
failure pattern, 115
fair execution, 9
fair message scheduling, 115
false root, 175
field, 145
FIFO channel, 7
FIFO queue, 137, 193
first-come, first-served, 150
Fischer's mutual exclusion algorithm, 152
fragment, 80
Franklin's election algorithm, 74
Frederickson's breadth-first search algorithm, 62, 204
frond edge, 7

Gallager-Humblet-Spira minimum spanning tree algorithm, 80, 207
garbage, 47
    cyclic, 47
garbage collection, 47
    generational, 51
    mark-compact, 51
    mark-copy, 51
    mark-scan, 51
    reference counting, 47
        indirect, 48
        weighted, 49
    tracing, 51
general, 127
generational garbage collection, 51
get-and-increment, 145
get-and-set, 145
graph, 7
    wait-for, 27

hard deadline, 181
hops-so-far controller, 66

ID, 7
IEEE 1394 election algorithm, 96, 210
indirect reference counting, 48
initial configuration, 8

initiator, 8
invariant, 9
Itai-Rodeh election algorithm, 89
Itai-Rodeh ring size algorithm, 94

jitter, 183
job, 181
    aperiodic, 182
    periodic, 182
    preemptive, 183
    sporadic, 182

Lai-Yang snapshot algorithm, 15, 194
Lamport's logical clock, 10
Lamport-Melliar-Smith Byzantine clock synchronization algorithm, 133
Lamport-Shostak-Pease authentication algorithm, 131
    Dolev-Strong optimization, 132
Lamport-Shostak-Pease broadcast algorithm, 128
Las Vegas algorithm, 88
least slack-time first scheduler, 184
lexicographical order, 3
lieutenant, 127
link-state packet, 67
link-state routing algorithm, 67
livelock-freeness, 146
liveness property, 9
local clock, 105
local snapshot, 13
lock, 146
    queue, 155
    test-and-set, 153
    test-and-test-and-set, 154
lockstep, 101
logical clock, 10
    Lamport's, 10
    vector, 10

Mahaney-Schneider Byzantine clock synchronization algorithm, 126
main memory, 145
mark-compact garbage collection, 51
mark-copy garbage collection, 51
mark-scan garbage collection, 51
MCS lock, 157, 216
Merlin-Segall routing algorithm, 55, 202
message, 7
    basic, 13
    control, 13
    valid, 131
message passing, 7
minimum spanning tree, 80
    Gallager-Humblet-Spira algorithm, 80, 207
minimum-hop path, 55
modulo arithmetic, 4
Monte Carlo algorithm, 88
multi-reader register, 145
multi-writer register, 145
multiset, 128
mutual exclusion, 135
    Agrawal-El Abbadi algorithm, 140, 215
    bakery algorithm, 150
    Dijkstra's token ring, 171
    Fischer's algorithm, 152
    Peterson's algorithm, 147
    Raymond's algorithm, 137, 213
    Ricart-Agrawala algorithm, 135, 212
        Carvalho-Roucairol optimization, 136
    test-and-set lock, 153
    test-and-test-and-set lock, 154

network, 7
    anonymous, 87
    bounded delay, 105
    bounded expected delay, 106
    complete, 7
    directed, 7
    undirected, 7
node, 7, 156
    blocked, 27
    child, 7
    core, 81
    parent, 7
null, 157, 217
NUMA architecture, 158

object, 47
    root, 47
object owner, 47
offline scheduler, 182
online scheduler, 183
order, 3
    lexicographical, 3
    partial, 3
    total, 3

outgoing edge, 80

padding, 156
parent node, 7
partial order, 3
passive process, 73
path, 7
   minimum-hop, 55
period, 182
periodic job, 182
periodic task, 182
Peterson's mutual exclusion algorithm, 147
pivot, 59
pointer, 47, 156
   null, 157
polling server, 186
postsnapshot event, 13
precision, 105
preemptive job, 183
presnapshot event, 13
priority ceiling, 189
priority inheritance, 189
privileged process, 135
probabilistic algorithm, 88
process, 7
   active, 73
   correct, 111, 121
   crashed, 111
   passive, 73
   privileged, 135
   safe, 102
process ID, 7
processor, 145
progress property, 146
property
   liveness, 9
   progress, 146
   safety, 9
pseudocode, 193
public-key cryptographic system, 130
pulse, 101

queue, 137, 193
queue lock, 155
   Anderson's lock, 155
   CLH lock, 156
   CLH lock with timeouts, 158, 217
   MCS lock, 157, 216
quorum, 140

Rana's termination detection algorithm, 40, 200
rate-monotonic scheduler, 183
Raymond's mutual exclusion algorithm, 137, 213
reachable configuration, 8
read-modify-write operation, 145
   compare-and-set, 145
   get-and-increment, 145
   get-and-set, 145
   test-and-set, 145
real-time computing, 181
receive event, 8
reference, 47
reference counting, 47
   indirect, 48
   weighted, 49
register, 145
   multi-reader, 145
   multi-writer, 145
   single-reader, 145
   single-writer, 145
relative deadline, 181
release time, 181
resource access control, 188
   priority ceiling, 189
   priority inheritance, 189
resource deadlock, 27
resuscitation election algorithm, 107
Ricart-Agrawala mutual exclusion algorithm, 135, 212
   Carvalho-Roucairol optimization, 136
ring size
   Itai-Rodeh algorithm, 94
ring traversal algorithm, 19
root, 7
   false, 175
root object, 47
rotating coordinator crash consensus algorithm, 116
routing, 53
   Chandy-Misra algorithm, 53, 202
   link-state algorithm, 67
   Merlin-Segall algorithm, 55, 202
   Toueg's algorithm, 58, 203
routing table, 53

safe process, 102
safety property, 9

Safra's termination detection algorithm, 42, 201
scheduler, 182
   earliest deadline first, 184
   least slack-time first, 184
   offline, 182
   online, 183
   rate-monotonic, 183
self-stabilization, 171
   Afek-Kutten-Yung spanning tree algorithm, 177, 218
   Arora-Gouda spanning tree algorithm, 175
   Dijkstra's token ring, 171
send event, 8
sense-reversing barrier, 161
server
   background, 185
   deferrable, 186
   polling, 186
   slack stealing, 185
   total bandwidth, 186
set, 2, 193
shared memory, 145
Shavit-Francez termination detection algorithm, 39, 198
simple synchronizer, 101
single-reader register, 145
single-writer register, 145
sink tree, 7
slack, 183
slack stealing server, 185
snapshot, 13
   Chandy-Lamport algorithm, 14, 194
   consistent, 13
   Lai-Yang algorithm, 15, 194
   local, 13
spanning tree, 7
   Afek-Kutten-Yung algorithm, 177, 218
   Arora-Gouda algorithm, 175
   minimum, 80
spinning, 147
sporadic job, 182
sporadic task, 182
starvation-freeness, 135
state, 8
   channel, 13
store-and-forward deadlock, 65
strongly accurate failure detector, 115

symmetric configuration, 87
synchronizer, 101
   α, 102
   β, 102
   γ, 103
   Awerbuch's, 102, 211
   simple, 101
synchronous communication, 8
synchronous system, 101

Tarry's traversal algorithm, 20
task, 182
   aperiodic, 182
   periodic, 182
   sporadic, 182
terminal configuration, 8
termination, 111
termination detection, 37
   Dijkstra-Scholten algorithm, 38
   Rana's algorithm, 40, 200
   Safra's algorithm, 42, 201
   Shavit-Francez algorithm, 39, 198
   weight-throwing algorithm, 39, 199
test-and-set, 145
test-and-set lock, 153
test-and-test-and-set lock, 154
thread, 145
time-to-live field, 67
token, 19
total bandwidth server, 186
total order, 3
Toueg's routing algorithm, 58, 203
tournament barrier, 165
tournament tree, 148
tracing garbage collection, 51
transition, 8
transition relation, 8
transition system, 8
traversal, 19
   breadth-first search algorithm, 55
   depth-first search algorithm, 21
   ring algorithm, 19
   Tarry's algorithm, 20
tree
   breadth-first search, 55
   depth-first search, 21
   sink, 7
   spanning, 7
      minimum, 80

tournament, 148
tree algorithm, 23, 197
tree edge, 7
tree election algorithm, 77

undirected channel, 7
undirected network, 7
utilization, 182

valid message, 131
validity, 111, 121

vector clock, 10

wait-for graph, 27
wave, 19
    echo algorithm, 24, 197
    tree algorithm, 23, 197
weakly accurate failure detector, 116
weight-throwing termination detection
    algorithm, 39, 199
weighted reference counting, 49
working memory, 146